Philosophy and the Interpretation of Pop Culture

Philosophy and the Interpretation of Pop Culture

EDITED BY WILLIAM IRWIN AND
JORGE J. E. GRACIA

ROWMAN & LITTLEFIELD PUBLISHERS, INC.
Lanham • Boulder • New York • Toronto • Plymouth, UK

Published in the United States of America
by Rowman & Littlefield Publishers, Inc.
A wholly owned subsidiary of The Rowman & Littlefield Publishing Group, Inc.
4501 Forbes Boulevard, Suite 200, Lanham, Maryland 20706
www.rowmanlittlefield.com

Estover Road
Plymouth PL6 7PY
United Kingdom

British Library Cataloguing in Publication Information Available

Library of Congress Cataloging-in-Publication Data

Philosophy and the interpretation of pop culture / edited by William
    Irwin and Jorge J. E. Gracia.
       p. cm.
    Includes bibliographical references.
    ISBN-13: 978-0-7425-5174-9 (cloth : alk. paper)
    ISBN-10: 0-7425-5174-1 (cloth : alk. paper)
    ISBN-13: 978-0-7425-5175-6 (pbk : alk. paper)
    ISBN-10: 0-7425-5175-X (pbk : alk. paper)
    1. Philosophy and civilization. 2. Popular culture—Philosophy. 3. Popular culture—
United States. I. Irwin, William, 1970–. II. Gracia, Jorge J. E.
B59.P56 2007
306.01—dc22   2006004801

Printed in the United States of America

∞™ The paper used in this publication meets the minimum requirements of American
National Standard for Information Sciences—Permanence of Paper for Printed Library
Materials, ANSI/NISO Z39.48-1992.

Contents

Part II: Interpretation and Popular Art Forms

Acknowledgments

This book grows out of a conference, "Philosophy and the Interpretation of Popular Culture," funded by the Samuel V. Capen Chair at the State University of New York at Buffalo in April 2004. In addition to the contributors to this volume, we are grateful to all of those who participated in the conference, including (but not limited to) Judith Barad, Gregory Bassham, David Baggett, Shai Biderman, Kimberly Blessing, Eric Bronson, David Carrier, Jason Eberl, David Hershenov, Thomas Hibbs, George Hole, Rebecca Housel, James Lawler, Bill Lawson, Peter Ludlow, Kevin Murtagh, David Schmid, Robert Thompson, Mark Wrathall, and Joseph Zeccardi. For their assistance in planning and supporting the conference, we are grateful to Audrey Anton, John Kearns, Eva Koepsell, Eileen McNamara, and Judy Wagner. Our student assistants Jamie McAndrew and Susan Smith were of great help in preparing the final manuscript. Last, but certainly not least, we are grateful to Tessa Fallon, who acquired this book for Rowman & Littlefield, and to Ross Miller and Sheila Zwiebel, who diligently saw the book through to publication.

1

Philosophy Engages Popular Culture: An Introduction

William Irwin

The walls and windows of the apartment rattle. Jake asks, "How often does the train go by?" Elwood responds, "So often you won't even notice it." As the Blues Brothers become deaf to the train, so we may ignore or become oblivious to popular culture, but it is there nonetheless. Even the conscious effort to avoid popular culture, whatever the motivation, is unlikely to succeed. Like the Matrix, "it is everywhere." This may always have been true to some extent, but popular culture is all the more dominant and commands more attention today thanks to mass production and distribution.

The medium influences our thought, as Marshall McLuhan and Neil Postman warned and worried. But the content is the message too. We reach out to one another and discuss life, current events, politics, and religion through popular culture. A 2004 *New York Times* article suggested that, rather than red states and blue states, America was divided into those who had seen Mel Gibson's *The Passion of the Christ* and those who had seen Michael Moore's *Fahrenheit 9/11*.[1] Indeed both films were part of a revitalization of religion and politics as elements of popular culture. Books for and against Bush and the war in Iraq and books for and against traditional Christianity occupied the best-sellers lists.

Somewhere between ossified idioms and newly coined phrases are the "metaphors we live by," the stock comparative descriptions we prereflectively use to comprehend the ever-changing world around us.[2] With such metaphors, we think *through* popular culture; it shapes the content of our thought. To be sure, popular culture does not supply all of "the metaphors we live by," but it does supply many. Just consider how much the language of baseball has become the language of America. Interviewers ask softball questions for politicians to knock out of the park. Teenagers try to get to second base on the first date. At work we strike out, we hit homeruns, we take one for the team. Our estimates are in the ballpark, but our adversaries are not even in the same league, and, as for football, that's a whole different ballgame. We describe our odd moments like *Seinfeld* episodes: we avoid close talkers, we eschew the pop in, we put things "in the vault," "not that there's anything wrong with that," and yada yada yada.

Popular culture itself is sensitive to our and its own proclivity to think through it. Nowhere is this clearer than in popular culture's practice of including allusions to other pieces of popular culture. *The Simpsons* is a prime example with its constant references to other television shows past and present as well as to popular music, movies, and so on. Rap music's "sampling" and its ubiquitous references to other rappers and gangster popular culture are practically constitutive of the genre.

As we continually adopt and internalize the references and metaphors of popular culture, we are reminded of the perennial question: Does art imitate life or does life imitate art? In the case of popular culture, often life does imitate art, as real wise guys mimic screen mobsters from *The Godfather, Goodfellas,* and *The Sopranos.* Less glamorously, some of us live in a *Dilbert* cartoon. Art imitates life as gossip and office politics is played out on a desert island on *Survivor* or—who would believe it?—in an office on *The Apprentice.* Realizing how much popular culture has taken over American culture, it becomes more understandable why those outside the United States commonly resent the way American popular culture, from Hollywood movies to Kentucky Fried Chicken, has colonized their lands.

Still, even people who despise American popular culture will, upon reflection, admit they like some of it for at least some reasons. Though a good number of the articles in this book deal with popular art in particular, popular culture is vast and encompasses more than just popular art. Among other things, sports, games, and hobbies are all part of popular culture. Few can honestly say they have no interest in or appreciation for any of these. Even if we restrict our focus to popular art, can many honestly say that they have no interest in or appreciation for any element of popular art? Some may dislike popular music; others may dislike television; fewer dislike movies; and fewer still dislike all of the above. Many are defensive about the popular art they like, quick to be clear that they don't take it seriously. As Richard Shusterman notes, such folks want to be clear that they consume popular art for diversionary, entertainment purposes only.[3]

With each generation in modern America, the tolerance for popular culture seems to increase. Surely the older generation may tend not to like or appreciate the popular culture of the younger generation, but importantly they tend not to despise its genres. Dwindling are the numbers of those who think rock music is inherently worthless. Some may think there hasn't been much, or any, *good* rock music since the '60s or any *good* movies since the '50s, but most are not opposed to rock or cinema per se. Likely rap music and video games will someday achieve similar acceptance, perhaps as rock and movies become practically elite art like jazz and theater. Acceptance takes time.

WHY ENGAGE POPULAR CULTURE?

Philosophy ignores popular culture at its peril. As a discipline, we have had a public relations problem for a couple of centuries now, so engagement with popular culture is not an opportunity we can afford to miss. And it is an opportunity other disciplines have already seized. Literature departments regularly teach courses in popular culture; Bowling Green State University has America's first Department of Popular Culture; and Syracuse University has a Department of Television, Radio, and Film. Film studies departments have become common, part of the establishment, in some places even part of the old guard.

But still, why should *philosophers* engage popular culture? Philosophy is the love of wisdom, and it is the philosopher's task to seek wisdom wherever it may be found, even on television. To exclude popular culture from philosophical consideration is to exclude much of the art and culture that is dear to people.

This book is the mirror image of books such as *The Simpsons and Philosophy*, which aim to bring people from popular culture to philosophy; this book invites philosophers to engage with popular culture. Contributors to this book all share the unstated premise that popular culture is worthy of consideration by philosophers. Still, the essays are not univocal in their reasons for taking this premise for granted.

Popular culture is the sea in which we swim, providing ample fodder for philosophical dialogue. Socratic pedagogy and public relations outreach are the most agreed-upon reasons that philosophy can and should consider popular culture. But perhaps philosophers themselves can actually learn from popular culture, and the narratives of popular culture may even provide means for doing philosophy. Engagement with popular culture can bring the philosopher back to the agora, or at least to the mall. To be a philosopher is to be engaged with the world around you and its culture, unless of course you're a cynic. Unfortunately, academic philosophy has become more and more remote from the life and concerns of ordinary people, and thus unable to properly serve humanity. Philosophy begins in wonder, and wonder remains the touchstone of the philosopher. As popular culture tends to be at the cutting edge of technology, philosophy, a discipline not often associated with the cutting edge, can keep current with what is wondrous and on guard against what is horrifying by reflecting on popular culture. Particularly in the realm of technology, it is not just ethics and aesthetics but metaphysics and epistemology that can benefit from engagement with popular culture.

Popular culture doesn't simply provide interesting objects of interpretation. It helps raise interesting philosophical questions about the nature of artistic production and interpretation. Popular culture also readily raises issues of taste and objectivity in judgment. To avoid popular culture is for philosophers to avoid an honest appraisal of what entertains and attracts us. Some see intelligent interest in popular culture as a bridge to interest in high art. Others see no real difference between high art and the art of popular culture.

For all of these reasons, philosophy should engage popular culture.

POPULAR CULTURE AND HIGH CULTURE

At first glance, joining popular culture and philosophy appears to be pairing the perishable with the perennial. The ancient quarrel between the philosophers and the poets speaks to philosophy's uneasy relationship with art in general. Though many philosophers continue to find art inferior to philosophy, few, if any, fully share Plato's worries about the corrupting influence of art. It is acceptable for philosophers to discuss Schönberg, but it is not clearly acceptable for them to discuss the Beatles, "nevermind" Nirvana. Philosophers generally consider high art ennobling and worthy of attention, but many philosophers continue to look on popular art and culture full of Plato's fears.

But we may wonder: Is there a real difference in kind between high art and popular art and culture?

Whether or not there is a difference, there are lots of labels. Thanks to Van Wyck Brooks, we have the colorful and class-conscious terms *highbrow* and *lowbrow*.[4] And at least since Dwight MacDonald coined the term *midcult* in 1957, the race has been on to subdivide culture.[5] Norman Rockwell paintings, by the way, are perhaps the paradigms of midcult.[6] In his seminal *Popular Culture and High Culture*, the sociologist Herbert J. Gans speaks of five taste publics and cultures: high culture, upper-middle culture, lower-middle culture, low culture, and quasi-folk low culture.[7] Sociologists aside, most culture critics seem content to deconstruct the dichotomy, breaking the binary of highbrow and lowbrow with middlebrow.[8]

Biting the binary bullet, the essays in this volume speak of popular culture and high culture, mindful of the problems with the terms and concepts. Akin to the analytic/Continental divide, the terms of the binary do not complement one another. To speak of high culture and low culture, as we sometimes do, would make more sense and would give at least the appearance of complementarity. "Popular culture" does not as readily suggest a companion concept, as the obvious "unpopular culture" is too negative. *Popular* suggests that many people like or partake of it. *Esoteric* might suggest its opposite but does not seem apposite. Perhaps *exclusive* would work, but then again, perhaps not, as its natural companion would be *inclusive*, which surely would not work. Add to this the use of *popular culture* interchangeably with *popular art*, as though they were synonymous, when in fact *popular culture* is much broader in its domain. Note, too, that *high art* may well be one of those unfortunate descriptive terms, such as *classical music* and *postmodern*, that does not accurately or informatively describe what it names. The point is clear: the terms are infelicitous. Still, we are stuck with them, at least for the moment.

While postmodernism has made fashionable the breakdown of the distinction between high and low art, most of the essays in this book presume that although there is no hard line or distinction between popular and high art, the distinction is helpful nonetheless. There are often typical or characteristic differences that make it worthwhile to speak of popular art and popular culture. Notably, high art tends to be difficult to access and comprehend whereas popular culture tends to be easy. Part of the appeal of popular culture is that it often strikes us as art that "I could do." The museumgoer who remarks—rightly or wrongly—of a painting in the Guggenheim, "I could do that," means, "that's not very good." But the legions of teenagers who heard the Beatles on *The Ed Sullivan Show* and said, "I could do that," meant, "This is terrific. Now I know what I want to do with my life."

Gans notes that "[t]he choice of high culture typically requires at least a high-quality college education with strong emphasis on the humanities."[9] While it is difficult to say what popular culture is, it is easier to say what it is not. Taking our cue from Gans and checking our intuition with ordinary language, we might say popular culture does not require for its proper appreciation money or education beyond the average or norm. This is not to say that it is necessarily easy or cheap, but simply that it does not project an aura of wealth or education that would exclude anyone.

With all the difficulty it involves, *popular culture* would seem a good candidate for elimination in favor of a more fitting term. Noël Carroll, for example, has argued for use of the term *mass art*.[10] Still, in this volume, we follow ordinary language in which *popular culture* remains, frankly, popular. Though Carroll and other authors included in this volume do employ *mass art* and other terms, we take *popular culture* as our point of departure.

THE HIGH AND LOW OF ART FORMS AND GENRES
To speak of culture in terms of "high and low" is, in part, to think in terms of "metaphors we live by," implying oppressor and oppressed.[11] Under the influence of Pierre Bordieu, who famously argues in *Distinction* that cultural capital serves the purpose of continuing the distinction between classes, John Storey maintains that the category of popular culture was actually invented as a way of preserving and legitimating class distinctions.[12] This may well be true, but it seems almost irrelevant. Today, at least in America, class is no longer the cultural divider it once was. As Gans notes, in the revised and updated version of *Popular Culture and High Culture*, most people today are "omnivores," not restricting their culture consumption to any of his five categories, nor, we might note, to either side of the high-low divide.[13]

Part of the reason for omnivorous taste may be, as Ted Cohen argues in "High and Low Art, and High and Low Audiences," that different people can like the same piece of high or low art for different, even mutually exclusive, reasons.[14] Being an omnivore does not imply slumming. A Bobo—bohemian bourgeois—may like *Pulp Fiction* for its urbane wit, whereas Joe Sixpack may like it for the graphic violence and uncensored language. There is nothing new in this, though; the groundlings and the seatlings tended to like the gravedigger's scene in *Hamlet* for different reasons too.

Even with the breakdown in the division between high and low, some still resent the intrusion of the popular on the high. Witness the clash between Oprah Winfrey and Jonathan Franzen when the queen of talk selected *The Corrections* for her fabulously successful book club. Franzen, who fancies himself a serious literary artist, had misgivings about being Oprah's selection, noting that he had not always admired her past choices. A public debate broke out in the media, and Franzen came off looking pretty bad.[15]

There are art forms and genres that currently exclude either the popular or the high. But genres that in the past excluded the high, such as theater, now include it, in fact are predominated by it. Genres that excluded the popular, such as twentieth-century orchestral music, now find twentieth-century rock music performed by leading philharmonics. Indeed, Haydn quartets, the epitome of high culture, were commonly played in pubs at one time.[16]

Opera seems safely outside popular culture, though this was not always the case. The operas of Mozart and Rossini were popular culture in their day.[17] Indeed, before the nineteenth century, and perhaps for most of it, opera was an element of popular culture.[18] If rock operas, such as The Who's *Tommy*, are indeed considered operas, then the genre is not as exclusive as it first appears. *Tommy* to the side, opera has been making a comeback as popular culture in recent years via advertising and the Three Tenors.[19] Concerts cut both ways. Rock concerts are part of popular culture, and symphony orchestra concerts are part of high culture. Interestingly, the ticket prices are for all intents and purposes the same.

Plays, though popular culture in the classical world, Middle Ages, and the Renaissance—Shakespeare was even popular culture in nineteenth-century America—are now nearly exclusively high.[20] Though the borders and boundaries are not nearly as firm as they once were, in present-day America, there continues to be some correlation between socioeconomic status and cultural tastes.[21] As Gans notes of theater, museums, and symphonies, "In the United States poor and moderate-income people often feel uncomfortable even at cultural institutions that charge no admission but are designed for the more affluent."[22] Here we do see the popular and the high strangely divided along socioeconomic lines. Most Broadway plays are not particularly difficult nor are they always extraordinarily expensive; some—such as *The Lion King*—are even overtly popular/low; yet their audiences skew wealthy and "cultured." Going to the theater is something wealthy, cultured people do, even when the tickets are free or reasonable.

With the advent of mass technology, plays have become inefficient cultural vehicles, as theaters hold only a limited number of people and usually charge admission. By contrast, a practically unlimited number of people can see a network television program at no upfront cost. Television would seem to be exclusively the domain of popular art. A television show, no matter how finely done, will not be regarded as fine art, at least not today. Yet the divisions blur again when we realize that some public broadcasting stations air opera and ballet performances.

Movies provide an interesting case. Certainly in the beginning they were all considered low or popular culture, but that is no longer so. Some filmmakers consciously make what are sometimes called art films. Indeed, small theaters often cater to screening these films, commonly made independently of big studios. On average, even commercially successful art films, such as *II* (pi), are more difficult and less accessible than are mainstream Hollywood movies, such as *A Beautiful Mind*.

Painting appears at first to be exclusively the domain of high art, though, for example, many medieval paintings were not considered high at the time. Original paintings find it hard to penetrate the popular. For example, pop art à la Andy Warhol, even when it engaged popular culture in the form of Campbell's Soup cans and Marilyn Monroe, did not itself become popular culture. It was too avant-garde and wittier-than-thou to have pop appeal. Norman Rockwell prints, by contrast, have major pop appeal. Still, folksy origin does not necessarily mean midcult or low status, as, for example, primitive paintings by Jamaican artists have become coveted by collectors. Today's inexpensive prints, notably the forested cottages of Thomas Kinkade, are often popular midcult kitsch. Some paintings even skew low, as for example the clichéd black velvet Elvis or dogs playing poker. And if we extend painting to include spray-paint graffiti and tattoos, clearly not all painting is high art. Sculpture, we might note, would seem to be the domain of high art, though certainly there is no reason we could not have pop sculpture.

The novel includes both the popular and the high. At one time, though, the novel was considered solely the domain of the popular and the common, and today many think of the novel as high. *The Da Vinci Code* is certainly not considered high art and is immensely popular. And, strangely, Oprah has made popular the classics *East of Eden* and *Anna Karenina*. Comic books and graphic novels may be exclusively the domain of popular culture, though works of literature have been adapted to fit their format, and it is conceivable that with time some comic books will come to be considered canonical works of art rather than mere popular art. Surely this has happened with film, though at one point few would have thought it likely or even possible.

QUESTIONS AND ISSUES

Much that may be true of popular culture may also be true of high culture and art, but we sometimes come to understand both better by examining each of them separately. The essays in part I of this volume, "Philosophy and Popular Culture," look at theoretical issues raised in engagement with popular culture. They include the use of popular culture as a vehicle for communicating philosophy, the possibility of doing philosophy through popular culture, the function of allusion in popular culture, the nature of our emotional ties to the characters of popular fictions, our aesthetic and ethical obligations to prefer the good, and the value of entertainment.

Can we learn from art? Does art have anything to offer philosophy? Ethical criticism, in which typically high-art narratives from the likes of *Middlemarch* and *Remembrance of Things Past* are used to discuss and illustrate ethical theory, brings some peace to the ancient quarrel. In "Philosophy and the Probable Impossible," Carolyn Korsmeyer argues that popular culture, with its probable impossible plot lines à la *The Matrix*, is an improbable but possible (indeed excellent) vehicle for the dissemination of philosophy. And the benefits flow both ways, as a strong line of philosophical thought can be a dramatic aid to a popular narrative. Korsmeyer takes *philosophy* as a success term referring to "works demanding imaginative engagement that results in the recognition, and perhaps the acceptance, of a philosophical position, such that what is done in philosophy proper that induces a plausible conclusion, is done in another genre by means appropriate to its appreciation." Given this understanding, Korsmeyer argues that philosophy itself can actually be conducted by narrative, including popular narrative. For example, the second season of the television show *Angel* makes the case for an existentialist ethics akin to, but independent of, Simone de Beauvoir's in *The Ethics of Ambiguity*.

But should philosophy, like watching *Angel*, be fun? The essays in books such as *Seinfeld and Philosophy* are generally written with tongue in cheek and nonacademics in mind. Is the commercial success of such books to be celebrated or feared? And what, after all, is popular culture? In "Philosophy as/and/of Popular Culture," I argue that popular culture comprises artifacts and subjects of mass interest and appreciation. Philosophy is *not* an element of popular culture, though in principle it could become one. Heeding warnings of "the closing of the American mind" and "the dumbing down of America," I consider whether any of the intellectual, political, or moral concerns about, or criticisms of, popular culture are such as to outweigh the good that can come of the philosophy *and* popular culture connection. I argue that they do not. Indeed, the example of Socrates makes clear that one must not only return to the cave but learn to see the shadows again in order to tell the prisoners about the world outside in terms they will grasp. I argue that *studying* popular culture *as* philosophy rather than *using* it for examples and communication would be abuse, at least abuse of philosophy, the kind of abuse that some mistakenly fear is already taking place in the philosophy *and* popular culture hybrid. There are methodological questions for the study of popular art that might come under the heading of "philosophy *of* popular culture," but these are just the same methodological questions and issues raised by aesthetics and its branches. The only unique question for "philosophy *of* popular culture" would be, What is popular culture?

Disposable references, allusions, and "in" jokes are an important part of popular culture. Much high art seems to be written or created "for the ages," whereas popular art seems to be written simply for the age, or, really, the moment, like a sandcastle to be enjoyed before the tide wipes it away. Noticing and understanding allusions is key to appreciation of high art. Through allusion, artists link, critique, and pay tribute. Does ubiquitous allusion in popular culture do more than adorn and entertain? Does it serve a better purpose?

In "Allusion and Intention in Popular Art," Theodore Gracyk distinguishes artistic from nonartistic allusion, specifying that in artistic allusion both the source text and the alluding text are works of art. Drawing examples from *The Matrix*, the Bangles, and Woody Allen, among others, Gracyk argues against Monroe Beardsley and Joseph Pucci that allusion is intentional. Grice's theory of conversational implicature and Randy Newman's "I Love L.A." aid Gracyk in arguing and illustrating that many popular artworks are intended to convey ideas they do not overtly present. In terms of speech act theory, then, an illocutionary intention to allude includes a perlocutionary intention to bring about an effect beyond mere recognition of the intention to allude—directing the audience to a specific source and suggesting a new interpretation of the alluding text. Characteristic of popular art is that its allusions are functional, working seamlessly even if not detected. In this way, allusions in popular art can be obscure without disrupting the text. For example, one does not have to catch the allusion to Lewis Carroll's *Sylvie and Bruno* to understand why Neo chooses the red pill in *The Matrix*. Gracyk concludes that the abundance of artistic allusion in popular art is a useful pedagogical link to high art.

Allusion aids in bonding audiences to authors and texts. Yet we react emotionally to fiction in part because we tie ourselves to characters. How do we become emotionally tied to them? The most ancient and still the most common explanation is identification. But in "On the Ties that Bind: Characters, the Emotions, and Popular Fictions," Noël Carroll argues that identification does not withstand scrutiny. If we truly identified with characters, we would expect to be in the same emotional states as they are in, but clearly this often is not the case. Carroll also considers simulation theory, according to which we understand others by simulating them. We do this with people in everyday life, so the theory goes, and we naturally transfer this to fictional characters. But, Carroll argues, simulation cannot explain how our emotions may diverge wildly from those of the character we're supposedly simulating. What's more, simulation would take more time than the pace of popular fictions ordinarily allows. Some of what is mistakenly thought of as identification or simulation may be explained by mirror reflexes, a biological tendency to mimic the expressive behavior of another as a way of gaining insight into the other's inner state. Carroll argues that most of our emotional ties to fictional characters are best explained in terms of sympathy, a nonpassing pro-attitude, which by definition is directed at another. Sympathy in popular fiction is most often elicited by characters who command the audience's moral endorsement.

Our ties to characters in popular fictions are often guilty pleasures. The popular is commonly assumed to be not as good as so-called high art. I once made the mistake at an aesthetics conference of bringing my knowledge of heavy metal to bear on a discussion of the blues, admitting my ignorance of the latter. One discussant offered me her scorn and pity. She clearly thought me aesthetically, and perhaps morally, deficient. Incidentally, it seemed to be lost on her that the blues was not long ago considered among the lowest of the low art forms. But this bad experience raises a good question: Is there an aesthetic obligation to like what is better? To prefer high art to popular art?

While at first it may seem there is such an obligation, in "Liking What's Good: Why Should We?" Ted Cohen argues that there is no argument that would lead from a premise such as "Mozart's *Don Giovanni* is better than The Who's *Tommy*" to "It is better to like *Don Giovanni* than *Tommy*." At most, we could say it shows better taste to prefer *Don Giovanni*, but this leads to the question, Why is it better to have better taste? Because you will like better things? But why is it better to like better things? Even if somehow we could find our way out of this circle, how could we establish that "Mozart's *Don Giovanni* is better than The Who's *Tommy*"? Cohen argues that there actually is no way to establish that conclusion when considering the artworks as art, rather than as instruments for other concerns. Any reason the critic could give for saying one artwork is better than another will be unacceptable, ultimately even to the critic himself.

Cohen proposes that instead of looking to what could make one artwork better than another, we should look for what joins us to one another, namely our appreciation of certain works of art. We form aesthetic communities in our appreciation for certain works of art. So what, for example, do all people in the aesthetic community of *South Park* fans have in common? The very same thing that all artworks I like have in common: nothing. Still, aesthetic communities are worthy of attention, if only to show us how alike and at the same time how different we are.

Whether we should like it or not, popular culture is entertaining. In fact, a Discovery Channel slogan implores "Entertain Your Brain." Is that possible? Does the Discovery Channel actually provide entertainment for the brain or just predigested brain food? If *Baywatch* entertains the eyes and Top 40 radio entertains the ears—and to some extent the whole body as we groove to the beat—perhaps the Discovery Channel does entertain the brain. It does not ordinarily give the brain the workout that solving differential equations might, but it can stimulate some thought.

Whether or not it's possible to "entertain your brain," can there be value in entertainment? Popular culture is highly entertaining; it has to be to remain popular. Some elements and examples of popular culture may have value beyond entertainment value, but is there anything wrong with a work of art having value simply for purposes of entertainment? Is entertainment a kind of opium for the masses of which we need to beware?

Whereas aesthetic value is generally conceived as intrinsic, entertainment value is generally conceived as instrumental. In "Popular Art and Entertainment Value," Richard Shusterman offers a theory of entertainment that steers a middle way between mere subservience to and sheer defiance of high culture. Entertainment is often associated with vulgar pleasure seeking, but the pleasures of art and entertainment help maintain and enrich life. Against G. E. Moore's isolationist account of intrinsic value, Shusterman offers a pragmatic account of transactional value. That is, all values, including intrinsic values, are subject to change. Intrinsic value is not so much "in itself" as "for itself." A movie, for example, has intrinsic value when we enjoy it for the pleasure it provides and not just as a means of passing the time. Shusterman argues that the intrinsic value of a movie may be objective, but this does not mean it is permanent. Rather, the intrinsic value is transactional, belonging to a situation that is subject to change. Thus entertainment value may be instrumental in providing relaxation and revitalization, but it can also be intrinsic, providing enjoyment that is valued for itself.

Part II of this volume, "Interpretation and Popular Art Forms," focuses attention on art forms and genres typical of popular culture. It is commonly and mistakenly assumed that the art of popular culture is transparent and requires no interpretation. But in fact popular culture requires interpretation and raises hermeneutic issues, perhaps not uniquely but nonetheless in a focused way. Surely much popular culture is rich and complex enough to require interpretation in a rigorous sense, and in the different sense in which interpretation is simply understanding, popular culture always requires interpretation. We miss this when dwelling solely on high art, which commonly requires interpretation because of its complexity or cultural and historical distance.

Interpreting television shows, films, children's stories, comic books, and pop songs, several essays in this section raise economic, aesthetic, ethical, and political issues. Bringing a hermeneutic of suspicion to bear on photography, one essay even questions our ordinary conceptions of reality and our knowledge of it.

Partly because of the way they are made, television shows are rarely even considered for their artistic merit. A team of writers, pressured by executives mindful of the bottom line, produce a script that a director must get actors to execute. Sounds like a recipe for disaster, and often it is. But not always. In "Popular Culture and Spontaneous Order, or How I Learned to Stop Worrying and Love the Tube," Paul Cantor debunks an idea that we have inherited from Romantic aesthetics, that a work of art must issue from an autonomous creative genius free from the demands of the marketplace. The solitary artist as a godlike central planner creating de novo and ex nihilo is just not television reality. Many hands and minds are involved, and fan feedback, particularly now on fan websites, impacts a show's development. Drawing on his own research for *Gilligan Unbound* and Friedrich Hayek's notion of "spontaneous order," Cantor argues that the market can be an ordering and creative force. This is not true just for the likes of *The X-Files* and *Buffy the Vampire Slayer*, but historically has been true for the likes of Shakespeare and Dickens. Shakespeare's plays gave people what worked before and were tailored to the actors of the company, and Dickens's serialized novels took into account reader reactions as they were written. As Cantor sums it up, "Just because a television show is a commercial success does not mean that it is an artistic failure."

When something succeeds commercially, you can be sure it will be tried again. So it is no surprise that Hollywood studios devote so much of their capital to sequels. Hollywood also commonly interprets earlier source material. The movie remake, for example, seems to be something unique to popular culture, though it can later become enshrined in high culture as Shakespeare's remakes have. Putting on film earlier stories such as the Trojan War, the Gospels, King Kong, and the legend of King Arthur requires interpretation both from the filmmakers and the audience.

How can we explain the appeal and success of the continuing incarnations of certain works of popular culture? In "From Horror to Hero: Film Interpretations of Stoker's *Dracula*," Jorge Gracia examines six films: Murnau's *Nosferatu* (1922), Browning's *Dracula* (1931), Morrisey's *Dracula* (1974), Herzog's *Nosferatu: The Vampyre* (1979), Badham's *Dracula* (1979), and Coppola's *Bram Stoker's Dracula* (1992). What is the relation between these six films and Stoker's famous novel? Gracia argues that the films are not simply independent works dealing with common subject matter; nor do they share essential core elements, or even a Wittgensteinian family resemblance. Rather, the films are "relational interpretations" of the Stoker novel that are still themselves works in their own right. A relational interpretation does not take understanding the work or its meaning as its primary goal. Instead, as the name implies, it relates the work or its meaning to something else. The Dracula films relate the work to contemporary culture and concerns, thus making new the old, appealing to audiences and succeeding at the box office.

Children's stories are sometimes appreciated for their literary merit, but could they have philosophical merit? As we learn so much from children, can we actually learn something from stories for children? In "Socrates at Story Hour: Philosophy as a Subversive Motif in Children's Literature," Gareth Matthews argues that there is a rich vein of children's stories that can lead to wonderful philosophical discussion if we're willing to subvert the dominant epistemological paradigm of adult authority. For example, do you know the essential and accidental differences between a deer and a moose? Reading and discussing *Morris the Moose* with children very naturally leads to discussion of real and conventional kinds. Who better than children to teach us and humble us to say with Socrates, "I don't know"? There is hope for the future when parents in the present admit when they don't know the answers to their children's questions and show them how to find the answers not just by Googling them but by debating them à la Socrates. Children's literature is not just for bedtime anymore, and it's not just for children either.

Clearly, comic books and graphic novels are for children, "children of all ages." But can they teach us anything worthwhile? What hope is there for us to lead happy, meaningful lives in the modern world of corruption, technology, and moral decay? In "Of Batcaves and Clock Towers: Living Damaged Lives in Gotham City," James South offers ethical criticism of Batman comic books and graphic novels. Examining the fictional world of Gotham, South draws out the lessons to be learned in answer to the question: How should we live under conditions of damage? It is true that Bruce Wayne was damaged by witnessing the senseless murder of his parents, but perhaps more importantly, he lives in a damaged world—one in which technology encroaches on daily life and everyone and everything has its price. Unlike most superheroes, Batman has no superpowers, yet for some reason he chooses to dress like a bat and fight crime. Why? South argues we can understand Wayne's motivation as an attempt to give meaning to his otherwise "damaged" life. Drawing on J. M. Bernstein's *Adorno: Disenchantment and Ethics*, South applies the notion of "fugitive ethics" to the fictional world of Batman. Fugitive ethical acts can bring happiness to otherwise damaged lives. Still, such fugitive ethical acts come always at a price. For whatever happiness and meaning Wayne manages in his life as Batman, much is lost in exchange.

Rock music is emblematic of what many believe is worst in popular culture, a cause of damaged lives. Much of it lacks in substance and morality, delivering only mindless, debasing entertainment. Given that self-reflection and self-criticism are difficult—some would say impossible—for all art forms and systems of thought, we would not expect rock music to fare very well on these scores. Far from critiquing itself and its milieu, rock would seem to wallow obliviously in its own decadence. In "'American Pie' and the Self-critique of Rock 'n' Roll," Michael Baur spins the record differently, arguing that Don McLean's 1971 anthem, "American Pie," is highly impressive for its self-reflection and self-criticism of rock 'n' roll in the medium of rock 'n' roll itself. The owl of Minerva may fly only at dusk, but the beat of rock 'n' roll can self-consciously pulse to the zeitgeist.

While the most obvious philosophical connections to popular culture are ethical, political, and aesthetic, let us not forget the epistemological and metaphysical. It is not only sci-fi movies like *The Matrix* that readily raise questions such as "What is real?" and "How do you know?" Photography has been a democratizing force and element of popular culture since its inception. In "Photography, Popular Epistemology, Flexible Realism, and Holistic Pragmatism," Peter Hare addresses the question, How are photographic images related to reality? Both the belief that a photographic image is a mirror image of reality and the belief that a photographic image is a manipulation of reality are, and always have been, embedded in the popular culture. The advent of digital cameras and software such as Photoshop has made people all the more aware of the ways in which a photograph can manipulate reality. To deal with photographs, Hare proposes a "flexible realism" in which we make the defeasible presumption that a photograph is genuine. To test the presumption, we consider the venue in which the photograph is published, context, and what is at stake, making adjustments in epistemic standards as needed. One size does not fit all when it comes to epistemic justification.

CONCLUSION

Aristotle took seriously and analyzed the popular art of his time, the tragedies and epics. Why should philosophers today not do likewise? While it is not the *Poetics*, this book is a beginning. Hopefully it offers some wisdom and insight and makes clear the importance and the value of philosophy's engagement with contemporary popular culture.

NOTES

1. Sharon Waxman, "Two Americas of 'Fahrenheit' and 'Passion'; Urban Moviegoers for Anti-Bush Documentary, Suburban Audience for Religious Epic," *New York Times,* July 13, 2004, E1.

2. George Lakoff and Mark Johnson, *Metaphors We Live By* (Chicago: University of Chicago Press, 1980).

3. Richard Shusterman, "Entertainment: A Question for Aesthetics," *British Journal of Aesthetics* 43 (2003): 289–307.

4. Van Wyck Brooks, *America's Coming of Age* (Garden City, NY: Anchor Books, Doubleday, 1958); and Russell Lynes, "Highbrow, Middlebrow, Lowbrow," chap. 13 in *The Tastemakers* (New York: Harper & Brothers, 1954).

5. Dwight MacDonald, "A Theory of Mass Culture," reprinted in *Cultural Theory and Popular Culture: A Reader,* ed. John Storey, 2nd ed. (Hemel Hempstead: Prentice Hall, 1998), 22–36.

6. Chris Lehmann, *Revolt of the Masscult* (Chicago: Prickly Paradigm Press, 2003), 22.

7. Herbert J. Gans, *Popular Culture and High Culture: An Analysis and Evaluation of Taste,* revised and updated (New York: Basic Books, 1999), 100–20.

8. John Seabrook, though, has given us "nobrow." See his *Nobrow: The Culture of Marketing and the Marketing of Culture* (New York: Vintage Books, 2001), which was roundly criticized by Curtis White, clearly a hair above all brows, in *The Middle Mind: Why Americans Don't Think for Themselves* (New York: HarperCollins, 2003).

9. Gans, 169.

10. Noël Carroll, *A Philosophy of Mass Art* (Oxford: Oxford University Press, 1998), 184–211.

11. Julian Johnson, *Who Needs Classical Music?: Cultural Choice and Musical Value* (Oxford: Oxford University Press, 2002), 111; Lakoff and Johnson, 15–16.

12. John Storey, *Inventing Popular Culture: From Folklore to Globalization* (Oxford: Blackwell, 2003), xi.

13. Gans, 9; Storey, 46.

14. Ted Cohen, "High and Low Art, and High and Low Audiences," *The Journal of Aesthetics and Art Criticism* 57 (1999): 141.

15. Lehman, 7–18.

16. Johnson, 49.

17. Johnson, 49.

18. Storey, 36–37, 77.

19. Storey, 74–75.

20. Storey, 35.

21. Gans, 18–19.

I

PHILOSOPHY AND POPULAR CULTURE

2

Philosophy and the Probable Impossible

Carolyn Korsmeyer

The suppressed term in the conjunction of philosophy and popular culture is "unpopular," which implicitly modifies philosophy. The popular-unpopular opposition is often used to measure artistic or intellectual quality by audience size: the more popular, the more suspect, a view suggesting a vaguely pessimistic assumption about human nature en masse. Together these implications seem to place philosophical texts alongside fine art in longstanding debates over the distinction between so-called high culture and low or popular culture—conceived as that which is designed to divert and amuse rather than to enlighten.[1] This theme with variations appears throughout the history of philosophy. Perhaps the most broadly based version emerged in the eighteenth and nineteenth centuries with theories of aesthetic judgment and taste. Taste is supposedly a common human sensibility that has the potential to be developed in virtually all audiences. Yet ironically, the wider the enjoyment, the more dubious the object enjoyed.[2]

There are indeed some ways in which the affinity between philosophy and fine art matches the high-low debate. The audiences for both high culture and philosophy are as a rule relatively small—meeting the approval of those for whom good taste is of necessity rare. Because they appear likely to draw upon similar kinds of educational demands, the audiences for high art and for philosophy might be presumed to share more members with each other than either does with audiences for popular culture, though this is a contestable empirical claim.[3] Certainly both fine art and philosophy arrogate to themselves a degree of seriousness and enduring value that they deny popular entertainment, and defenders of the latter are apt to share critic Ian Shuttleworth's view of "genre snobbery," which is "the snobbery of a sense of mainstream high culture: that works in certain areas cannot speak as valuably about various subjects as deliberately self-consciously literary or cultural works can."[4]

Despite certain parallels, however, there are also numerous differences between the philosophy–popular culture issue and the high-low debates. First of all, many of the same problems arise with the relationship between philosophy and high or fine art that arise between philosophy and popular art. Debates over whether philosophy can be well conducted in a narrative form are apt to ponder literary works of decidedly "high" status, such as *Middlemarch, The Golden Bowl, Antigone,* or *The Remembrance of Things Past.* (Or to invoke more contemporary works: the difficult—sometimes near unreadable— works of authors such as Calvino, Borges, and Eco.)[5] Doubts about such works' claims to philosophical status are the same as those that arise with *Star Trek, The Matrix,* or *Winnie the Pooh.* Therefore the relationship of philosophy to artistic works is similarly problematic whether those works count as high or low, though there is one important exception: the approach to literature that goes by the name of "ethical criticism" defends some narrative texts as complements to philosophical ethics on the grounds that extended absorption in works of worthy artistic vision sensitizes the imagination to moral complexity and the points of view of others.[6] The works that serve as exemplars for ethical critics are as a rule narratives whose qualifications as high art are indisputable. Popular cultural forms such as blockbuster movies and television series do not receive much defense from ethical criticism. These genres will be the focus of my consideration.

A rather crude argument that would in principle remove philosophy from popular culture pursues a line of reasoning something like this: Popular culture is fun. Fun things are easy.[7] Easy things are never philosophy. Therefore popular culture can't be (or do) philosophy. Philosophy is vulnerable to a lot of criticisms, but it has never been accused of being easy. Moreover, difficulty is supposedly a signal of worth. As Spinoza observes at the close of the *Ethics,* "All things excellent are as difficult as they are rare." Pierre Bourdieu more skeptically relates the easy to the difficult when he remarks, "In cultural consumption, the main opposition . . . is between the practices designated by their rarity as distinguished . . . and the practices socially identified as vulgar because they are both easy and common."[8] However, even if one deems items of low culture to be easy and vulgar, they may still beguile. As Ovid remarks in *Metamorphosis* 7:20, "We scan and approve of the better; we go for the worse." In this case, the "we" is general. It does not separate the audiences of high from low culture but suggests a lazy or perverse tendency in everyone to let go of a perilous cling at the top of prickly cultural peaks and slide comfortably down to smoother terrain. Ovid reminds us of the phenomenon of aesthetic *akrasia*: *valuing* things that we recognize as fine, but *preferring* to spend our time with that which is less demanding. In such a way, the culture wars become internal strife.

Since pop culture is not a candidate for the defense mounted by ethical criticism, genre snobbery places it twice removed from philosophy, a long step below high art, which is itself already removed from the properly philosophical. The rest of my remarks will be devoted to examining several hierarchies assumed in the relationship between philosophy and popular culture, including the notions of entertainment and learning, easy and difficult, and the complex and stubborn opposition between emotional response and rational deliberation. A good deal of appreciative response to any art, but perhaps especially to popular art, comprises emotional arousal. Noël Carroll opens his essay in this volume by noting, "The emotions, to an arresting degree, are the ties that bind us to popular fictions." The engagement of emotions is one of the venerable features of entertainment that supposedly separates it from philosophy.

ENTERTAINMENT AND EDUCATION: THE FUN AND THE NOT SO FUN

One of the several ways to parse the relationship between philosophy and popular culture is to consider pop culture as a vehicle for philosophy, and this is the reading I shall pursue. The metaphor "vehicle" is suitably multipurpose, for philosophy might simply be carried along like luggage, or even more incidentally like a stone picked up by a tire that taps along for a while before dropping off. But sometimes philosophy can also be identified with the engine or the wheels, the ideas inseparable from the conveyance.

Currently, the accessibility of philosophy when approached by means of popular culture is being exploited by teachers and publishers; witness titles such as *Philosophy Goes to the Movies* and *Philosophy through Film*, in addition to the success of the books in Bill Irwin's Popular Culture and Philosophy series.[9] In these cases, stories—and "stories" is shorthand here for the pop narratives of TV and movies—deftly point in the direction of philosophies whose abstract or austere style is initially daunting.[10] Recognizing the mutual illumination of philosophic and narrative texts is by no means new: the style of Sterne's *Tristram Shandy* comes into focus when aligned with Locke's empiricism and the theory of associated ideas, and Elizabethan Neoplatonism sufficiently pervades Shakespeare's plays to reward comparison of his works and Plato's, to mention two now somewhat unfashionable examples. Protectors of disciplinary distinctions, however, worry that the nuances of theoretical issues will nearly always be lost without the space of standard philosophical discourse in which they are best articulated. But the worry travels in both directions: defenders of entertaining narrative recognize that patches of extended argument become didactic and boring, and they too may believe that the very forms of these genres are incompatible. The genre snobbery of philosophy cannot be palliated with an appeal to the high quality of some popular narrative arts, for it is precisely the fact that they are narratives at all that raises the issue. So we find ourselves back in the center of the very oldest dispute in philosophy of art: whether an object, experience, or event that is an engaging story can also be an object, experience, or event that is a pathway to philosophical understanding. So we might as well begin at the beginning.

Plato's famous warnings against mimesis in the *Republic* pit the (difficult) activities of the rational soul against the (easier) pleasures that attend the senses and the emotions, warning that enjoyment is never harmless because it diverts the mind and weakens the intellect's governance over the whole person. Aristotle's counterpoint sees philosophy and poetry as closer allies, for while Plato stodgily held a literalist criterion of truth for poetic imitation, Aristotle on occasion found fiction superior to fact. As he puts it in a famous passage from the *Poetics*, poetry is more philosophic than history, since it explores universals (what could happen) rather than particulars (what actually did happen). He even goes on to declare, "Events which are impossible but plausible should be preferred to those which are possible but implausible."[11] Or to put it in the words of an older, somewhat hyperbolic translation which I prefer for its tongue-twisting charm: when faced with the choice, a poet should opt for the probable impossible over the possible improbable. In this usage, "probable" refers to a psychological effect, describing plots and scenarios that are emotionally and dramatically compelling but might not survive scrutiny of fact—or perhaps even of logic. Aristotle licenses pursuit of the philosophic in the realms of imagination and fantasy, including by (long) extension the popular contemporary "probable impossibilities" of science fiction and horror so prevalent in movies and television.

VEHICLES OF LEARNING

While some, such as Horace in *Ars Poetica*, praise the pleasure afforded by art as an invitation to learning, others suspect that entertainment is only a cheap and easy route around the pains of real education. We can dismiss outright the stricter versions of this suspicion because they are simply silly. Think of Alexander Pope's snobbish declaration from the *Essay on Criticism*: "A little learning is a dang'rous thing / Drink deep, or taste not the Pierian spring: / There shallow droughts intoxicate the brain, / And drinking largely sobers us again."[12]

But a little learning is not a dangerous thing. Nobody can know everything. And unless one wants to limit oneself to Plato's perplexingly narrow specializations (for he claims that no one can do more than one thing well), the only alternative to a little learning about a lot of things is complete ignorance about all of them. And precisely because they are "easier" in some sense of that term, popular cultural forms furnish marvelous ways to learn about a host of things that are the proper purview of some academic discipline, including not only philosophy but also history, medicine, and the various sciences. To take a random sampling from my own informal education, I learned about worm holes, warp speed, nanotechnology, Napier's constant (the basis of logarithms), the Crusades, fifteenth-century Italian banking, the legend of El Dorado, and the Yukon gold rush from, respectively, *Star Trek*, *The X-files*, Scott's *Ivanhoe*, Dorothy Dunnett's *House of Niccolo* novels, and Scrooge McDuck comic books. In fact, my favored rendition of the line from the *Poetics* quoted above was suggested to me by Lord Peter Wimsey.[13] I'm sure we could all furnish our own lists. A few things one discovers from such diverting entertainment might be areas to which one later returns to drink deep from the relevant section of the Pierian spring, but most are not. They do, however, furnish breadth to imagination and recognition of the knowledge of others.

Where does philosophy fit into this mode of learning? How shallow is the Pierian rivulet that dispenses philosophy in a popular form? There are obviously many fields of study that are invoked as part of plot and drama, whether accurately or inaccurately, clumsily or with flair. Do philosophy's popular forms pose any special worries? It is surely not the most difficult or intellectually demanding field of learning to be integrated into popular narratives, nor is it the most readily misunderstood. One of the sciences frequently employed in television dramas, for comparison, is physics in its most recondite varieties. Relativity, string theory, quantum mechanics, and cosmology are pressed into service in science fiction and fantasy—indeed, without them, there would be no way to propel certain plots, such as those involving time travel, portals to alternate dimensions, or visits of aliens from other galaxies. I suppose sometimes the discoveries of physics are used more or less accurately for entertainment purposes, though probably more frequently they are invoked just quickly enough to establish the impression of a plausible plot line and then glossed over with a device that I call the "Mulder-somehow." The Mulder-somehow is an indispensable tool for presenting the probable impossible. It is a script segue that moves quickly from one element of dialogue to the next without leaving time for skepticism, as in statements such as "somehow there must have been a tear in the space-time continuum" to explain how two bodies can occupy the same space; or declarations that Einstein predicts the possibility of "some kind of time warp, a rift in space" to explain how a ship enters the Bermuda triangle in 1939 and emerges in 1998; or—an egregious case—"somehow you got into my dreams . . . and through that you got access to my memories."[14] This *somehow* is not the exclusive property of Fox Mulder, of course, nor is it always expressed explicitly. It is a symptom of a narrative moment when a difficult idea from science that one dimly recognizes is invoked quickly and briefly to lend plausibility to an otherwise fairly lunatic plot. For instance, we see it in an episode of *Buffy the Vampire Slayer* with Rupert Giles's revelation as to how a slighted teenager unkindly ignored by her peers could have become actually invisible: "Of course!" he exclaims, "I was looking for a mystical solution when I should have been thinking of the quantum-mechanical!"[15] It helps a great deal with the Mulder-somehow that hardly anyone truly understands a verbal account of phenomena that are properly expressed in lengthy mathematical formulae. In fact, mathematics itself provides another version of the Mulder-somehow: chalkboards full of mathematical symbols have become a visual stand-in for the fact that someone in a story is about to discover something crucial that itself will not receive any additional explanation. A scientist who appears in an episode of *Angel* scribbles a cascade of calculations that will make it possible for him to freeze time by "removing an infinitesimal space-time aggregate from all that surrounds it."[16] He can't get the math right, but a demon comes along and rewrites his formula successfully; thus do math and magic align . . . somehow. Nor is this use of math limited to science fiction or fantasy; plots of the crime drama *Numbers* depend almost entirely upon a rapid dazzle of mathematics.

It may be a disadvantage that philosophy does not have an equivalent of the Mulder-somehow, that tag on a comment that indicates there is much knowledge alluded to that "somehow" in an undisclosed way explains a crucial bit of plot. It appears that complex philosophical ideas are so rooted in terminology and arguments that they are hard to extract from their precise formulations. But if extended argumentation is dramatically impossible, an anxious concern might go, then philosophy is distorted by appearing to be complete in the story in which it is evoked. Is this a significant worry? Perhaps so. It is certainly more than mere genre snobbery, for unlike physics or mathematics, which are importantly alluded to by plot gestures that refer to a body of knowledge *external* to the story, philosophy is a candidate for actually being *conducted by* the narrative itself; philosophical ideas sufficiently integrated into narrative are *internal* to the work—at least when they are effectively and cleverly developed.[17]

DRAMATIC PHILOSOPHY AND PHILOSOPHICAL DRAMA

The most obvious connection of philosophy and popular culture is pedagogical: movies and TV shows can be used to illustrate a number of philosophical problems or positions. Thinking computers such as Hal and R2-D2 enliven questions about the nature of mind, plots that feature a switch of bodies or bodily appearance prompt speculation about the conditions of personal identity, and so forth. Indeed, considered simply as illustrations that illuminate standard philosophical issues, story lines are usually superior to the examples commonly introduced into philosophical texts, such as familiar farfetched thought experiments about brains in vats, twin earths, and runaway trolleys.

However, stories are not merely illustrations of independently articulated philosophical positions. The closer union of the two is indicated by the fact that a well-developed philosophical position in a story makes the *story* better—not just more educational, but *better narrative art*. For just as compelling examples and illustrative cases *enhance philosophical analysis*, so a strong philosophical line of thought is a *dramatic advantage*. This is worth emphasizing: if philosophical essays are clarified and made persuasive with the judicious inclusion of illustrative examples to explain and convince (and most certainly they are), it is also the case that a story is made stronger and more compelling if the philosophy it evinces is presented thoughtfully and thoroughly, as well as cleverly. Not to grant this is to fall into a sort of reverse genre snobbery: assuming that a persuasively structured sequence of ideas is irrelevant to the power of a theoretical position. Such reverse snobbery is in fact the deceptive pose of Socrates, who slyly claimed to be a poor speaker, although Plato's dialogues themselves stand out for their dramatic structure and poetry. Indeed, some of Plato's most persuasive arguments rely heavily on strong story lines. The most famous passage of the *Meno* pictures the wealthy citizen Meno, slightly huffy and impatient, watching as Socrates scratches lines in the dust and an enthusiastic young slave discovers that he (more or less) knows the Pythagorean theorem. Without this story structure, where readers are led to hope that the boy demonstrates the knowledge that Socrates says sleeps within him, I doubt very many would be persuaded for a minute of Plato's preposterous conclusion regarding the doctrine of recollection.

There has been a good deal of admiration for the aptly placed and sustained skepticism about the distinction between dreaming and veridical experience that is woven into *The Matrix*.[18] This movie bolsters dream skepticism partly because at times the audience—along with the characters—is not sure which state is being portrayed. Similar episodes occur in shows such as *The X-files* and *The Twilight Zone*, in which hallucinated scenes are presented as if they were veridical. These plots mimic the experience of false-awakening dreams, and hence effectively evoke what we call in another context Cartesian doubt. Contrast them to the notorious first episode of the 1986 season of *Dallas*, in which it is declared that the entire previous year had been a bad dream. This ludicrous plot device for allowing an actor to resume a character who had died two seasons previously should have scuttled the whole show. What is more, it could never be used to supplement Descartes' already barely credible dreaming argument.

However, there is no *logical* preferability for *The Matrix* over *Dallas*. If Descartes is right that at any given moment we have no certain warrant that our experiences are veridical and not dreamt, then any of the plot contrivances that yield the claim that sometimes a character takes a dream for reality have equal plausibility, logically speaking. That is to say, both are equally improbable (with a probability approaching zero, in fact). But dramatically speaking, *The Matrix* provides an Aristotelian probable impossible, whereas *Dallas* delivers the worst combination: an improbable impossible.

The *Dallas* contrivance is an obvious failure because it is tacked on to the plot and not sustained by anything else in the drama. It is both philosophically and dramatically bankrupt. But there are plenty of examples of compelling narratives that are the ideal combination, yielding a "philosophical" probable impossible, at least for a segment of the story. The action sci-fi movie *Predator* is a good example of this, for in the course of discovering, tracking, and killing an alien hunter who is visiting a South American jungle for sport, both the characters and the audience gradually infer something about how the world must appear to a creature with an entirely different perceptual system. By the time the camera shows us the alien's own visual field (sensitive to the infrared spectrum and motion), this unlikely being is a thoroughly probable impossible. (In contrast, we might criticize as an improbable possible an extended plot in which two of the characters leave the jungle, go home, and are elected state governors.)

The examples I have approvingly reviewed above still might be considered only lengthy illustrations of a problem that is properly worked out in standard treatise form, entertaining supplements to less entertaining philosophy. In many instances, the relationship of philosophy and popular culture is just this: mutually enlightening texts. Skeptics might still maintain that no matter how clever the plot and how dramatically well integrated the philosophical issue, the hierarchy of genres remains: the movie form is fun; it is the easier entry to a path that leads to difficult territory. I grant that it is fun; whether it is aptly labeled "easy," however, demands reflection. Possibly it is considered intellectually easier because it is readily grasped by most members of an audience, but that ready grasp might chiefly be the result of the fact that an extended story can be a *better example* that sharpens understanding of an issue. If this is so, then the pop culture item is not necessarily easier than the kind of example standardly included in an essay or treatise; it is just dramatically superior.

What is more, intellectual demand does not have a monopoly on difficulty. If one were to rank the demands placed on emotional and affective tolerance, popular culture—as well as high art—would come out considerably more difficult than philosophy. Tragedy, horror, and the tensions of drama can be so painful that many people avoid emotionally strenuous art. Incidentally, here too there is precedent for admiring the difficult over the easy. In an influential essay written at the beginning of the twentieth century, Bernard Bosanquet distinguished what he called "easy" from "difficult" beauty to describe art that severely taxes the audience.[19] Among the qualities of difficult beauty, he identifies intricate structure, sensitive content, and discomforting emotional arousal; such features characterize not only classically difficult genres such as tragedy and the grotesque, but also some popular movies and television series.

Moreover, on occasion a work of entertainment may raise and explore the same questions that philosophy considers its purview as such a deep element of its plot, characters, and structure that the philosophy is intrinsic to the narrative. It is not ever purely philosophy—not just because it lacks extended argument and analysis, but also because it does so many other things: it captures the imagination, arouses emotions, and presents exciting plots that distract attention from the fact that there is a philosophical agenda at work. If some works from popular culture are to count as philosophical vehicles absent the adjunct status that the hierarchy of genres presumes, then we have to countenance the idea that conclusions may be reached not only by analysis and argument, but also by the more complicated and indirect route provided by plots and characters, including the most obvious influence they exert: the arousal of appreciative emotions.[20] This comparison is *not* intended to describe philosophy as purely rational argument and popular culture as simply emotional arousal. Nor is it meant to separate utterly reason and emotion. At the very least, emotions are a brand of mentation requiring cognitive elements, and cogent argumentation requires that one care about the conclusion. Nonetheless, it is the imbalance in the comparative roles of emotion in these genres that is the venerable subject of concern, not because emotions are free from reason, but because they can divert reason from critically reaching the conclusions that it might come to in their absence. I have already claimed that thorough philosophical treatment enhances both the content and the form of a story. Now we need to consider the reciprocal of that claim: Can the affectively engaging elements of a story also enhance its philosophy such that the story stands alone as a fully developed philosophical position?

In order to take this question seriously, we need to entertain the possibility that the term *philosophy* has a legitimate usage beyond being a label for a particular type of theoretical writing. Otherwise the answer is analytically negative, since philosophy as a matter of fact is a distinct genre.[21] This investigation probes much deeper than matters of pedagogic strategy. It addresses how the mind becomes sensitized to questions that demand philosophical answers, and what form those answers assume. For the purpose of argument, I propose to treat *philosophy* as a success term to refer to works demanding imaginative engagement that results in the recognition, and perhaps the acceptance, of a philosophical position, such that what is done in philosophy proper that induces a plausible conclusion is done in another genre by means appropriate to its appreciation. Of course, straight philosophy does not always persuade a reader that its conclusions are correct, nor does it always culminate in a clear position on an issue. Sometimes the most profound philosophy ends in aporia—a recognition that one does not know the answer to a question that seemed at first to have an answer.[22] So when I refer to "the recognition and perhaps acceptance" of a philosophical position, I mean to include among those "positions" all conclusions that reflect on the limits of the answers available to philosophical inquiry.

Another way to describe philosophy as a success term is to acknowledge distinctions among "having a philosophy," "being a text of philosophy," and "doing philosophy."[23] Therefore I expand the distinction that Bill Irwin has drawn between *philosophy* and *philosophical*, which permits art (his focus is literary texts) to be "philosophical" but not "philosophy."[24] I agree that no literary text, movie, or television show is itself philosophy; the genres are distinct. But this does not answer the question: might a television show conduct philosophy in its own way, such that viewers are led to contemplate, take seriously, and perhaps accept a genuinely philosophical problem, dilemma, or position with the same depth of understanding offered by a work of the genre of philosophy? If and when this were to occur, philosophy would be conducted by a nonstandard vehicle. Are there works of popular culture that qualify to be called philosophy, using that label as a success term?

VEHICLES EN ROUTE

I shall explore this issue with two instances of ethical theorizing in which virtually the same philosophical position is reached by a treatise and by a television series, but with no mutual references or allusions to link the two texts. The two examples are Simone de Beauvoir's *Ethics of Ambiguity* and the television show *Angel*, particularly its second season (2000–2001). I shall present their deliberations and conclusions separately and, of necessity, briefly.

Beauvoir's *Ethics* (1947) was written in defense of the philosophy that she and Sartre had developed, specifically the ideas that he published in *Being and Nothingness*.[25] That book was widely assailed for the apparent absence of any possibility for a moral philosophy that could be established if the tenets of existentialism were accepted. In a world where values have absolutely no foundation in divinity, society, or law, critics challenged, what prevents existentialism from sanctioning the whims of individuals to do whatever they please? As Beauvoir summarized the criticism, existentialism "encloses man in a sterile anguish, in an empty subjectivity. It is incapable of furnishing him with any principle for making choices."[26] Her answer to this challenge is somewhat Kantian in its tenor, although she faults Kant for overrationalizing human nature. She argues that only a philosophy that recognizes that the sole possible source of value is autonomous human action can truly articulate the nature of moral duty and obligations to oneself and others.

Central to Beauvoir's ethics is recognition that what she labels *ambiguity* pervades existence. Ambiguity obtains because the human condition comprises irreconcilable elements. Human beings are born but to die; we are rational mind and animal body; each of us is both subject and object; we have consciousness and thingness; a person is both an end in itself and an instrument to be used, a unique individual and a cipher in larger collectivities, free in mind and unfree in physical limitations. Ambiguity is a profoundly uncomfortable situation, which is why bad faith—the relinquishing of one's autonomy to follow the guides of religion, law, custom, or passion—is so tempting. There is no external rule or power that can resolve the tensions of ambiguity: we are inescapably free, and therefore the weight of responsibility falls upon each of us to bring value into the world through action. Beauvoir describes this condition in classic genre terms: it is "tragic"—tormenting and inescapable. Once one recognizes and accepts ambiguity, then one realizes that there is no recourse to justify the values we invest in action other than our own decisions. Rather than freeing the individual to act as he or she wishes, an ethics of ambiguity forces one to acknowledge responsibility for the smallest act, for it is these that bring the only value there is into being.

> The [person] who seeks to justify his [or her] life must want freedom itself absolutely and above everything else. At the same time that it requires the realization of concrete ends, of particular projects, it requires itself universally. . . . To will oneself moral and to will oneself free are one and the same decision.[27]

The Ethics of Ambiguity is not a staple in philosophy courses; indeed, outside of the community of Beauvoir scholars, it is rarely read. (It has my vote for being one of the two most neglected ethical works of the twentieth century, along with Iris Murdoch's *Sovereignty of Good*.) For my purposes at present, the relative obscurity of the book is an advantage, for recognizing the existential ethics in *Angel* is hardly apt to proceed from a previous acquaintance with a classic text. While there are several slight allusions to French culture and to existentialism in the show (Angel quotes Baudelaire and reads Sartre, apparently in French), by themselves they are philosophically negligible. Therefore, the relationship that *Angel* bears to Beauvoir is markedly different from the relation that obtains between *The Matrix* and Descartes, or between *Tristram Shandy* and Locke, or *The Tempest* and Plato. The moral theory emerges entirely from the character and the development of his actions over weeks, even years—and these are weeks and years not only in the life of the character but in the life of the viewer, for a television series is by nature an interrupted and extended event.

Angel is a spin-off of another of Joss Whedon's television dramas, *Buffy the Vampire Slayer*. For the first three seasons of the latter, the strongest story arc involves Buffy—a high school girl chosen by destiny to be the champion who fights the forces of evil—and her doomed relationship with the vampire Angel. After they conclude that their hopeless love is too strong for them to be together, Angel departs for Los Angeles, where he sets up shop as a detective whose motto is "We help the helpless." *Angel*'s Los Angeles foregrounds sophisticated desperation, loneliness, and anomic fakery. This L.A. is also liberally outfitted with demons and vampires—and with the impossible presented with dramatic probability.

At first glance, the metaphysics that underlies both *Angel* and *Buffy* is more-or-less Christian, though it is highly embellished by an eclectic global demonology. Churches are hallowed spaces that vampires fear to enter; they are burned by crosses and scalded by holy water. However, despite these religious trappings, the show depends in no way whatsoever on faith in God. In fact, the opposite is true.[28] Whedon's California provides all of the fears and tortures of a Christian hell, but little of its promise of heaven. What is more, the characters must fight an occult evil that is not publicly acknowledged, and so they cannot rely on law, ordinary social relations, or family to support or justify their actions. Their situation, therefore, is suitably described as an existentialist universe—one of lonely anxiety and perpetual effort.

These uncomfortable elements, however, are masked by the form of the series. Many scripts have a light, ironic tone and ingeniously meshed multiple plot lines. The dialogue is literate and clever; both the characters and plots display a comic side. As such, any philosophical content might be expected to be only philosophy lite. But the weight of both shows is provided by the fact that despite the wit, both Angel and Buffy are tragic figures.[29] They are tragic in a classic sense: singled out by fate for heroic roles they cannot escape, the reasons for which surpass human understanding, and which doom them from entry into the normal rhythms of a lifetime. Therefore, neither can even entertain the common hope that she or he might eventually be happy.

This is an especially strong theme of the character Angel: a vampire nearing his 250th birthday, who began life as a dissolute young eighteenth-century roué, was "sired" in an intoxicated seduction, and turned into "Angelus," a vampire legendary for his devilish cruelty. After a century and a half wreaking havoc across Europe, he makes the error of killing the favorite daughter of a gypsy clan. In revenge, the gypsies curse him by returning his soul—and hence his moral conscience. He is forever condemned to suffer the guilt for all that Angelus did. His previous sins are unforgivable, and his guilt cannot be assuaged; what is more, the gypsy curse has a nasty twist. If Angel ever achieves even a moment of pure happiness, he loses his soul and becomes again the terrible Angelus. This "moment of pure happiness" is dramatically encapsulated in sex, which with a few exceptions Angel avoids after a disastrous night of passion with Buffy. But what he really cannot experience or even pursue is consummate *love*, which is true happiness. His terrible loneliness is mostly treated comically, as with his comment: "There are three things I don't do: tan, date, and sing in public."[30] But the comedy is in the form of the story, not its meaning.

Vampires turn out to be especially good exemplars of ambiguity, adding to our common existential ambiguities the fact that they are hybrids of demon and human. The metaphysics of identity in this myth is a bit hard to chart.[31] Vampires feed on blood, and if they permit their victims to drink of their own blood after the first killing bite, then the victim is "turned" and becomes another vampire. When the vampire kills, the soul of the victim leaves his body and a demon takes its place. Thereafter, the vampire only looks like the original human; it is another individual altogether, and it is dead (or more precisely, undead). An evil being, it cannot show itself to the light of day, for sunlight ignites vampires. But the vampire retains all the memories of his human host and in some ways still matches that person. Thus a vampire both is and is not identical with itself.

What is more, Angel is a vampire with a soul. Although he is a different individual from Angelus, he must suffer for the latter's wrongdoing, which would make no sense unless their difference is compromised by a residual sameness. As Spike (the other vampire with a conscience in the two shows) puts it, he can be neither monster nor man. The special discomfort of this ambiguity is dramatically realized in the worrisome nostalgia that Angel occasionally expresses for the purity of the single-minded pursuit of evil from his conscienceless past. Notably, it is only in the disambiguated evil state that such purity is possible.

Flashbacks permit us from time to time to review the wicked career of Angelus and to compare the intoxicating exuberance he brought to killing with the brooding reflection of Angel. At times, his sense of the eternal struggle that he faces leads Angel to despair of the worth of any effort at all. His recovery of purpose returns us to the ethical theory he dramatizes, which is a particular theme of the second season. Especially explicit is one episode which ends with an acknowledgment that there is no greater scheme in the universe, no big picture, and ultimately nothing means anything at all. Angel concludes,

> If there's no great, glorious end to all this and nothing we do matters, then all that matters is what we do. Because that's all there is—what we do, now, today. . . . Because if there is no bigger meaning, then the smallest act of kindness is the greatest thing in the world.[32]

From time to time the same moral refrain is repeated, as two seasons later when Angel says to his son,

> Nothing in the world is the way it ought to be. It's harsh and cruel. But that's why there's us. Champions. It doesn't matter where we come from, what we've done or suffered. Or even if we make a difference. We live as though the world were the way it should be. To show it what it can be.[33]

Absent the language of phenomenology, this is very like Beauvoir's own thesis. Here we have two works—a philosophy book and a TV series—with similar perspectives and nearly matching conclusions arrived at by entirely different means. Two vehicles, one destination. Naturally, to discover a philosophical position dramatically established is no guarantee of its correctness, although it does demonstrate a measure of coherence. (It is, after all, a probable impossible.) But have we really got a philosophy here? Or, to pose the question more precisely, assuming that the positions are equally well articulated, is there any reason philosophically still to prefer one vehicle over the other?

Grounds for answering "yes" to this question might include the following:

The philosophical conclusion will be clearer and better developed in the treatise form; it cannot be anything but a pale and partial version in the popular plot vehicle. Since this reason merely restates genre snobbery without advancing any new defense, we can set it aside.

Secondly, perhaps the entertainment value of a TV show is too strong to foreground philosophy. No matter how well articulated, the philosophical position extracted from this show will be easily overlooked by the casual viewing audience. This reason has a little more cogency, for viewers bring to entertainment a habit of relaxation and an expectation of amusement that might blunt alertness to philosophical content. But one can also read a philosophical work and miss the point, and so I don't believe that the fact that the conclusion might be missed is a reason to prefer one vehicle over another. What is more, since (as I have argued) narrative drama is only strengthened by coherence of philosophical content, the philosophical conclusion is the sort of thing one notices simply by following the plot. The example I have chosen is pretty hard to miss, because it is an element of the entire series and an explicit story line for close to sixteen episodes in a single season.

The third and most important worry is harder to appease: The dramatically engaging means by which one realizes the philosophical conclusion of the television show might adventitiously be a means to philosophical insight. But it is an unsound and perhaps even a dangerous way to get there. Standard philosophical style positively invites critical reflection on its arguments, its methods, and its conclusions. This is only possible if an idea is stripped of all that makes one desire its truth. Emotional engagement induces the audience to anticipate and wish for a certain kind of conclusion. Therefore, an affectively powerful drama may sweep one away with such intensity that one affirms a set of propositions that would not bear up under cooler scrutiny. What is more, because the object of experience is fiction, one is not critically alert to the imaginative affirmation of the philosophical position induced.

This concern should be distinguished from one with which it is easily conflated: the practical influence that art might exert upon audiences. Addressing the behavioral consequences of popular culture is beyond my purpose here, though it is indirectly related to the more focused issue I have been addressing: the status of a philosophical position presented in popular culture. The shared issue concerns the antecedents that induce belief.

I have argued that it is a mark of good philosophy to be dramatically convincing in the presentation of problems and solutions, and some forms of pop culture clearly possess this feature. Therefore, some of them merit being called vehicles for "philosophy"—if that category is taken not just as a genre label but as a success term. The fact that the success may be the outcome of liminal persuasion is not a trivial worry, and it raises a final question: Can one be seduced into a philosophical position when the vehicle is fictional, and if so might that be a position that one would not deliberately endorse? At first this possibility sounds unlikely, for we tend to think of philosophy as a self-conscious and reflective activity. But if *philosophy* is a success term, our ears may not be finely attuned to its implications, and one of the implications of the view I have argued is the possibility that philosophy can come in disguise, as it were, persuading one to a conclusion in the course of diversion and emotional engagement.

Perhaps there is nothing to worry about here. Some philosophers have asserted that the prior beliefs that one takes to entertainment are proof against philosophic *akrasia*, such that when a work of fiction violates one's prior moral and epistemic precepts, it will no longer be an object of conviction or enjoyment. Kendall Walton, for instance, invokes what he calls a "reality principle," according to which, works that violate moral precepts and other strongly-held beliefs break through the imaginative thrall of art and interrupt appreciation.[34] Noël Carroll argues that the narratives of popular art activate beliefs already held and clarify them by providing "an opportunity for us to deepen our grasp of the moral knowledge and emotions already at our command."[35] I am not confident that this is always the case, and one can imagine Plato admonishing premature complacency. For even though it is unlikely that engagement with fictions could take one very far from one's considered beliefs, when the impossible appears probable, those beliefs may falter.

NOTES

1. Richard Shusterman, "Entertainment: A Question for Aesthetics," *British Journal of Aesthetics* 43 (July 2003): 289–307. See also Shusterman's essay in this volume.

2. Larry Shiner, *The Invention of Art: A Cultural History* (Chicago: University of Chicago Press, 2001), chap. 7. Ted Cohen makes a similar observation in his essay in this volume.

3. Extrapolating from the essays in this book, one might conclude that the claim is false. Ted Cohen's aesthetic communities mingle both high and popular art and audiences, and Ted Gracyk demonstrates the numerous crossover allusions to high art within the popular or "mass" arts.

4. Ian Shuttleworth, "Buffyworld," interviewed by Mary O'Connell, "Ideas," CBC broadcast, January 20, 2003.

5. *Literary Philosophers: Borges, Calvino, Eco*, ed. Jorge Gracia, Carolyn Korsmeyer, and Rodolphe Gasché (New York: Routledge, 2002).

6. Ethical criticism is most prominently associated with Martha Nussbaum, *Love's Knowledge: Essays on Philosophy and Literature* (New York: Oxford University Press, 1990); and Wayne Booth, *The Company We Keep: An Ethics of Fiction* (Berkeley and Los Angeles: University of California Press, 1988).

7. Noël Carroll includes "easy" among his criteria for mass art in *A Philosophy of Mass Art* (Oxford: Oxford University Press, 1998), 196.

8. Pierre Bourdieu, *Distinction: A Social Critique of the Judgement of Taste*, trans. Richard Nice (London: Routledge, 1984), 176.

9. Christopher Falzon, *Philosophy Goes to the Movies: An Introduction to Philosophy* (London: Routledge, 2002); and Mary M. Litch, *Philosophy through Film* (New York: Routledge, 2002). Other teaching texts mix classic texts with pop culture discussions, such as Adam Morton, *Philosophy in Practice* (Malden, MA: Blackwell, 2003). Irwin's multivolume series is published by Open Court, and he has begun a new series with Blackwell.

10. I focus here on relations between particular works of art and specific philosophies. Popular culture may also be regarded as a general manifestation of cultural trends with philosophic significance: viz. Paul Cantor, *Gilligan Unbound: Pop Culture in the Age of Globalization* (Lanham, MD: Rowman & Littlefield, 2001).

11. Aristotle, *Poetics*, 1451b, trans. Stephen Halliwell, in *Aesthetics: The Big Questions*, ed. Carolyn Korsmeyer (Malden, MA: Blackwell, 1998), 236.

12. Alexander Pope, *Essay on Criticism*, Part I: Line 215.

13. Dorothy L. Sayers, *The Unpleasantness at the Bellona Club*, chap. 15 (1928; New York: Harper & Row, 1971), 113.

14. These quotes are from the episodes "Dreamland I" (6:4), "Triangle" (6:3), and "Paper Hearts" (4:8). See also Alec McHoul, "How to Talk the Unknown into Existence," *Deny All Knowledge: Reading the X-Files*, ed. David Lavery, Angela Hague, and Marla Cartwright (Syracuse, NY: Syracuse University Press, 1996), 142.

15. "Out of Mind, Out of Sight," *Buffy the Vampire Slayer* (1:11).

16. "Happy Anniversary," *Angel* (2:13).

17. History may be even more vulnerable than philosophy for the power of the distortions produced for dramatic ends.

18. See several essays in *The Matrix and Philosophy: Welcome to the Desert of the Real*, ed. William Irwin (Chicago: Open Court, 2002).

19. Bernard Bosanquet, *Three Lectures on Aesthetic* (1915); (Indianapolis, IN: Bobbs-Merrill, 1963), lecture 3.

20. The arousal of emotions by art is a complicated subject with its own field of argument. For a sampling of some of the issues, see Noël Carroll, "On the Ties That Bind," this volume.

21. Several articles in *Literary Philosophers* make this point: Deborah Knight, "Intersections: Philosophy and Literature," 15–26; William Irwin, "Philosophy and the Philosophical, Literature and the Literary, Borges and the Labyrinthine," 27–45; Jorge J. E. Gracia, "Borges; 'Pierre Menard': Philosophy or Literature?" 85–107.

22. As Gary Matthews points out, this is the important outcome of many of Plato's dialogues.

23. These distinctions were suggested to me by Ted Gracyk.

24. Irwin, "Philosophy and the Philosophical," cited in note 21.

25. Although Beauvoir always ceded the leading position to Sartre, many scholars credit her contributions to what is now called "Sartrean existentialism." See Kate Fullbrook and Edward Fullbrook, *Simone de Beauvoir and Jean-Paul Sartre: The Remaking of a Twentieth-Century Legend* (New York: Basic Books, 1994); Claudia Card, ed., *The Cambridge Companion to Simone de Beauvoir* (Cambridge: Cambridge University Press, 2003).

26. Simone de Beauvoir, *The Ethics of Ambiguity*, trans. Bernard Frechtman (Secaucus, NJ: Citadel Press, 1980), 10.

27. Beauvoir, 24.

28. This is implicit in many episodes and explicit in at least two. When asked by a chatty vampire whether her sojourn in the afterlife established the existence of God, Buffy replies "the jury's still out." "Conversations with Dead People" (7:7).

29. Series are cumbersome "works" to assess. The indeterminate shape of a television show means that there cannot ever be a truly tragic series. A grim one, yes (like *The Sopranos*). A tough one (like *NYPD Blue*). One that features an inveterately

sad character (such as the BBC's Inspector Morse mysteries). But tragedies require a shaping that series do not permit, even if one extends the genre far beyond Aristotle's antique prescriptions. Thus the tragic aspects of Buffy and Angel are masked in comedy and adventure plots, though it is their tragic positions that contribute weight to their characters and their situations.

30. "Judgment" (2:1).

31. Gregory J. Sakal, "No Big Win: Themes of Sacrifice, Salvation, and Redemption," in *Buffy the Vampire Slayer and Philosophy: Fear and Trembling in Sunnydale*, ed. James B. South (Chicago: Open Court, 2003), 242–43.

32. "Epiphany" (2:16).

33. "Deep Down" (4:7). The entire series ends on the same theme: the perpetual requirement to do right despite the fact that there will be no ultimate triumph. In the last scene of the final episode of the series, Angel and his friends enter battle with an army of demons with the words "Let's get to work." There is no reason to think they survive.

34. Kendall Walton, *Mimesis as Make-Believe: On the Foundations of the Representational Arts* (Cambridge, MA: Harvard University Press, 1990), 154–61.

35. Carroll, *A Philosophy of Mass Art*, 325.

Philosophy as/and/ of Popular Culture

William Irwin

WHAT IS POPULAR CULTURE?

Before we can usefully consider philosophy's engagement with popular culture, we need to know what popular culture is. Is popular culture the same as low culture? The fleeting (as opposed to the classic)? Popular art? Mechanically produced art? Mass art? Mass culture?

Woody Allen once quipped that art is entertainment for intellectuals.[1] Of course this oversimplifies the point, but it nicely reflects the elitist connotations of *art*.[2] Following Allen, perhaps popular culture is entertainment for the people, "art" for the masses. "Intellectuals" do sometimes enjoy popular culture, but perhaps they are just "slumming" when they do so. High culture includes high art, and low culture includes low art, and popular culture is just another name for low culture and its art. Does that make sense? As Ted Cohen captures this reasoning, "What makes the high art high? Is it that its appeal is mostly to high audiences? Then what makes the audience high? That its taste is for high art? Well, of course, that makes a circle. Is something wrong with that?"[3] While it might be possible to mark an audience as high on the basis of something other than its taste for high art, such as socioeconomic status or level of education or familiarity with the art world, this approach nonetheless does not hold much promise.

Even if we were to excuse the circularity, the facile dichotomy between high and low art is problematic in its application to borderline cases. Though Rachmaninov and Beethoven are unambiguously high art, while *Rocky and*

Bullwinkle are unambiguously low art, other cases are not so clear. Where does jazz fit? Clearly jazz was at one time (not long ago) regarded as very low art indeed, though this perception has changed or is changing. We may dare to think that the same fate awaits rock music, at least some of it.[4] Today's low-brow can be tomorrow's highbrow.

Indeed, much that we think of as paradigmatic high art was once popular, low art. Attic comedy and tragedy survived thanks to a shift in its perception from low to high art, or, more accurately, some of the most extraordinary instances of Attic drama survived while the most ordinary have been lost, probably at no great aesthetic loss.[5] The same may be said with regard to the survival of the extraordinary plays of Shakespeare and the loss of most ordinary Elizabethan drama. Perhaps the examples of Aeschylus and Shakespeare simply show that we do not always recognize high art—the classic—when we see it. Popular culture, by contrast, is fleeting, not classic, not timeless, so the argument goes. But Dickens, for example, undoubtedly wrote for the people and was popular, though he has survived to become classic. We must be mindful that there can be instances of good (popular) low art, such as *The Simpsons*, and there can be instances of bad high art, such as Stoppard's *Jumpers*.[6] And, of course, not all high art, not even all good high art, is classic. Most is lost and forgotten. So popular culture is not simply that which is not classic, because much that is not classic is not necessarily popular, and some that is popular may indeed become classic.

Another way of salvaging the distinction between high and low is in terms of availability and means of production. The value of high art might be said to derive in part from its one-of-a-kind status with its attendant aura, as Walter Benjamin calls it. There is only one *Mona Lisa*, one (Michelangelo's) *David*, one Parthenon, etc. Similarly, theatrical and orchestral performances are always unique. By contrast, popular culture "in the age of mechanical reproduction" is generally mass produced and ready for virtually identical mass consumption.[7] Movies and television shows are seen in essentially the same way by people in theaters and living rooms around the world; rock music is heard on CDs in essentially the same way by people all over the world. By contrast, mass production copies of the *Mona Lisa* or *David* do not provide essentially the same experience as the originals; they are mere copies, not tokens of types.

So should discussion of "popular culture" be replaced by discussion of "mass art"? Mass art would presumably be what Benjamin speaks of as "art in the age of mechanical reproduction," art that is mass produced and distributed for mass consumption. But although most (if not all) the art of popular culture is mass art in this sense, not all mass art in this sense is popular culture. With modern technology, new symphonic music can be mass produced for mass consumption in just the way rock music can, if not ordinarily with the same commercial success.[8] Discussion of mass art would make sense if, as Benjamin believes, the use of mass technologies does something to essentially change the kind of art that is produced. Benjamin valorizes distraction and lack of concentration in perceiving mass art, free from aura, as empowering the audience.[9] But it is clear neither that all mass art encourages distraction nor that distraction is necessarily a salutary effect. Unfortunately, then, Benjamin's account specifies nothing essential about the art he considers.

Noël Carroll does not believe mass art is essentially different from art in general. Nonetheless, he holds that it is useful to speak of mass art as "roughly popular art produced and distributed by mass technology,"[10] "a necessary feature of [which is] that it is designed to be accessible to masses of people."[11] Carroll's account distinguishes mass art from the popular art of past eras, which (generally) was not produced and distributed by mass technology, and from folk art, which is often not produced and distributed by mass technology. With its necessary condition of mass production and distribution, "mass art," unlike "popular culture," would unfortunately exclude some works that do not fit neatly into the ordinary language categories of folk or avant-garde, such as unrecorded, unbroadcast punk rock, tattoos, and graffiti.

The necessary condition of accessibility is meant to distinguish mass art from what most regard as contemporary high art, the avant-garde.[12] But by defining mass art as necessarily accessible, Carroll embraces ease as a criterion of mass art. As he says, "avant-garde artworks are not structured for ready assimilation and reception by mass audiences."[13] "Mass art, in contrast, is designed to be easy, to be readily accessible, with minimum effort, to the largest number of people possible."[14] Carroll is explicit in stating that, despite the ease associated with it, he does not regard *mass art* as a derogatory term.[15]

Photography, then, which Benjamin takes as paradigmatic of art "in the age of mechanical reproduction," would not necessarily be mass art for Carroll. Despite its reproducibility, a photograph without ease of accessibility would not be mass art. This would seem to define mass art in such a way as to make it a misnomer, but perhaps that is not a problem.

Most mass art is readily accessible in precisely the way Carroll specifies; think of Top 40 radio and television sitcoms. Still, some of what should surely count as mass art is not readily accessible. There is no a priori reason why popular, or mass, art cannot be difficult and inaccessible. With a large enough public, mass art can aim to appeal to a small fraction of the public rather than as many as possible.[16] Some popular musical artists, for example Slipknot, Dimmu Borgir, the Sex Pistols, (early) Metallica, and (much) Frank Zappa, actually aim at being inaccessible to most, thus generating great appeal among others, largely because of that inaccessibility.[17] Carroll says, "Mass art has to be comprehensible for untrained audiences, virtually on the first go-around,"[18] but virtually no one in 1976 could claim to comprehend the Sex Pistols "on the first go-around," or, mutatis mutandis, Dimmu Borgir and Slipknot today. Yet they have vast followings. We might then be tempted to classify the songs of the Sex Pistols, Dimmu Borgir, and Slipknot as avant-garde, but surely they are both too popular and too unlike other avant-garde artworks, even those produced and distributed by mass technology, such as the works of John Cage. "The question is about what *masses* of untutored people find easily accessible,"[19] Carroll says. But what does it mean to be tutored? And what exactly does it mean for an artwork to be accessible? Surely a Dimmu Borgir or Slipknot fan is in some way tutored to appreciate their music in a way that the average person is not.[20] Is Carroll's accessibility criterion akin to acquired tastes in food? Appealing to an untutored palate? If so, isn't *Buffy the Vampire Slayer* an acquired taste that some take to quickly while others never find palatable? Perhaps the Sex Pistols, Dimmu Borgir, Slipknot, and *Buffy* are avant-garde mass art. Certainly this could be correct if all we mean by "mass art" is art produced and distributed by mass technology, but this is not what Carroll means. He considers mass art and the avant-garde to be mutually exclusive categories, necessarily differentiated in terms of ease of accessibility.[21]

In response to John Fisher's objection that most examples of important rock music, notably the work of the Beatles, Bob Dylan, and Jimi Hendrix, do not satisfy the accessibility condition,[22] Carroll clarifies: "According to my theory, accessibility is a cognitive affair. It is a matter of whether audiences comprehend the works in question without tutoring, not whether they approve of or like the works."[23] So, Carroll is saying, while the contemporary audience may have needed repeated listening to acquire a taste for, say, the experimental sound of *Sergeant Pepper's Lonely Heart's Club Band*, or Hendrix's use of feedback on *Are You Experienced*, these works were cognitively accessible. People may not have liked them the first time they heard them, but they nonetheless understood what they were about.

I believe Carroll is mistaken. The average person in the contemporary audience for rock music of any vintage is untutored in the sense of lacking the knowledge and cognitive delicacy required to comprehend some of the best and most important music of the genre. There simply is no meaningful sense of *accessible* in which *all* popular music is accessible. The very reason that many among the contemporary audience for the Beatles and Hendrix did not like their music is precisely the same reason that many among the contemporary audience for the Sex Pistols did not like their music and that many among the contemporary audience do not like Slipknot. They did not fully comprehend what the music is about. They had only a partial comprehension of the music, which in fact was a misunderstanding of the music, leading to a negative evaluation of the music. Although they were panned by many benighted music critics at the time, no one knowledgeable of rock music today would gainsay the greatness of the Sex Pistols. Much the same, mutatis mutandis, can be said of Black Sabbath and Metallica. There is no guarantee, of course, that proper comprehension will lead to proper appreciation, but in notable cases, full appreciation is impossible without proper comprehension.

The cognitive and the affective are linked. The Sex Pistols, for example, like many bands before and since, were misunderstood as simply loud, rebellious, and obnoxious for the sake of it, and thus were easily dismissed by rock fans and non-rock fans alike. The music requires repeated listening and background information to "get it." There is more to understanding the music than simply realizing that it is intended to be transgressive and offensive. One did indeed need to be tutored to comprehend the conventions the Sex Pistols were employing and the icons they were smashing in the attempt to recapture the true spirit of rock music. While the tutoring was part of the subculture for some young punks, it would require for others an advance placement course at Jack Black's "School of Rock." Though much of what was revolutionary about the Sex Pistols has today become nearly mainstream, many among the untutored continue to miscomprehend and dismiss the authentic punk of the Sex Pistols, as if it were cut from the same cloth as the pseudo-punk of Green Day. Worse, the untutored often miscomprehend and thus like Green Day and reject the Sex Pistols. Still worse, the truly soulless comprehend and nonetheless like

Green Day, who, to mix a metaphor, are but shadows on a wall standing on the shoulders of giants.

If we are to disagree with Carroll, we are left with the unhelpful understanding of mass art, à la Benjamin, as simply that which is produced and distributed by mass technology, a definition that does nothing to essentially differentiate mass art from other art. We return, then, to the distinction between the high and the low (or popular).

The low is the popular in the sense of being what the people like, even if it isn't what the people, in the sense of the *Volk*, produce.[24] It seems we can't live with or without the distinction between high and low art; it is, as Ted Cohen says, indefensible but indispensable.[25] Even if we could neatly delineate between high art and low art, by whatever names, equating popular culture with low art would not be correct. *Culture* refers to leisure, things done or made for entertainment or interest (Aristotle's *schole*): "things which are not done or made for explicitly practical, utilitarian, or survival-related concerns."[26] Accordingly, popular culture includes, but is not limited to, popular art. Rather, it includes baseball, fast food, fashion, cars, commercials, crystals, astrology, self-help, home design, dieting, UFOs, video games, cell phones, blogs, Disneyland, Las Vegas, serial killers, pornography, televangelists, court TV, spring break, Halloween, Mardi Gras, wrestling, and reality TV, among other things. While some of these examples may arguably involve art, not all do.[27] Perhaps they all involve entertainment, and so popular culture is "mass culture," entertainment for the masses? But it would be inaccurate to say that entertainment motivates consumption of fast food and interest in crystals, astrology, self-help, and UFOs. We are left with a vague notion of popular culture as often, though not necessarily, involving entertainment and art.

We can loosely define popular culture as artifacts and subjects of mass interest and appreciation.[28] Popular culture does not exclude people from appreciating it on the basis of class or formal education. This is perhaps a necessary, though not a sufficient, condition of popular culture. "Mass interest and appreciation" is admittedly indeterminate, though hopefully not troublesome. How popular does the popular have to be? No fixed answer can be given. One size does *not* fit all. The British sense of "pop" sheds light on the issue. In the British sense, Ozzy Osbourne and the Grateful Dead, for example, are considered "pop stars," even though they have cult followings. Cult followings may be large or small, but they are still part of popular culture as I conceive it.

As long as we have a general idea of the extension of "popular culture," as this preliminary survey has provided, this definition, though imperfectly specifying the intension of the term, will be enough to begin. We need not worry the vexed question of whether it is possible, and if so how, to differentiate between popular culture and high culture (if that is even the appropriate name for the companion concept). Without any theoretical advantages to the contrary, it makes sense to follow ordinary language, speaking of *popular culture* rather than *mass art, mass culture*, or any other alternative.

PHILOSOPHY AS POPULAR CULTURE?

Philosophy[29] is *not* popular culture, not an artifact or subject of mass interest and appreciation, but it could be. At various times in the past, indeed, it was. Arguably rocketry and the U.S. space program were elements of popular culture for a time in America, as dinosaurs and the Internet are now. Astronomy and computer programming *could* become popular culture. So could philosophy. Freud and Einstein were among the *People*/VH-1 top two hundred popular-culture icons.[30] Why not Russell and Sartre?

Consider books such as *The Tao of Pooh, The Consolations of Philosophy, Wittgenstein's Poker, Sophie's World, Socrates Café, Plato not Prozac, If Aristotle Ran General Motors*, and *The Metaphysical Club*. Arguably, none of these is either philosophy or popular culture, but their very existence evinces some popular interest in philosophy. So how can we get people further interested in philosophy? The answer, to paraphrase a British philosopher, is "we need a spoonful of sugar to help the medicine go down." We need to start with popular culture and use it to bring people to philosophy. This is what I have attempted to do in editing *Seinfeld and Philosophy* and related books. Even if these books are, in some loose sense of the word, philosophy, they are surely not in themselves popular culture. They simply make use of popular culture.

There is no instance of philosophy that is also popular culture in America now. Is there any reason to want philosophy *as* popular culture? The obvious objection is that it would cheapen great treasures. "Books for all the world are always foul-smelling books," Nietzsche said.[31] Though it may often be true, only the most cowardly snob could believe Nietzsche's statement is necessarily true. Actually, there is a long tradition in philosophy of making exoteric the esoteric, carried on by the likes of Socrates, Aristotle, Boethius, and Descartes.

Is there any harm in Americans knowing a lot about popular culture and relatively little about philosophy?[32] Yes. Americans hungry for knowledge and wisdom have turned to sources such as astrology, motivational speakers, and self-help books. While these sources are of varying value, none matches what philosophy has to offer. Philosophy needs to replace pseudo-philosophy (crystals, astrology, tarot cards) as science must replace pseudo-science (often surrounding interest in things such as bigfoot, the Loch Ness monster, UFOs, and other paranormal phenomena). Pseudo-philosophy, like pseudo-science, is attractively packaged and readily available, and so philosophy needs similar packaging and availability if it is to compete.

Shortly after World War II, with interest in science low, the United States found itself falling behind the Soviet Union. Thanks to a government-sponsored public relations campaign, rocketry was popular culture for a time in the 1950s and 1960s. But it is foolish and precarious to rely on the government to spark interest in science. As Carl Sagan says,

> In all uses of science, it is insufficient—indeed it is dangerous—to produce only a small, highly competent, well-rewarded priesthood of professionals. Instead, some fundamental understanding of the findings and methods of science must be available on the broadest scale.[33]

Sagan's point about science is well taken. Science must be made available to all, and it is scientists, not governments, who must take science to the people.[34]

Part of the difficulty in interesting people in philosophy is that it deals in abstractions. Of course, so do physics and mathematics, but people more readily and easily see the payoff for studying math or physics, with their clear applications to technology that makes life easier and supposedly better. The value of living the examined life through the pursuit of philosophy is much more difficult to demonstrate than the technological and pecuniary payoff of studying science.[35] Still, for the benefit of the individual and the discipline, though not everyone needs to be a scientist, ideally everyone should be scientifically literate. Similarly, though not everyone needs to make a vocation of formal philosophical study, ideally everyone should be philosophically literate, having a sense of the history and questions of philosophy.[36] Citizens of a democracy are better citizens for their knowledge of philosophy, as it teaches them to think critically and encourages them to dissent responsibly. Unenlightened elected officials will never see it as in their best interest to encourage the popular study of philosophy, so philosophers must take the message to the people. To sample Chuck D. of Public Enemy, we have to rock the bourgeoisie and the boulevard.

Philosophy as popular culture would be of tremendous service in this regard, and such democratization of philosophy need not be dumbing down. Popular science is not necessarily pseudo-science; in fact, it rarely is, as the magazine *Popular Science* attests. Most popular science simply explains scientific theories and discoveries sans mathematics. Of course popular science risks oversimplifying and misrepresenting the science, but that is a much lesser risk than depriving the public of a comprehensible account. Popular philosophy does not have to be pseudo-philosophy, as the periodicals *Philosophy Now* and *The Philosophers' Magazine* attest. To democratize philosophy is not necessarily to "dumb it down" but to make it available in at least some form for all. Wouldn't it be wonderful if the lives of Socrates and Buddha, the thought of Aristotle and Descartes, were better known as a result of being related in pop-cultural art forms? Though not a panacea, such sources would not only inspire philosophical musing but would foster critical, skeptical thinking.[37] And by starting with children, we have a greater chance of interesting future generations of adults in philosophy, whose increased interest in philosophy cafes is a good sign.[38]

The fact is that currently neither popular science nor popular philosophy is popular culture or a subject of mass interest. The reality is that we may not need, or at least may not realistically hope for, philosophy *as* popular culture. We may be satisfied with increased and increasing popular awareness of and interest in philosophy. And for that, all that may be necessary is the successful combination of "popular culture *and* philosophy."

"THE CLOSING OF THE AMERICAN MIND," OR JUST "THE END OF THE WORLD AS WE KNOW IT"?

Before we advocate philosophy *and* popular culture, we should consider the potential partner more closely. Despite the promise of popular culture for spreading philosophy, it may just be too dangerous a liaison. Warnings of the closing of the American mind and the dumbing down of America have been heard for some time; we would be foolish to ignore them. To be clear, my aim is not to defend popular culture or popular art per se.[39] Rather, I am considering whether any of the intellectual, political, or moral concerns about, or criticisms of, popular culture are such as to outweigh the good that can come of the connection.

From the beginning, there has been disagreement among philosophers about leisure-time stimulation and entertainment. Plato condemns Homer; Aristotle champions Homer. Aristotle advocates going to the theater; Epictetus cautions against it. Ironically, Plato makes ample use of Homer, and Epictetus uses the metaphor of the actor in a play. One doesn't have to approve of popular culture to make use of it.

One serious concern is that America has become a nation entranced by popular culture, devoid of interest in classical liberal learning and art. Students come to high school and to college less and less well prepared, with less and less interest in and respect for the treasures of the Western tradition they are asked to study. "Here we are now, entertain us," they seem to say, as Neil Postman prophesied and Kurt Cobain sang. Entertainment is the opiate of the masses;[40] the problem is not Big Brother but soma. As Postman paraphrases Huxley, "People will come to love their oppression, to adore the technologies that undo their capacities to think."[41] Everything is entertainment, or it had better become entertainment if it would survive.

> Our politics, religion, news, athletics, education and commerce have been transformed into congenial adjuncts of show business. . . .[42]
>   . . . It [television] has made entertainment itself the natural format for the representation of all experience.[43]

As the argument goes, when we pander to passing interest, replacing the rigorous study of canonical texts with the "anything goes" discussion of the philosophy of the latest fad, we only devalue what has classic, enduring value. All of life becomes entertainment, and teaching, an amusing activity.[44] The very existence of the pop-culture-philosophy hybrid devalues the traditional, posing as a fast, easy, genuine substitute. The rigor of classical liberal education is lost to the languor of phast-phood philosophy's empty-calorie high. To combine philosophy with popular culture is to give in, to concede, and to do harm to those we are trying to help.

While concern with the pervasive American demand for entertainment is well founded, it is not sufficient reason to dismiss the pairing of philosophy and popular culture. No one, least of all myself, wants or advocates that the pop-culture-philosophy hybrid be a substitute for the study of canonical texts any more than we want watching television to be a substitute for reading books. Nor is there serious danger of this becoming an unintended consequence of the hybrid.

Difficulty is not a virtue in its own right. Ease isn't always necessarily bad when it comes to art; nor is difficulty necessarily good. The same is true, mutatis mutandis, of philosophy. Philosophy written in cumbersome, abstruse prose is not necessarily profound. Teaching and lecturing is not necessarily better when it makes learning and understanding more difficult. But fervent interest in something, even a bad situation comedy or wrestling, can encourage critical thinking about it, rather than intellectual passivity.

We are "amusing ourselves to death," Postman laments. A steady diet of popular culture leaves us weak and vulnerable, not just to outside threats but to internal deceptions. An educated and philosophically astute citizenry is the friend of a vital democracy but the foe of the elected official. Marxists such as Adorno have warned that popular culture is beset with traps and controls. For example, in "Revolutions Reloaded," Slavoj Žižek argues that the *Matrix* films, rather than suggesting and inspiring political and economic solutions, simply perpetuate capitalist ideology.[45] Far from freeing our minds, popular culture ensnares them, making them weak and colonizing them with capitalist ideology.[46] The prepackaged, predigested art of popular culture disables our ability to think for ourselves and leaves us vulnerable to the techniques of mass persuasion.[47] First we lose sight of political and economic reality, and eventually we blur the very line between fiction and reality.[48] Ironically we become prisoners of a Matrix or unwitting stars of our own *Truman Show*.

What better way to expose capitalist traps in popular culture than to bring philosophy to bear in discussion of the very traps?[49] Retreating from the battleground of popular culture is no way to win the war. As Danny Goldberg argues in *Dispatches from the Culture Wars: How the Left Lost Teen Spirit*, popular culture is too important to American youth to be ignored.[50]

To suppose that popular culture is apt to brainwash us into accepting an ideology we would otherwise reject is misguided. As Carroll says,

> For audiences who do not already accept the ideological propositions and concepts of a given mass artwork, and who realize that they do not accept them, the ideological address of the mass artwork, no matter how skillful rhetorically, is

apt to seem unintelligible or ridiculous or distorting and, perhaps, worthy of indignation.[51]

Much popular art can be used as fodder for philosophical discussion, and
some naturally inspires thought and political resistance. For example, Douglass Kellner argues that *The X-Files* presents a critical vision of the U.S. government, that the show "instill[s] distrust towards established authority"[52]
and "articulates fear and distrust of dominant institutions."[53] Carroll offers
Spike Lee's *Do the Right Thing* as leaving the audience actively questioning
whether Martin or Malcolm had it right. I would add the music of Rage
Against the Machine. Adorno would likely reject these and other such examples as works of pseudo-criticism,[54] a note that rings hollow, a pseudo-
criticism itself.[55]

Even if we could intellectually and politically survive the pop-culture-
philosophy hybrid, perhaps we could not morally survive it. While in the *Republic* Plato was worried about morality connected with the emotions of
pity and fear, contemporary Platonists tend to be worried about morality
connected with aggressiveness and sexuality.[56] Indeed, this is a concern of
Allan Bloom, who takes Mick Jagger to be symbolic of all that is corrupt
about popular culture in *The Closing of the American Mind.*[57] While Bloom's
use of (the now grandfatherly) Jagger is dated, his concern is timely, as Brit-
ney Spears, Janet Jackson, and gangsta' rap attest (examples which soon will
themselves become dated). Images of sex, violence, and immoral behavior
fill the big screen and the small screen; they pour from the speakers of CD
players and iPods. Undoubtedly these images have at least some detrimental
influence on their—often young—audience. So perhaps the moral costs of
partnering with popular culture are more than philosophy can bear.

The concern that popular culture is too morally corrupt is well founded.
Plato thought the popular culture of his time, Homerica, too corrupt, and
perhaps he was right; the depiction of the gods in the *Iliad* and *Odyssey* leaves
much morally to be desired. To some extent, the story of popular culture in
twentieth-century America was the cyclical tale of the older generation railing
against the moral corruption of the younger generation's music and movies,
which often depicted the moral failings of the elder generation. That there is
a long history of generational disagreement about the morality of popular
culture certainly does not mean we may simply dismiss concerns about the

morality of current popular culture. Though the cause-and-effect relationship between art and morality remains difficult to establish,[58] these concerns are indeed valid. But taking the moral high ground of rejecting popular culture has the unwanted result of rejecting its fans, to whom it is often dear. We must meet people where they are. Philosophy combined with the most popular, and often the most morally dubious, popular culture reaches the audience that needs it most. Taking philosophy to the public through liaison with popular culture even provides some small hope that future popular culture will not be as immoral.

Concern about the pairing of popular culture and philosophy is not much ado about nothing; it is a genuine concern. But it is not indicative of "the closing of the American mind." "It's the end of the world as we know it, and I feel fine."

PHILOSOPHY AND THE USE OF POPULAR CULTURE

Reflecting on the pernicious influence television has had upon American thought and communication, Postman Platonically purports, "In courtrooms, classrooms, operating rooms, board rooms, churches and even airplanes, Americans no longer talk to each other, they entertain each other. They do not exchange ideas; they exchange images."[59]

The most neglected part of the celebrated allegory of the cave is the escaped prisoner's return. Once he has come to true knowledge in and of the higher world, he is not to remain there but to return from whence he came to "share the knowledge." This is the duty of the philosophically educated guardian in Plato's *Republic*, it is the way of Socrates, and it is the duty of philosophers generally. Plato tells us that the returning prisoner must be prepared to be mocked and persecuted, for he will be talking of a strange and unlikely world. What's worse, he will appear to be damaged goods, as he will no longer be able to see clearly the shadows on the wall as he once did. How then is he to succeed in conveying his message? Plato offers little hope that he will. For the answer, we must turn to Socrates, who, despite losing his life to the cave dwellers, was able to communicate with some.

What did Socrates do, start off talking about a higher level of reality? Of course not. He met his interlocutors where they were, often using agricultural analogies and references to Greek culture, commonly known at the time, though the stuff of scholars today. He then gradually led them from what they knew or thought they knew to higher knowledge. The example of Socrates makes clear that one must not only return to the cave but must learn to see the shadows again in order to tell the prisoners of the world outside in terms of the shadows.[60] They are unlikely to understand or listen if the message is delivered any other way. Those who criticize Americans for being immersed in popular culture but show them no way out and provide no motivation are like escaped prisoners who simply sneer at those stuck in the cave, haranguing and ridiculing them. Why would they listen?

But isn't there too much danger in sinking back to the level of the troglodytes? Adorno worries that the prefab art of popular culture encourages only further passive reception rather than active learning.[61] Isn't the pop-culture-philosophy hybrid so prefab and predigested as to thwart real thought? Postman worries that *Sesame Street* doesn't so much encourage children to like school as to want school to be like *Sesame Street*.[62] Does *The Simpsons and Philosophy* make philosophy attractive? Or does it just encourage the demand that philosophy be phun? Hannah Arendt cautions, "The danger of mass education is that it may become very entertaining indeed; there are many great authors of the past who have survived centuries of oblivion and neglect, but it is still an open question whether they will be able to survive an entertaining version of what they say."[63]

Jeremiads aside, popular culture *and* philosophy is like a bike *with* training wheels. The idea is to become comfortable enough to no longer need the training wheels. We kick away the ladder once we have ascended. Popular culture and philosophy is akin to a philharmonic orchestra performing Beatles songs. People will come to the philharmonic who might not otherwise. They'll enjoy it, and some, who would not otherwise, will come back to hear Beethoven. There is a pragmatic, American spirit in using popular culture to spread philosophy. It works.

It is not just that we can or may, but that we should and must bring philosophy to the public in terms that they will know and find attractive and interesting, not for the sake of joining the crowd in the cave but for the sake of showing them the way out. Willie Sutton was a criminal mastermind, a genius of sorts. Once asked, "Willie, why do you rob banks?" he replied pragmatically, "Because that's where the money is." Why would a philosopher write about popular culture? Because that's where the people are. And as the goal is to bring the prisoners from the shadows to the light, so it is the goal to bring the public from popular culture to philosophy. In his controversial book *Cultural Literacy*, E. D. Hirsch contends that there are certain pieces of cultural information that "every American needs to know" to communicate effectively and comprehend others.[64] I contend that this can be extended to the realm of pop culture. The idea of adding pop-cultural literacy to cultural literacy may seem contrary to the intentions of the father of intentionalism, but it is not. Hirsch never intended cultural literacy to be a conservative notion, despite its embrace by political conservatives. Hirsch duly recognizes and accepts that the shared body of knowledge—that is, cultural literacy—is not stable but changing.[65]

Popular culture is the common language of our time, and knowledge of popular culture has become necessary for effective communication, like it or not, good or bad. Goldberg makes this clear concerning politics in *Dispatches from the Culture Wars: How the Left Lost Teen Spirit*. American presidential candidates are obliged to display some knowledge of popular culture and appear on certain television shows: *Oprah*, Letterman, Leno, and *Saturday Night Live*.[66]

Assuming that, like politicians, philosophers have a vested interest in using popular culture to reach the public, what is the proper use for this purpose? It is the same as the proper use of literature, which, as Peter Jones argued well in *Philosophy and the Novel*, is to open the imagination and to aid philosophy by providing vivid examples.[67] Martha Nussbaum has argued for the importance of literature in theorizing ethics.[68] Good literature may be more helpful than bad literature or shallow popular culture in displaying the intricacy of moral problems and moral reasoning, but not always and not necessarily.[69] There is a virtue in appealing to what is commonly known; what is not great literature or fiction can still be a great example. Metaphysics, epistemology, and other areas of philosophy have been neglected. They, too, benefit from the use of literature—particularly science fiction (if it is classed as literature)—and popular culture. Thought experiments have long been valued in philosophy, and popular culture can supply us with thought experiments that are sometimes more helpful and less contrived than those cooked up by philosophers. Certainly they tend to be at least more entertaining and better known,[70] sparking thought and argument. People are often very knowledgeable about their favorite piece of popular culture, and in very sophisticated ways, whether it be comic books or baseball. And this can be used to lead them to sophisticated thinking about philosophy.[71]

PHILOSOPHY AND THE ABUSE OF POPULAR CULTURE

What constitutes the abuse of popular culture in philosophy? *Studying* popular culture *as* philosophy rather than *using* it for examples and communication would be abuse, at least abuse of philosophy. It is the kind of abuse that some mistakenly fear is already taking place in the pop-culture-philosophy hybrid, an understandable mistake, given that other academics, notably literary theorists, have begun study of popular culture for its own sake, or, more correctly, for the sake of interpretation. Cultural studies,[72] as it is commonly called, takes popular culture too seriously, often just telling bad stories about (sometimes bad) stories.[73] Practitioners take themselves and their subject matter too seriously. The tendency to value a creative reading of a text[74] more highly than the text itself leads to accepting that the text itself need not even be aesthetically valuable as long as the interpretation is aesthetically pleasing, interesting, or ideologically correct.

Such interpretation for the sake of interpretation has become the bane of literary studies, though thankfully it seems to have made no inroads into philosophy. In philosophy, we can justify examining a piece of popular culture, even inferior popular culture, to illustrate a philosophical point or issue, but we cannot justify *studying* an inferior piece of popular culture for the sake of philosophical interpretation. And when we do offer a philosophical interpretation of popular culture, we must be clear that we are offering the philosophical significance of the film, show, or song, not its authorially intended meaning, lest we misrepresent its creator(s), truly abusing popular culture.[75] Some literature, for example *Nausea*, may be philosophy, and it is theoretically possible that some element of popular culture could be philosophy, but to my knowledge, no instance yet exists.[76] Until and unless someone manages to create a piece of popular culture that is also philosophy (or vice versa), we must limit ourselves to interpretations that give the philosophical significance of popular culture.

PHILOSOPHY *OF* POPULAR CULTURE

Dictionaries and encyclopedias of philosophy and aesthetics have no entry under "philosophy of popular culture." Although "philosophy and popular culture" may some day be worthy of an entry, the addition of "philosophy of popular culture" will not be necessary. We could for practical purposes have a "philosophy of popular culture," but that would likely have the undesirable consequence of perpetuating the distinction between the high and the popular. There are methodological questions for the study of popular art that might come under the heading of "philosophy of popular culture," such as the nature of fictional worlds, expression, and interpretation, but these are just the same methodological questions and issues raised by aesthetics generally and the philosophy of literature, painting, theater, film, music, and so on more specifically. There are interesting ontological issues related to popular art, but these are the issues owing to mass production raised by Benjamin and Carroll under the heading "philosophy of mass art." Questions raised by pop-cultural phenomena other than popular art, such as baseball and fast food, can be studied under the headings of philosophy of sport and philosophy of food.

Let's close with a note of caution: "philosophy of" is not for the public but for the academic. The surest way to lose a comedy fan's attention is to discuss philosophy of comedy, and so too the surest way to lose the public's attention is to talk about philosophy of popular culture, if there even is such a thing. And if there is, I suspect its only unique question is the one we began with: What is popular culture?

NOTES

For helpful feedback and discussion, thanks to Greg Bassham, Kimberly Blessing, Per Broman, Eric Bronson, Noël Carroll, Ted Cohen, Mark Conard, Jorge Gracia, Ted Gracyk, Jim Lawler, Megan Lloyd, Abby Myers, Read Mercer Schuchardt, Aeon Skoble, and James South.

1. Stig Björkman, *Woody Allen on Woody Allen* (New York: Grove Press, 1993), 103.

2. Though we here consider "intellectual" status as the potential distinguishing criterion between high and low, class status could also be considered and similarly rejected. Cf. Noël Carroll on "Elimination Theory," *A Philosophy of Mass Art* (Oxford: Oxford University Press, 1998), 176–84.

3. Ted Cohen, "High and Low Art, High and Low Audiences," *The Journal of Aesthetics and Art Criticism* 57 (1999): 142.

4. For some excellent, serious aesthetic consideration of rock music, see Theodore Gracyk, *Rhythm and Noise: An Aesthetics of Rock* (Durham: Duke University Press, 1996); and *I Wanna Be Me: Politics and Identity in Rock Music* (Philadelphia, PA: Temple University Press, 2002).

5. Paul Cantor, "The Art in the Popular," *Wilson Quarterly* (2001): 26–39.

6. Or choose your own example of bad high art. See the Museum of Bad Art, www.museumofbadart.org, for food for thought.

7. Walter Benjamin, "The Work of Art in the Age of Mechanical Reproduction," in *Continental Aesthetics: Romanticism to Postmodernism*, trans. Harry Zohn, ed. Richard Kearney and David Rasmussen (Oxford: Blackwell Publishers, 2001), 166–77.

8. Carroll would not count such music as mass art. Cf. (1998), 189.

9. Benjamin, 176.

10. Carroll (1998), 3.

11. Carroll (1998), 8; cf. 196.

12. Not from high art from all eras. Carroll (1998) takes mass art and avant-garde to be mutually exclusive categories, 224.

13. Carroll (1998), 190.

14. Carroll (1998), 192.

15. Carroll (1998), 186–87.

16. Though the examples I'll give are from music, the same can be said to some extent of television. *Buffy the Vampire Slayer* would be one example. For another, see Douglass Kellner, "*The X-Files* and the Aesthetics and Politics of Postmodern Pop," *Journal of Aesthetics and Art Criticism* 57 (1999): 161–75.

17. Carroll (1998) has a straw man in considering supposedly inaccessible mass art using Guns N' Roses as an example, 205; cf. 202. Guns N' Roses clearly aimed at a mainstream audience with radio-friendly singles and MTV-friendly videos.

18. Carroll (1998), 192.

19. Carroll (1998), 228.

20. For some tutoring, see Judith Grant, "Bring the Noise: Hypermasculinity in Heavy Metal and Rap," *Journal of Social Philosophy* 27 (1996): 5–30.

21. Carroll (1998), 224.

22. John Andrew Fisher, "On Carroll's Enfranchisement of Mass Art as Art," *The Journal of Aesthetics and Art Criticism* 62 (2004): 58.

23. Noël Carroll, "Mass Art as Art: A Response to John Fisher," *The Journal of Aesthetics and Art Criticism* 62 (2004): 64.

24. In a subsequent section, we shall discuss Adorno's rejection of *popular culture*, a term he thinks is misleading in suggesting the art and culture comes "from the people." Adorno prefers to speak of the "culture industry." Cf. Robert W. Witkin, *Adorno on Popular Culture* (London: Routledge, 2003), 2.

25. Ted Cohen, "High and Low Thinking about High and Low Art," *The Journal of Aesthetics and Art Criticism* 51 (1993): 151–52.

26. Douglas R. Anderson, "Culture," in *A Companion to Aesthetics*, ed. David Cooper (Oxford: Blackwell Publishers, 1992), 101.

27. Carroll recognizes that his treatment of mass art does not include these other cultural phenomena but believes much of what he says about mass art can be applied to other mass cultural productions. Cf. Carroll (1998), 210.

28. This could include some elements of folk art, those in which there is sufficient mass interest, paintings of tigers or Elvis on black velvet, for example. Much of what in the past was or would have been folk art has become popular culture thanks to mass technology—the blues, for example.

29. I believe that what I say holds for nearly any definition or understanding of philosophy. Elsewhere I have argued that *philosophy* is a kind of family resemblance term, "Philosophy and the Philosophical, Literature and the Literary, Borges and the Labyrinthine," in *Literary Philosophers: Borges, Calvino, Eco*, ed. Gracia, Korsmeyer, and Gasché (New York: Routledge, 2002), 27–45.

30. *People and VH-1 Special Collector's Edition, 200 Greatest Pop Culture Icons* (New York: People Books, 2003).

31. Friedrich Nietzsche, *Beyond Good and Evil*, trans. Walter Kaufmann (New York: Vintage Books, 1989), sec. 30.

32. On American distaste for philosophy, see Richard Hofstadter, *Anti-intellectualism in American Life* (New York: Vintage Books, 1962); and Aeon J. Skoble, "Lisa and American Anti-intellectualism," in *The Simpsons and Philosophy: The D'oh! of Homer*, ed. William Irwin, Mark T. Conard, and Aeon J. Skoble (Chicago: Open Court, 2001), 24–34.

33. Carl Sagan, *The Demon Haunted World: Science as a Candle in the Dark* (New York: Ballantine Books, 1997), 37.

34. See Sagan, 37, 333–36, 362–63.

35. I largely assume I am here preaching to the choir concerning the value of philosophy. For an opposing point of view, see Stanley Fish, "Truth But No Consequences: Why Philosophy Doesn't Matter," *Critical Inquiry* 29 (2003): 389–417.

36. Elsewhere, I have argued that basic philosophical literacy can be accomplished in an introduction to a philosophy course. "Philosophical Literacy: Are There Things Every Philosopher Needs to Know?" *American Philosophical Association Newsletters* 98 (1998): 128–130. The ideal I am arguing for here is for mass philosophical literacy well before college.

37. Philosophy may be more readily embraced by German and French society, though obviously it wasn't enough to prevent their involvement in the worst atrocities of the twentieth century. Still this does not obviously speak against the value of philosophy and the benefits increased philosophical literacy would have for American society.

38. On philosophy cafes, see Christopher Phillips, *Socrates Café: A Fresh Taste of Philosophy* (New York: W. W. Norton & Company, 2002). On the importance of philosophy for children, see Christopher Phillips, *The Philosophers' Club* (Berkeley, CA: Tricycle Press, 2001); Jostein Gaarder, *Sophie's World: A Novel About the History of Philosophy* (New York: Berkley Publishing Group, 1997); and Gareth Matthews, *Philosophy and the Young Child* (Cambridge, MA: Harvard University Press, 1982).

39. Carroll has already ably defended such phenomena against concerns about emotions, morality, ideology, and freedom. See also Richard Shusterman, "Popular Art," in *A Companion to Aesthetics*, ed. David Cooper (Oxford: Blackwell Publishers, 1992) for discussion of six arguments against popular culture, 337–39.

40. Cf. Neal Gabler, *Life: The Movie: How Entertainment Conquered Reality* (New York: Vintage Books, 1998), 16–17.

41. Neil Postman, *Amusing Ourselves to Death: Public Discourse in the Age of Show Business* (New York: Penguin Books, 1985), vii.

42. Postman, 3–4.

43. Postman, 87.

44. Cf. Postman, chap. 10.

45. Slavoj Žižek, "Reloaded Revolutions," in *More Matrix and Philosophy: Revolutions and Reloaded Decoded*, ed. William Irwin (Chicago: Open Court, 2005), 198–208.

46. Cf. Witkin, 29.

47. Cf. Shusterman on Gans, 337.

48. Cf. Gabler.

49. See Norah Martin, "Peterman and the Ideological Mind: Paradoxes of Subjectivity," in *Seinfeld and Philosophy: A Book about Everything and Nothing*, ed. William Irwin (Chicago: Open Court, 2000), 139–47; James M. Wallace, "A (Karl not Groucho) Marxist in Springfield," in *The Simpsons and Philosophy: The D'oh! Of Homer*, ed. William Irwin, Mark T. Conard, and Aeon J. Skoble (Chicago: Open Court, 2001), 235–51; Martin A. Danahay and David Rieder, "*The Matrix*, Marx, and the Coppertop's Life," in *The Matrix and Philosophy: Welcome to the Desert of the Real*, ed. William Irwin (Chicago: Open Court, 2002), 216–24; and Martin A. Danahay, "*The Matrix* is the Prozac of the People," in *More Matrix and Philosophy: Revolutions and Reloaded Decoded*, ed. William Irwin (Chicago: Open Court, 2005), 38–49.

50. Danny Goldberg, *Dispatches from the Culture Wars: How the Left Lost Teen Spirit* (New York: Miramax, 2003). Cf. Postman against politicians entering the arena of entertainment, 132. Also cf. Gabler on politicians on late-night talk shows, 115–16.

51. Carroll (1998), 407.

52. Kellner, 169.

53. Kellner, 173–74.

54. Cf. Witkin, 65.

55. Popular culture may be criticized as contributing to a pernicious globalization à la *Jihad vs. McWorld: Terrorism's Challenge to Democracy* (New York: Ballantine Books, 1995), but even if this criticism holds, it would not serve to invalidate the pop-culture-philosophy hybrid. See Paul A. Cantor, *Gilligan Unbound: Pop Culture in the Age of Globalization* (Lanham, MD: Rowman & Littlefield, 2001).

56. Cf. Carroll (1998), 251. In *The Laws*, Plato, too, is worried about music-induced sexuality.

57. Allan Bloom, *The Closing of the American Mind* (New York: Simon & Schuster, 1987), 78–79.

58. Cf. Carroll (1998), 300–305.

59. Postman, 92–93.

60. Thanks to Bill Van Camp for that insight.

61. Witkin, 129.

62. Postman, 142–43.

63. Hannah Arendt, "Society and Culture," in *The Human Dialogue*, ed. Floyd
Mason and Ashley Montague (Glencoe, IL: Free Press, 1967), 352. Cf. Postman, 124.

64. E. D. Hirsch Jr., *Cultural Literacy: What Every American Needs to Know* (Boston:
Houghton Mifflin, 1987).

65. It must be, as cultural literacy is empirical and descriptive, not prescriptive. See
Hirsch, xiv, 82–93.

66. Goldberg argues that the left will continue to have difficulty as long as they
continue to alienate the youth vote through neglect of popular culture. Bill Clinton,
who actually appeared on MTV, successfully used popular culture. By contrast, Gore
and Lieberman seemed unhip. Though it is nearly forgotten, Gore even had the
anti–popular culture connection to the PMRC via his wife Tipper. Lieberman has
taken a moral stand against much of Hollywood and popular culture.

67. Peter Jones, *Philosophy and the Novel* (Oxford: Clarendon Press, 1975).

68. Martha Nussbaum, *Love's Knowledge* (Oxford: Oxford University Press, 1990).

69. On Nussbaum's elitism, see Jennifer L. McMahon, "The Function of Fiction: The
Heuristic Value of Homer," in *The Simpsons and Philosophy: The D'oh! Of Homer*, ed.
William Irwin, Mark T. Conard, and Aeon J. Skoble (Chicago: Open Court, 2001),
220–21. And see Judith Barad and Ed Robertson, *The Ethics of Star Trek* (New York:
HarperCollins, 2000).

70. See, for example, Richard Hanley, *The Metaphysics of Star Trek* (New York: Basic
Books, 1997).

71. See Karen Bennett's review of *Buffy the Vampire Slayer and Philosophy* for
discussion of the different ways to do "and philosophy." *Notre Dame Philosophical
Reviews* October 10, 2003, http://ndpr.nd.edu/review.cfm?id=1320.

72. For a useful discussion, see Deborah Knight, "Aesthetics and Cultural Studies," in
The Oxford Handbook of Aesthetics, ed. Jerrold Levinson (Oxford: Oxford University
Press, 2003), 783–95.

73. Although I do not wish to be negative, putting down what others have done
with pop culture, cf. Rhonda V. Wilcox and David Lavery, eds., *Fighting the Forces:
What's at Stake in Buffy the Vampire Slayer* (Lanham, MD: Rowman & Littlefield,
2002). For critical discussion of *Fighting the Forces*, see Michael P. Levine and Steven
Jay Schneider, "Feeling for Buffy: The Girl Next Door," in *Buffy the Vampire Slayer
and Philosophy: Fear and Trembling in Sunnydale*, ed. James B. South (Chicago: Open
Court, 2003), 294–308.

74. Or a nontext, as the tendency of cultural studies is to take everything capable of interpretation to be a text. Cf. Knight on cultural studies' pantextualism, 787.

75. See my *Intentionalist Interpretation: A Philosophical Explanation and Defense* (Westport, CT: Greenwood Press, 1999); and E. D. Hirsch Jr., *Validity in Interpretation* (New Haven, CT: Yale University Press, 1967).

76. Not by my understanding of philosophy. But in her essay in this volume, "Philosophy and the Probable Impossible," Carolyn Korsmeyer argues that the second season of the television show *Angel* meets her definition of philosophy. Stephen Mulhall, in *On Film* (London: Routledge, 2002), argues that the *Alien* series of films constitutes philosophy by his lights, 2.

4

Allusion and Intention in Popular Art

Theodore Gracyk

ACCESSIBILITY

While there is much to admire in David Carrier's *The Aesthetics of Comics*, one passage in chapter 5 puzzles me. "The interpretation of comics (and other genuine mass-culture art)," Carrier argues, "differs in kind from analysis of museum paintings." While art historians continue to debate "the intended significance" of "many old-master pictures," Carrier thinks no such interpretive problem confronts the audience for comics, movies, and presumably other mass art. For "almost everyone understands a commonplace comic strip without any need for explanation. You don't need to know anything, apart from that shared knowledge we all possess about contemporary life, to interpret comics."[1] In contrast, museum-based high art is relatively esoteric, and it therefore appeals to a limited audience. We cannot understand most Renaissance paintings or even recent works by Jasper Johns "by merely looking."[2]

Carrier appears to endorse Noël Carroll's analysis of mass art. This analysis holds that mass art involves artworks that have multiple instances, are produced and distributed by a mass technology, and are intentionally designed to provide accessibility "with minimal effort, virtually on first contact, for the largest number of untutored (or relatively untutored) audiences."[3] Almost everyone with passing familiarity with the medium can grasp a particular work's meaning without effort on first exposure. Although Carrier does not propose a general account of popular art, his comments on the accessibility of comics lead him to the topic of popular films, leaving it open what else in popular culture is likewise "obvious to everyone in the culture."[4]

There are strong arguments against equating mass art and popular art. William Irwin reviews them in his contribution to this volume, so I will not repeat them. These arguments remind us that we should not generalize too broadly about popular culture when we are actually discussing mass art. Like Carrier and Carroll, I will focus on identifiable works of mass art fixed in a medium and capable of being known by a broad range of people at various times and places. Movies and recorded music will furnish my primary examples. In contemporary life, they constitute paradigm cases of popular art.

Many popular movies are unlike the daily comics in inviting interpretation, some of it as obscure as is the meaning of Carrier's example, Nicolas Poussin's *Landscape with Diana and Orion* (1660–1664). I was recently talking with some students about Ridley Scott's *Alien* (1979). One of them mentioned another philosophy professor's reading of the film, a reading based on the film's many references to "mother," its position as the first of four, and the importance of the "mother" theme in the other three. I responded that I'd just listened to the director's commentary on the DVD and was more inclined to follow Scott's lead in seeing it as a quasi-existentialist meditation on individual choice.[5]

I am not proposing that we embrace a simple intentionalism and treat Scott's intentions as trumping all other interpretations. I am recommending that we embrace Carroll's point that accessibility for "everyone" should not be taken to include those with no knowledge of anything.[6] So adjusted, I agree with Carrier and Carroll that mass art differs from high art in being aimed at a mass audience, and mass art is designed accordingly. However, the accessibility condition of mass art does not preclude the presence of complex messages that require sophisticated interpretation. Some plausible interpretations will not be obvious to the majority of the mass audience. Obviously, one cannot give *Alien* an existentialist reading unless one has some grasp of existentialism. But *Alien* is a mass artwork, and almost everyone can follow its plot. Doing so does not require a college course in philosophy.

In suggesting that the accessibility condition is compatible with the presence of interpretative challenges, I am not proposing that difficult art is always better than simplistic art. As Carroll argues, it is doubtful "that the quality of art varies in proportion to its difficulty."[7] Instead, I am proposing that, all other things being equal, works of art that present certain kinds of challenges

are aesthetically richer than those that do not present the same species of challenge. My present focus is the richness generated by artistic allusion, and my
primary aim is to show that mass and popular art regularly employ such allusion. In this respect, popular art introduces some of the esoteric elements that
Carrier treats as the province of antipopulist, museum-based high art. Although some allusions are simple and accessible to almost everyone, many allusions in popular works require the same critical insight that Carrier reserves
for high art. Allusions involve hermetic background conditions for their understanding and appreciation. In other words, many works of popular art are
not fully understood unless the audience can supply some very specific information that it presupposes but does not supply to the audience.[8] Like knowledge of the legend of Orion and Diana in Carrier's example of museum-based
art, a lot of popular art rewards a suitably informed audience.[9]

In short, my main point is that although popular art is designed to be accessible to the widest possible audience, allusion introduces hermetic conditions into popular art without interfering with accessibility. Allusion is a
means by which accessible works remain accessible while generating interpretative problems and a consequent aesthetic richness. If I can show this much,
it will reconcile the presence of interpretive challenges for understanding with
the position that mass art is designed to be "easily accessible, virtually on first
exposure, to mass untutored audiences."[10]

ALLUSION IN *THE MATRIX*

Examples can be an obstacle as well as help. What examples can I use without
having to provide enough material and context for the examples to be useful? I
would have to describe a large chunk of the film *Alien* if I wanted to defend the
existentialist interpretation. In discussing allusion, I will concentrate on a small
group of relatively simple examples.[11] Consider *The Matrix* (1999), the first film
in the trilogy. Recall the scene in which Morpheus offers Neo the choice to learn
what the matrix is. "I imagine," says Morpheus, "that right now you're feeling a
bit like Alice, tumbling down the rabbit hole." Here we have an allusion to the
opening chapter of Lewis Carroll's *Alice's Adventures in Wonderland*. The allusion is obvious and signals that strange things are likely to happen. Clearly, we
are supposed to understand that Morpheus knows *Alice's Adventures in Wonderland*, and he expects Neo to know it, too. Lewis Carroll and his books exist
in the fictional world of *The Matrix*. While it is fictional that Morpheus alludes

to Lewis Carroll, because everything Morpheus does is fictional, the film alludes to a very real book by way of this fictional interaction.

But Morpheus extends his allusion. He offers Neo two pills. "After this, there is no turning back. You take the blue pill, the story ends. You wake up in your bed and you believe whatever you want to believe. You take the red pill, you stay in Wonderland, and I show you how deep the rabbit hole goes." This additional allusion to Wonderland and the rabbit hole adds no new information to the scene. But suppose we pause and ask why the pills are blue and red, and why blue means "stop" and red means "continue." After all, Morpheus and Neo are operating in a simulation of "the end of the twentieth century," where red means "stop" and green means "go." But the film narrative continues past this minor point, never to return to it.[12] The choice of colors for the two pills appears to be arbitrary.

Except that the color choice is not arbitrary, and it deviates from twentieth-century practice because it is an allusion to a nineteenth-century text. It alludes to chapter 6 of Lewis Carroll's *Sylvie and Bruno*. Sylvie is invited to choose one of two lockets.[13] One locket has a blue gem and the other has a red gem. The blue locket is engraved with the phrase "All—will—love—Sylvie," while the red is engraved with "Sylvie—will—love—all." Seeing the difference, Sylvie selects the red locket. "It's very nice to be loved," she said, "but it's nicer to love other people!" (On a side note, Sylvie never uses the magic locket in *Sylvie and Bruno*. But the locket introduces the theme of love, central to the book and its sequel, for love is the thing that transforms empty ritual into something of genuine significance.) We might also notice that the opening words of *Sylvie and Bruno* are a short poem. It begins, "Is all our Life, then but a dream?"

So Neo's choice parallels Sylvie's in crucial respects. Each is offered something red and something blue, and each chooses the red one. Since it is obvious that this scene in *The Matrix* alludes to one Lewis Carroll novel through its verbal allusion to *Alice's Adventures*, it seems apparent that the same scene contains an equally important, although less obvious, allusion to a second Lewis Carroll novel. However, there is no reason to think that Morpheus is making an allusion to *Sylvie and Bruno*. That novel is no longer widely read, and there is no reason to suppose, in this fictional world, that Morpheus would know it and would expect Neo to know it, too. So in this case, the film makes the allusion without having a character fictionally allude. This subtle allusion to *Sylvie and Bruno* is ingenious, and those who discovered it received a foreshadowing of what was to come at the end of the *Matrix* trilogy. In choosing the red pill, Neo would not escape fate. Fate, remember, was what Neo wants to escape by taking the red pill. Despite his rejection of self-sacrifice in *The Matrix Reloaded* (2003), Neo would ultimately be the one to love all. In short, this allusion suggests at the outset that Neo is a Christ figure who must die for humankind.

So I think that the same scene contains two allusions, one obvious and one subtle. In the vocabulary I'll adopt, the scene with the two pills is the alluding text.[14] The scene intentionally alludes to both *Alice's Adventures* and to *Sylvie and Bruno*, which are its two source texts. What analysis of allusion is broad enough to count the references to Alice and to the lockets as allusions despite their many differences?

STANDARD CONDITIONS FOR ALLUSION

I will employ a variant of the analysis of allusion defended by William Irwin. Following Irwin, an allusion is an intended reference that calls for associations that go beyond mere substitution of a referent.[15] Breaking this proposal into its constituent parts, there are three necessary conditions for the presence of allusion. The three conditions are jointly sufficient. They are the presence of indirect reference, authorial intention to allude, and the possibility of detection in principle.[16] Since I am sympathetic to Irwin's arguments for these three conditions, I will now concentrate on extending them beyond Irwin's consciously limited scope of verbal allusion.

On this model, *The Matrix* alludes to *Sylvie and Bruno* in advance of audience recognition of the connection. The audience discovers the allusion (as opposed, say, to creating it through an act of recognition). Although few viewers of the film detect the subtle allusion to *Sylvie and Bruno*, it satisfies the condition that an allusion must offer the audience the possibility of its recognition. Its reference to a source text is established by textual similarity that makes the allusion capable of detection. Citing a verbal joke in a *Simpsons* episode, Irwin says, "This is clearly intended as an allusion to *Forrest Gump*."[17] Although Irwin does not emphasize the point, the joke alludes to the film as source text, and only secondarily to the fictional character of Forrest. Similarly, the first verse of the David Bowie song "Ashes to Ashes" (1980) is an extended allusion to two different verses of a Buddy Holly song, "Peggy Sue Got

Married" (1959). Bowie alludes to the earlier song, but he does not allude to the character, Peggy Sue.[18]

However, Stephanie Ross's work on allusion reminds us that it is dangerous to treat verbal allusion as typical of all allusion. Our tendency to emphasize literary allusion limits recognition of allusion throughout popular culture, where it is frequently visual or aural. To return to one of my earlier examples, my daughter and I recently watched the movie *Alien*. One of the film's first images is an establishing shot of the exterior of the spacecraft. My daughter's immediate response was that the image was remarkably like the opening frames of *Star Wars* (1977; what we now know as episode 4, *A New Hope*). Since I assume that Ridley Scott knew that his opening sequence mimics the opening sequence of *Star Wars: A New Hope*, it seems to be a case of nonliterary artistic allusion to an identifiable source text.

Ross also reminds us to look for cross-modal allusion, that is, allusion between two arts that appeal to two sensory modalities. *The Matrix* offers a cross-modal allusion to *Sylvie and Bruno*, taking us from the visual prompt of two colors to the literary text and its verbal description of two lockets. One of my favorite cross-modal allusions is the photograph on the front of the Rolling Stones album *Get Yer Ya-Ya's Out!* (1970). It illustrates Bob Dylan's lyric "jewels and binoculars hang from the head of the mule" from "Visions of Johanna" (1966).

Irwin acknowledges that there are nonverbal allusions, but only in passing. Focusing on verbal allusion, he divides allusion into the literary and the nonliterary.[19] T. S. Eliot's line, "I am not Prince Hamlet," alludes to the character of Hamlet in the play *Hamlet*. So it is a literary allusion. In a courtesy sense, so is David Bowie's allusion to the Buddy Holly song. Popular culture is rife with nonliterary allusion, but it is important to notice that their nonliterary status may derive from either of two situations. On the one hand, the allusion may be musical or visual or otherwise nonverbal. If you have seen the movie *Shrek* (2001), it is likely that you will recall the moment that visually parodies *The Matrix*. Princess Fiona leaps into the air and freezes in the same pose that Trinity adopts in the opening fight sequence of *The Matrix*. Just like Trinity, Princess Fiona delivers a vicious martial arts kick to her opponent. Because it is a visual allusion, it is not a literary allusion.

On the other hand, allusion may be verbal but nonliterary by failing to allude to an identifiable source text. For instance, Irwin provides the verbal example of

"He is no Mr. October" in sports writing, a nonliterary piece of writing that alludes to a nonliterary subject. It refers to a person, but it does not refer to any source text. Paul Simon employs this type of nonliterary allusion when the song "Mrs. Robinson" refers to baseball great Joe DiMaggio as "Joltin' Joe."

For my purposes, the important distinction is between artistic allusion and nonartistic allusion. With artistic allusion, both the source text and the alluding text are works of art.[20] With nonartistic allusion, either the source text or the alluding text is not a work of art, or there is no identifiable source text. If we examine popular culture with this distinction in mind, artistic allusion is widespread in mass art. Only a small portion of it is literary allusion.

On this analysis, artistic allusion is distinct from genre parody, where such parody does not assume audience familiarity with any specific source text. *This is Spinal Tap* (1984) features songs that lampoon heavy metal music, and while it seems that the idea arose as a spoof of the band Black Sabbath, none of the jokes depend solely on allusions to that band. In contrast, *The Rutles* film and album (1978) features artistic allusion, for each song parodies a specific Beatles song. The song "Ouch" parodies "Help," "Piggy in the Middle" parodies the psychedelic style of "I Am the Walrus," and the album jacket parodies four different Beatles albums. Some of these jokes rely on aural similarities. Others are visual allusions.

So my first major point is that artistic allusion intentionally refers the audience to another text, an identifiable source text. I will argue that this relationship places normative conditions on audience interpretations of such allusions, in principle limiting the associations that carry from source text to alluding text. If a property cannot be independently assigned to the source text, then associating that property with the alluding text cannot be an association justified by the presence of the allusion. If we do not treat the allusion as intentional, then there is no normative force to our recognition that two texts are similar. If we do not treat the allusion as intentional, there is no interpretative error in anachronistically supposing that the 1994 film *Forrest Gump*'s "Run, Forrest, run" alludes to the 1999 film *Fight Club*, when it is really the other way around.

ALLUSIVE ASSOCIATIONS

Artistic allusion does more than refer us to a source text. It also refers us to something in the source text that is beyond the immediate point of overlap between the source and derivative texts.[21] The goal of this reference is to call attention to something that is not actually said in it. In a successful allusion, a different referring expression with the same reference would not call for the same associations. I am going to expand on this point by employing Paul Grice's position on conversational implicature.

Allusive associations vary when we substitute different referring terms. And this is so even if the alluding text is a popular text: the same couplet from T. S. Eliot's "The Love Song of J. Alfred Prufrock" is alluded to by the Sisters of Mercy's song "Amphetamine Logic" (1986) and by the Bangles' song "Dover Beach" (1984): "In the room the women come and go / Talking of Michelangelo." In the film *Love and Death* (1975), Woody Allen's character alludes to the same poem, but to a different couplet. Settling down after his marriage, Allen's character takes up poetry. Scribbling a line, he reads it aloud: "I should have been a pair of ragged claws / Scuttling across the floors of silent seas." He pauses, crumbles it up, and tosses it on the floor, saying, "Too sentimental." Each of these works of popular art cites Eliot's "Prufrock" with an artistic allusion.

But why quote one famous line, and not the other? If the Bangles and Woody Allen merely wish to allude to T. S. Eliot, they can quote "Let us go then, you and I" instead of later lines from the poem. Here, I think, we arrive at the necessity for introducing authorial intention into the analysis of allusion, because consideration of the authorial decision is relevant to its normative force and to the richness of the resulting allusion.

AUTHORIAL INTENTION

Some analyses of allusion reject the necessity of citing authorial intention.[22] The distinction between genuine and accidental associations is a strong basis for responding to anti-intentionalist analyses. Let us look at two anti-intentionalist arguments in greater detail.

Influenced by literary poststructuralism, some anti-intentionalists argue that authors do not intend any "specific interpretation" of the allusion when they introduce one. Authors cannot control the reader's associations, so "no specific interpretation of the allusion can be demonstrated in any convincing way to be intended by the author." An author or artist can create an allusion and can intend that we find it, but the author can neither "direct" nor "control" its meaning or "what sorts of interpretations arise from it."[23] Therefore, an allusion "gains a meaning only through the reader's actualization of it."[24] Each member of the audience "assumes complete interpretive power over the allusive moment."[25] Far from displaying artistic intention, allusion reveals "the transference of meaning's authority from writer to reader."[26]

However, the fact that a speaker cannot control the associations in the audience's mind is no evidence against the relevance of authorial intentions. If I advise you that the brakes on the car are faulty and warn you against driving it, my words might cause you to think about a near accident that you had yesterday. I didn't intend for you to think about this incident, for I tried to get you to think about the future, not the past. My inability to control your thoughts is no evidence that you have complete interpretive power over the meaning of my words. If you take my words about the car's brakes to be an invitation to think about yesterday's events, your "interpretive power" amounts to nothing more than the freedom to misunderstand. The fact that some associations are subjective, arbitrary, or unexpected does not show that artists cannot intend to suggest one set of associations rather than others.

Monroe Beardsley offers a very different argument against authorial intentions. He dismisses references to intentions as unnecessary appeals to private mental events. Tokens of a text are public objects, and the text does what it does apart from its author's intentions. Beardsley notes that one line in T. S. Eliot's "The Waste Land" alludes to a line written by Edmund Spenser.[27] Beardsley proposes that Eliot's text alludes to Spenser's, and that it does so even if "Eliot never read or heard a line of Spenser." In other words, allusiveness is a literary quality. *Texts* allude, not authors, and texts allude by virtue of their place in an artistic tradition.[28]

Beardsley's position is well known. Among the many rejoinders made to Beardsley, I think that the best response is to call attention to conversational implicature.[29] Conversations are full of sentences that convey more information than is actually said. Suppose Sue asks Miranda if she wants to go to lunch, and Miranda answers, "I'm not hungry." Miranda might be telling Sue that she does not plan to go to lunch, or perhaps she is suggesting that she does not want to have lunch with *Sue*. The declarative sentence states neither of these things, but Miranda's answer certainly *intends* more than it says. When Sue wonders whether Miranda is rejecting lunch with Sue or merely rejecting lunch, Sue is pondering Miranda's intentions.[30] Actual conclusions about what is meant beyond what is said are constrained by Grice's cooperative principle, which is the general assumption that each utterance in a conversation will advance "the accepted purpose or direction of the talk exchange in which you are engaged." Among its subprinciples are requirements to be relevant and to be sufficiently informative.[31]

Similarly, artworks pose interpretive challenges that require audiences to regard them as designed to convey ideas that they do not overtly present.[32] With ordinary conversational implicature, remarks that do not seem directly relevant will, on the assumption of relevance, be taken to *imply* something relevant. Likewise, many cases of artistic meaning are enriched by the seeming irrelevance of some of their features. Randy Newman's song "I Love L.A." (1983) names several major thoroughfares in Los Angeles, concluding the list with "Sixth Street." But why Sixth Street? It's not famous. It is an unremarkable street in downtown Los Angeles. Its inclusion invites those of us who've driven on it to reconsider the rest of the list, and it suggests that Randy Newman included it in order to make the whole list ironic. Pride about Santa Monica Boulevard is made to look foolish, as foolish as pride in Sixth Street. The song says one thing, but Randy Newman intends us to understand something more.[33]

Artworks, including mass artworks, invite us to reflect on the intentions of their designers. Consequently, if I had reason to think that "Eliot never read or heard a line of Spenser," then I would conclude that there is no allusion at this point in the poem. Likewise, if the codirecting Wachowski brothers were not aware of *Sylvie and Bruno*, then *The Matrix* does not allude to the two lockets. In that case, my claims about the relevance of the lockets constitute a misunderstanding of the film. In his contribution to this book, Noël Carroll observes that many popular films and stories are similar because they recycle the same basic schemas and prototypes—"the sensual woman who loves sex" describes both Samantha in *Sex and the City* and Chaucer's Wife of Bath.[34] But if the similarity ends there, we do not interpret *Sex and the City* as an *invitation* to think of Chaucer.

Allusion requires highly specific overlap between an alluding text and a source text. When we detect this, we become aware of intentions advising us to consider the content of the work from a certain perspective. The intention to allude is thus an illocutionary intention; it succeeds when the audience recognizes the presence of the intention to allude.[35]

But artistic allusion also involves a perlocutionary intention, that is, an intention to bring about an effect beyond mere recognition of the intention to allude. The additional effect is twofold: the audience is directed to a *specific* source text, and there is a new interpretation of the alluding text. The fact that the audience supplies this interpretation does not negate the possibility that specific meanings are part of this authorial intention, as some suppose. When you do a crossword puzzle and the clue for 5 across is "feline," the perlocutionary intention is that the reader will fill in the appropriate horizontal spaces with some appropriate word. If there are three spaces, and the first two are already filled in with a *c* and an *a*, most people will fill in the third space with a *t*. And this is the intended perlocutionary effect of the clue. Granted, this effect is not one that the crossword puzzle writer can dictate or control. But it does not follow that the author has surrendered all power over meanings in this situation. The author has provided a puzzle and has invited the audience to solve the puzzle. Some clues will be misinterpreted, and some responses to the puzzle will be full of errors and dead ends. But the activity of solving such puzzles can be a source of great pleasure.[36]

In artistic allusion, the textual similarity that refers the audience to the source text is like a clue in a crossword puzzle. It alludes, but it also authorizes some associations and proscribes others.[37] I have proposed that this normative aspect of allusion would be absent if allusion did not require authorial intention. Recognition of allusion requires recognition of an intention to allude, and this recognition is recognition that the author, in alluding, asks us to make it relevant to the current situation. In the same way that understanding an invitation to go to lunch requires you to recognize the speaker's illocutionary intention to invite you, you cannot claim to have found an allusion unless you also recognize the author's intention to allude. Again, as with a luncheon invitation, the success of the illocutionary act does not guarantee that the perlocutionary intention will be realized. A luncheon invitation may be understood but declined. The presence of the allusion may be *recognized*, in which case the illocutionary intention succeeds, but the invitation to make associations may be declined. And even if the invitation is accepted, there will be many cases where the clues are not understood. The perlocutionary intention does not guarantee successful perlocutionary effect.

Yet a failure of the allusion's perlocutionary intention does not mean that the allusion was wasted on the audience. The most significant feature of a mass-art allusion is that it simultaneously presents two illocutionary intentions, only one of which carries the perlocutionary intention that the audience do something with the indirect reference. In mass art, an artistic allusion authorizes and proscribes various meanings in the alluding text, meanings that are accessible even if one is not aware of the presence of allusion. A viewer of *Alien* who hasn't seen *Star Wars* will understand the narrative purpose of the alluding shot. One can understand Neo's decision in taking the red pill without noticing the allusion. But for those who catch the allusion, it authorizes and proscribes additional meanings that arise from associations with the source text. This doubling of illocutionary intention explains how mass art can satisfy the accessibility condition endorsed by Carrier and Carroll, while at the same time it can incorporate references that are not accessible to much of the mass audience.

INTEGRATING ALLUSIONS INTO TEXTS

When the allusion is recognized and the audience makes connections under the auspices of Grice's cooperative principle, different aspects of the allusion will limit the range of associations appropriate to it. An artistic allusion reflects two artistic decisions: the choice of a source text and the choice of an "echo," quotation, or paraphrase from among the many that might be employed. The two decisions are closely related.

In mass art, a good allusion will serve as a functional element of the alluding text independent of its alluding function. Apart from their indirect reference, the red and blue pills allow us to see Neo's choice without his having to announce it. Two different mass artworks may allude to the same source text but will choose different allusive elements, ones appropriate to their own direction. When Jefferson Airplane's Grace Slick wrote a song alluding to both of Carroll's Alice books, she chose to mention the rabbit (but not the rabbit hole), Alice, changes in size, the caterpillar with the hookah, the Red Queen, and the pieces on the chessboard coming to life. *The Matrix* mentions Alice and the rabbit hole but not the rabbit, and I can't recall any references to caterpillars, chess, or hookahs. Grace Slick and her band, Jefferson Airplane, were interested in elements that could serve as drug references in the absence of detailed knowledge of the Alice books. *The Matrix* explores altered realities, but not the sort that comes about by ingesting psychoactive drugs. When the Bangles and Woody Allen allude to Eliot's "Prufrock," they choose different couplets. The Bangles want to create a positive bond between two characters, while Woody Allen wants to make his poet look absurd. Each chooses accordingly, and the words contribute sense to the alluding text even in the absence of recognition that it alludes.

This strategy also holds for nonverbal allusion. Irwin mentions the case of the banjo theme from the movie *Deliverance* (1973) appearing in the "Colonel Homer" episode of *The Simpsons*, humorously foreshadowing danger. This burst of banjo must function even if viewers do not "get" the full allusion. Thanks to prevailing connotations of banjo music, viewers who do not recognize the banjo tune as the theme from *Deliverance* will not laugh, but the mere *sound* of the banjo tells the audience "that Homer has entered a backward, redneck area."[38] Those who recognize the link to the source text will be authorized to read more into the moment, based on additional associations that might be made. Viewers of *Kill Bill: Vol. 1* (2003) who don't know that Uma Thurman's yellow jumpsuit is an allusion to Bruce Lee's final film (*Enter the Dragon*, 1973) don't expect her to be naked, so the outfit has a purpose apart from the allusion. It also makes her stand out from the multitude of attacking villains in a big fight scene. In mass art, virtually all allusion satisfies this twofold function. But when allusions occur, there is the possibility of recognition (in principle) that two distinct decisions must have been made. A source text was chosen, and an element from that source text was chosen, subject to conventions that allow its integration into the alluding text without diminishing access for those who miss the allusion.

The same integration strategy is employed in the traditional fine arts. It would be silly to suppose that fine-art allusions are present solely for the sake of their allusive effects, creating incomprehensible elements for those who do not grasp their reference to a source text. Visually, Edouard Manet's painting *Olympia* (1863) packs its punch independently of its allusion to Titian's *Venus of Urbino* (1538). Eliot's "The Love Song of J. Alfred Prufrock" contains a subtle allusion to John Donne's "The Relic." (Eliot's "arms that are braceleted and white" echoes Donne's "a bracelet of white hair.") Yet Eliot's line has its own descriptive function, independent of the fact that it alludes. Two lines of Bob Dylan's song "Maybe Someday" are equally subtle in alluding to two lines of Eliot's "Journey of the Magi." While creators of both high and low art enhance their work with allusion, recognizing that they do so is not essential to the enjoyment of either the poem or the rock song. The audience for fine art may be more open to avant-garde techniques and so more tolerant of disruptive allusions, with no function except as allusions. But the popular arts are not special in designing allusions that contribute to the alluding work apart from their functions as allusions.

For those who successfully grasp an allusion, the artistic decision to use one element of the source text rather than another provides interpretative direction. It directs the search for relevant associations, suggesting elements of the source text that are to be brought to bear on the alluding text. In light of the cooperative principle, this decision serves as a clue to allusive relevance. How and where does the alluding element appear in both texts? *The Matrix* alludes to *Sylvie and Bruno* at the moment of Neo's choice. Any associations that arise should be relevant to his choice. Morpheus prefaced the allusion with a discussion of fate. It is likely that the associations will tell us about Neo's fate. Subsequent discussions of fate will then invite application of Sylvie's reason for choosing the red locket (e.g., when the Oracle warns Neo that he is fated to sacrifice himself or Morpheus). The Bangles want to play with an ambiguity of gender, which is accomplished by changing Eliot's "women" to "we." Knowledge of Eliot's original line is required to grasp that the narrator is addressing another woman, something that cannot otherwise be determined from the lyric. Woody Allen wants to make us aware of the anachronism of putting a modernist passage into a poem a hundred years before it could work. The couplet about the women and Michelangelo would allude to the same poem but would lack the unsentimental jolt of the "ragged claws / Scuttling across the floors of silent seas."

But it is also important to acknowledge that the allusion underdetermines the associations it invokes. The source text has many features that are not relevant to the linking of the two texts, and the mechanism by which allusion operates will always leave us with the interpretative problem of which features of each text are relevant when importing associations from one to the other. Hence there is always a possibility that the perlocutionary intentions will be unsatisfied even when the allusion is noticed.

COVERT ALLUSIONS IN POPULAR ART

The source text for an allusion may be overt (obvious to most of the audience) or covert. We might assume that high art is more likely to contain covert allusion, and that popular culture is more likely to exploit overt, obvious allusions. But I do not see any reason to generalize in this way. Popular culture is full of covert allusion too. These are generally cases where the source text is not as well known as the alluding text. Although I would speculate that millions of music fans have seen the Foo Fighters' video for "Everlong" (1997), relatively few viewers are likely to notice its allusions to *Andalusian Dog* (*Le Chien Andalou*), for the obvious reason that relatively few rock music fans have ever seen the 1929 short film by Luis Bunuel and Salvador Dali. But the visual connections are there in plain sight, as is the allusion to Lewis Carroll's *Sylvie and Bruno* in *The Matrix*.

Generational change can rapidly move an allusion from the overt to the covert. I was surprised when my son asked me if I know of a rock song called "Stairway to Heaven." "Of course," I said, "by Led Zeppelin." At first, I thought he knew the song and wanted to know who performed it. But then it became clear that he wanted to know if such a song existed at all. I pointed out to him that he'd heard the song before, even if he didn't know its name. His interest was that "Stairway to Heaven" is the original name of a Japanese film from 2001, a spin-off of the Cowboy Bebop anime television series. A fan, my son knew that every episode of Cowboy Bebop has a title that alludes to a rock song. (Early episodes include "Sympathy for the Devil" and "Honky Tonk Women.") Fans of the TV series knew that the lack of such a title for the film was a marketing decision: the original Japanese film was *Cowboy Bebop: Stairway to Heaven*, but the subtitle vanished when it received international release. Knowing all of this, my son knew that the film made an allusion to a song, but he did not know if he knew the source text. Twenty years ago, it would have been difficult to find an American male teenager who did not know "Stairway to Heaven." But listening habits have changed, and now there are many teenage music fans who have never heard Led Zeppelin. In 1968, the Kinks inserted relatively obvious allusions to both "Smokestack Lightning" and "Train Kept A Rollin'" in their recording of "Last of the Steam-Powered Trains." Today, all three songs are largely forgotten. As the audience changes, an obvious allusion can gradually become one for which there is merely the possibility of detection in principle. It takes very little time for an allusion to become as obscure as the high-art reference to the legend of Diana and Orestes.

But a second reason that overt allusions become covert is that popular culture is no longer folk culture. Both the construction and economics of mass art encourage the consumption of artworks in cultural contexts distinct from their origins.[39] Audiences throughout the world see American films. Americans, in turn, can watch *Cowboy Bebop*. Looking at a fan's website that catalogues allusions in Cowboy Bebop, I find that the majority of the nonmusical allusions are simply unknown to me, but not because of historical distance.

Both cultural difference and the sheer quantity of mass art ensure that no audience member will grasp all the allusive references that they encounter in mass art. I am a great fan of Elvis Costello, but I listened to the *Armed Forces* album (1979) for years before I learned that "Senior Service" (a song title) is a British brand of cigarettes, a nonartistic allusion that greatly enriches the song's theme of youthful dissatisfaction.[40] In mass art, it is inevitable that seemingly overt meanings and allusions will be erased as the mass-art text makes its way to new audiences.

SOME COMPLICATIONS

I will conclude by suggesting two additional points about mass-art allusion. One concerns the perlocutionary intention of placing an allusion in a mass artwork. The other concerns the possibility of extended allusion.

Irwin proposes that the chief aesthetic effect of allusion "is that it strengthens the connection between the author and the audience, cultivating intimacy and forging a sense of community."[41] While this is certainly important in the case of one-on-one, face-to-face conversation, I am not clear how it works with mass art. Irwin is borrowing a page from Ted Cohen's analysis of jokes. However, Cohen treats joke telling as a direct human encounter, not as one mediated by mass media.[42] When I see a Woody Allen film and I recognize its allusion to T. S. Eliot, the intimacy and community that I share with Allen is extremely shallow. I would be a fool to think that Allen has tried to establish an intimacy with me. I would be like Charles Manson, who infamously thought that the Beatles were talking to him through their albums. Reading Christopher Rick's recent book on Bob Dylan, I recognize hundreds of allusions to Dylan's lyrics in Rick's prose.[43] But I feel no intimacy with the author, for I know that most readers will be Dylan fans and will recognize them too, while nonfans won't care.

While there are many situations in which allusion can create intimacy among members of the audience who find one another responding to the same allusion, mass art is not a forum for instilling a genuine sense of community. There may be "a sense of community" for a small group in front of the television, laughing at the same joke, or for friends and coworkers who debate the merits of a film they've seen (whether together or, more likely, separately). But there is nothing special about allusion here. We get the same sense of connection with others by being fans of the same sports team or by finding that we watch the same late-night talk show.

If the feeling of intimacy and community is neither a major nor a unique source of pleasure in mass-art allusion, we might shift our focus to the pleasure that comes from recognition and understanding of allusions. Irwin proposes that while we do not want allusions to be too obvious, it "should not be a riddle to be pondered for an extended time." We should get it "all at once" by remembering something we already know.[44] Part of his evidence is that this immediacy is essential to the effect of intimacy and community.[45] But since I've cast doubt on *that* effect with mass-art allusion, perhaps their gamelike quality is more important than Irwin allows. If we admire the wit and skill behind a good allusion, we may think a good deal about the associations that are intended. Most of the audience for mass art returns to the same text, watching their favorite films many times and listening to the same music again and again. Allusions that were overlooked may suddenly appear, in part because the audience member will have learned new things in the meantime. The first time I saw Woody Allen's *Love and Death*, I'd never heard of T. S. Eliot and Prufrock. The second time I saw it, I was studying literature in college, and I got the joke. Watching *The Matrix* after learning of the *Sylvie and Bruno* allusion, I became more aware of how the theme of choice and fate was introduced at other points in the plot, and I looked to see how the theme of love might be related to each of them. The allusion's pleasurable prompt of recognition (my awareness that the author intends to allude) is not at odds with its puzzle pleasure.[46] The pleasure of recognition is sometimes an invitation to a puzzle, a puzzle that may be solved over time and after multiple experiences of the same text.

Finally, I'd like to note that the analysis of mass art that I've endorsed is neutral about the saturation of the alluding text by the source text. Are allusions necessarily local, small-scale aesthetic effects?[47] Is this more likely to be the case with popular art? Some authors insist that allusion is a local event within a text. This view is reinforced by the assumption that allusions please through their immediacy. However, Irwin endorses the possibility of a sonnet that alludes, as a whole, to Shakespeare's sonnet 55. But at this point, I think we have thousands of real cases where a long stretch of a work or even a whole work alludes. Gus Van Sant's film *My Own Private Idaho* (1991) is an obvious example. The stilted quality of many scenes derives from extended borrowings from Shakespeare's *Henry IV*, parts 1 and 2. Many fans of actor Keanu Reeves have seen the film, and they can follow the story despite their ignorance of Shakespeare. But much of its aesthetic richness comes from the extended allusion.

Saturation is also present through music sampling and in remakes of films and songs. Remakes, in which an entirely new version is created, can satisfy the conditions of allusion. Consider the phenomenon of tribute albums, in which an assortment of pop musicians contributes "covers" of songs by the same artist. One of my favorites is the British package, *The Last Temptation of Elvis: Songs from His Movies* (1990), in no small part because of the allusion of the title. When Bruce Springsteen covers "Viva Las Vegas" and the Jesus and Mary Chain covers "Guitar Man," each renders the song in their own style. But the musicians intend that we compare what they have done with the "originals," the Elvis Presley versions, and we are invited to interpret each new performance in light of the Elvis source text. I will leave you to think about film remakes, and how later versions are purposely enriched by our memories of the source films.

To sum up, allusions involve both illocutionary and perlocutionary intentions, and the pleasure that comes from recognition of an allusion is not always resolved in the immediate recognition of its significance. As in high art, many mass-art allusions are invisible to much of the audience. Some are puzzles even for those who notice their presence. But a successful work of mass art must satisfy an accessibility condition. For those who "get" a small-scale allusion, part of its aesthetic richness is how it dovetails into the alluding work without disrupting accessibility for those who don't grasp it.

A PRACTICAL BENEFIT

When works of popular art are enriched by artistic allusion, their interpretation does not differ in kind from that of many works of fine art. While this result is not a trivial one, it should not be taken to imply that there are no important differences between popular art and museum masterpieces, or between accessible entertainment and challenging works of art. Many works of mass art remain trivial, shallow, or juvenile, including ones enriched by allusion. So critics of mass art are unlikely to be impressed by the presence of artistic allusion in *The Matrix*, cover songs, and Woody Allen movies.

But here is one valuable result of observing artistic allusion in mass art. In a culture saturated with mass art, it can be difficult to give neophytes an entry point into the process of interpreting and appreciating traditional art. This problem torments art educators and museum curators. Audiences who have not received the education necessary to deal with fine art often respond to it

ALLUSION AND INTENTION IN POPULAR ART

with some combination of embarrassment, frustration, and hostility. But mass culture ensures that almost everyone already understands and enjoys artistic allusion. So most people already possess one of the central interpretive skills needed for understanding and enjoying fine art. Highlighting artistic allusion might be a useful bridge in moving audiences from mass art to fine art.[48]

NOTES

1. David Carrier, *The Aesthetics of Comics* (University Park: Pennsylvania State University Press, 2000), 84–85.

2. Carrier, 85.

3. Noël Carroll, *The Philosophy of Mass Art* (Oxford: Clarendon, 1998), 196.

4. Carrier, 85.

5. For an interesting discussion of DVD commentaries, see Deborah Parker and Mark Parker, "Directors and DVD Commentary: The Specifics of Intention," *The Journal of Aesthetics and Art Criticism* 62 (2004): 13–22.

6. "After all, when I spoke of 'untutored audiences,' I did not mean to refer to wolf children." (Carroll, 227.)

7. Carroll, 100.

8. Ted Cohen, *Jokes: Philosophical Thoughts on Joking Matters* (Chicago: University of Chicago Press, 1999), 12–21.

9. An interesting example is a pair of songs, "Diana—Part 1" and "Diana—Part 2," featured on Paul Kantner and Grace Slick, *Sunfighter* (Grunt Records, 1971). As with Poussin's *Landscape with Diana and Orion,* the songs provide a richer experience for those who grasp their reference to the myth of the goddess Diana.

10. Carroll, 227.

11. For extended consideration of a single example, see Michael Baur, "*American Pie* and the Self-Critique of Rock 'n' Roll," in this volume.

12. The next film, *Matrix Reloaded,* returns to it in the scene where the Oracle offers Neo a red candy.

13. My son, Thelonious Gracyk, provided this example to me. As I wrote this essay, I could find no commentary on *The Matrix* acknowledging it. An account has now been published by James Lawler, "Only Love Is Real: Heidegger, Plato, and *The

Matrix Trilogy," in *More Matrix and Philosophy:* Revolutions *and* Reloaded *Decoded,* ed. William Irwin (Chicago: Open Court, 2005), 26–37. Lawler became aware of the allusion when Irwin (with my permission) shared my essay with Lawler. My interpretation directly conflicts with that of Richard Giles, who claims that the color choice derives from the colors assigned to fire and water in "The Chinese classical Five Elements," www.astrologycom.com/matrix2.html (accessed February 18, 2006).

14. I am using *text* in order to emphasize the overlap between two structural types. But since a source text must historically precede and influence an alluding text, the source text is part of the historical context of the alluding text. Following the common practice of using *text* to indicate an abstract structural type and *work* to mean a historically situated type, it should be understood that I am at all times claiming that an alluding *work* refers to a source *work.*

15. William Irwin and J. R. Lombardo, "The Simpsons and Allusion: 'Worst Essay Ever,'" in *The Simpsons and Philosophy: The D'Oh! Of Homer,* ed. William Irwin, Mark T. Conard, and Aeon J. Skoble (Chicago: Open Court, 2001), 82.

16. William Irwin, "What Is an Allusion?" *The Journal of Aesthetics and Art Criticism* 59 (2001): 294. Although Irwin correctly objects to small details in the definition of allusion defended by Stephanie Ross, Ross provides strong supporting argument for the second and third conditions of Irwin's definition. See Stephanie Ross, "Art and Allusion," *The Journal of Aesthetics and Art Criticism* 40 (1981): 59–70. Following Ross, we should note that our usage (e.g., "*The Matrix* alludes to *Sylvie and Bruno*") is shorthand for the claim that the author of the former alludes to the latter (Ross, n2).

17. Irwin and Lombardo, 82.

18. The "Ashes to Ashes" allusion is an interesting case, because the lyric alludes to another song, Bowie's own "Space Oddity" (1969), while "Peggy Sue Got Married" alludes to Holly's early hit, "Peggy Sue" (1957). Thus Bowie suggests an additional allusion, one that arises from his mirroring the allusive technique of the Holly source text. The parallel creates one of the rare cases where allusion is transitive, so that an allusion to a source text that itself alludes carries the allusion back to that earlier source text. But such transitive allusions seem the rare exception, not the rule.

19. William Irwin, "The Aesthetics of Allusion," *The Journal of Value Inquiry* 36 (2002): 522.

20. It need not be an *individual* source text. Many popular texts are serials. In the television show *The Nanny,* one episode has a joke with the punch line "I look like John-Boy Walton." If one has seen any of the many episodes of *The Waltons,* the joke

succeeds. No specific episode serves as a source text. This allusion back to a reoccurring element of a series is not unique to mass culture. Ross notes that Roy Lichtenstein's cathedral paintings allude to a series done by Claude Monet, but not any *one* Monet. Many mass art texts are part of a series of works (e.g., the *Star Wars* or *Alien* films, comic books, Nancy Drew novels) with recurring features that can be the object of an allusion.

21. As Irwin puts it, with allusion, "we are supposed to make unstated associations, and in this sense the reference is indirect." Irwin, "What Is an Allusion?" 288.

22. For my purposes, it does not matter whether the intentions are the actual intentions of the artist, or merely the intentions that well-informed audiences are most justified in attributing to that artist. That debate has to be decided on grounds other than these.

23. Joseph Pucci, *The Full Knowing Reader: Allusion and the Power of the Reader in the Western Literary Tradition* (New Haven, CT, and London: Yale University Press, 1998), 41.

24. Pucci, 40.

25. Pucci, 43.

26. Pucci, 256.

27. Eliot's "Sweet Thames, run softly till I end my song" alludes to Spenser's "Prothalamion." Monroe C. Beardsley, "Intentions and Interpretations," in *The Aesthetic Point of View: Selected Essays*, ed. Michael J. Wreen and Donald M. Callen (Ithaca, NY, and London: Cornell University Press, 1983), 200.

28. Beardsley, 198.

29. H. P. Grice "Logic and Conversation," in *Syntax and Semantics*, vol. 3, ed. P. Cole and J. Morgan (New York: Academic Press, 1975), 41–58.

30. There are various versions of this argument, and mine derives from Robert Stecker, *Artworks: Definition Meaning Value* (University Park, PA: Pennsylvania State University Press, 1997), 172–73, and *Interpretation and Construction: Art, Speech, and the Law* (Malden and Oxford: Blackwell, 2003), 29–50. See also Peter Lamarque, *Fictional Points of View* (Ithaca, NY, and London: Cornell University Press, 1996), 178–80.

31. Paul Grice, *Studies in the Way of Words* (Cambridge, MA: Harvard University Press, 1989), 26–31.

32. However, artworks routinely violate the submaxim of the Cooperative Principle that directs us to avoid obscurity. (Grice, *Studies in the Way of Words*, 26.) In this respect, popular art is more like conversation than is high art.

33. My thanks to Tom Gracyk for detouring to Sixth Street in order to make this point.

34. Noël Carroll, "On the Ties That Bind: Characters, the Emotions, and Popular Fiction," this volume.

35. The classic source on illocutionary and perlocutionary acts is J. L. Austin, *How to Do Things with Words* (Cambridge, MA: Harvard University Press, 1962).

36. The cognitive pleasure of discovery plays an important role in Noël Carroll's theory of "horror-pleasure." But where Carroll emphasizes narrative structure as the source of our curiosity and subsequent enjoyment, the cognitive satisfactions of crossword puzzles and allusions are independent of narrative drama. See Noël Carroll, *The Philosophy of Horror or Paradoxes of the Heart* (New York and London: Routledge, 1990), 180–85.

37. This idea is a variant of Kendall Walton's well-known position in *Mimesis and Make-Believe* that representational art offers props that mandate imaginings in games of make-believe. (Kendall Walton, *Mimesis and Make-Believe* Harvard University Press, 1990, 69–72). In saying that props "mandate imaginings," Walton makes them normative with respect to our imaginings.

38. Irwin and Lombardo, 85.

39. For an extended discussion of other ramifications of this process, see Theodore Gracyk, *I Wanna Be Me: Rock Music and the Politics of Identity* (Philadelphia, PA: Temple University Press, 2001), pt. 2.

40. In her contribution to the present book, "Philosophy and the Probable Impossible," Carolyn Korsmeyer observes that popular culture can call attention to and thus encourage learning about a wide variety of specialized information that we would not otherwise encounter. Allusions can be part of this process.

41. Irwin, "The Aesthetics of Allusion," 523. See also Irwin and Lombardo, "The Simpsons and Allusion," 86.

42. Notice Cohen's emphasis on occasions for joke telling; Cohen, chap. 4.

43. Christopher Ricks, *Dylan's Visions of Sin* (London and New York: Viking, 2003).

44. Irwin, "The Aesthetics of Allusion," 528.

45. Irwin is constructing a very close parallel between allusion and joking. Cohen argues that a joke that is not immediately understood cannot generate the intimacy that is intended in joke telling.

46. Irwin suggests a conflict between the two pleasures; Irwin, "The Aesthetics of Allusion," 528–29.

47. Irwin, "What Is an Allusion?" 288. Irwin is responding to Michael Leddy.

48. I thank Ted Cohen for getting me to think about this last point.

5

On the Ties That Bind: Characters, the Emotions, and Popular Fictions

Noël Carroll

THE ISSUES

From Plato to Collingwood, philosophers have regarded the arousal of emotions as the characteristic calling card of the popular arts. Though far from pleased by this aspect of popular fictions—for Plato, the tragedies of his own day—he nevertheless was convinced that this was the inevitable destiny of any art that aspired to popularity, since the general populace, he believed, lives by its guts rather than by its mind. Consequently, Plato reasoned, anyone who wished to curry favor with the common run of the citizenry would have to appeal—Plato would say *pander*—to their emotions instead of to their brains.

Whether or not one shares Plato's low estimates of the emotions and those who allegedly live by them, one can agree that addressing the emotions is a central feature of what are called the popular arts, and perhaps even concur that these arts are popular in large measure because they engage the emotions, especially the garden-variety emotions, as effectively as they do.[1] This is particularly obvious with popular fictions—whether literary or visual; whether novels, short stories, plays, films, comic books, or graphic novels; whether a song or an entire musical; or whether still photos, sculptural ensembles, radio broadcasts, or TV shows. Popular fictions command our attention by provoking emotional responses which, in turn, keep us riveted to them as they unfold. The emotions, to an arresting degree, are the ties that bind us to popular fictions. This chapter is about the affective address of popular fiction.[2]

Needless to say, Plato not only noticed that arousing the emotions was a primary strategy for absorbing audiences in popular fictions; he also realized that an indispensable means for doing so—for holding onto audiences affectively—was via their relationships to fictional characters. And though this is clearly not the only mechanism by which popular fictions enlist audiences in their agenda, I have to agree with Plato that it is, indisputably, a major channel for securing our attention emotively. Thus, for the remainder of this chapter, I will follow Plato in attempting to limn the ways in which popular fictions engage their audiences emotionally by exploring the various kinds of affective relationships popular fictioneers propose between viewers, readers, and listeners, on the one hand, and the fictional characters whose adventures preoccupy us, on the other hand.

In short, this chapter is an examination of the emotive address of popular narration in terms of the way in which that process is implemented through our relation to fictional characters. Of course, it goes virtually without saying that there is no *one* relation here, but many.[3] How many exactly? I must confess that I do not know. Thus, this chapter is only a preliminary sketch, offering several crude distinctions that will undoubtedly benefit from future refinement. My only justification for presenting such an unfinished project at this time is that one has to start somewhere.

In order to begin this exploration of the affective bonds between characters and popular audiences, I will start with the most ancient and maybe still the most popular proposal about the nature of this relationship—namely, that it is a matter of identification. I will critically review both simple and sophisticated versions of the notion of identification, not merely for the sake of dismissing this idea, but, more importantly, in order to reveal how much more diverse and complicated our relationships with fictional characters really are than is suggested by the identification model.

Next, I will examine and reject the recently fashionable concept of simulation as a comprehensive account of our relation to fictional characters. I will argue that we rarely, if ever, resort to simulation in trying to understand the emotions of fictional characters or to explain and/or to predict their behavior.[4]

Like the idea of identification, that of simulation promotes the notion that sharing the selfsame or congruent emotive states with fictional characters is key to our affective bond with at least the protagonists in popular narratives. However, I will maintain that a much more comprehensive model of our emotional

stance to characters is captured by concepts such as care, concern, and sympathy—pro-attitudes that we have *for* others rather than emotional states we share
with them. That is, whereas we feel sympathy for the immiserated family, that is
not an emotion they bear toward themselves, and it therefore is not an emotion
that we *could* share with them. Thus, pace the identification and simulation approaches, it would appear that the most frequently recurring relationships between ourselves and fictional protagonists are not ones in which we reproduce
the same emotional states but ones in which we, the audience, mobilize an affective stance toward the relevant characters that is different from the one, if any,
that they are undergoing. Or, so I shall argue.

Before concluding, however, I will also consider one sort of audience-
character interaction where it does seem that we should concede that there is
an undeniable degree of shared affect. This is the case where the audience automatically mimics the facial and/or postural expressions of the characters in
order to ascertain approximately what they are feeling. These may be called
mirror reflexes. These reactions play a significant role in popular audiovisual
fictions. Moreover, understanding the way in which these processes operate
may also suggest the grain of truth that makes notions like identification and
simulation seductive.

IDENTIFICATION

Perhaps the earliest theory of our emotional bond with fictional characters
was proposed by Plato in his *Republic*. There he hypothesized that audiences
take on board the emotions—notably pity and fear—of the characters they
encounter in tragedies. Plato did not think this politically advisable, since
guardians who pitied either themselves or the enemy, or who feared for their
own death, would scarcely make ideal warriors. Although most have parted
company with Plato's worries about the civic danger of taking on these emotions, the idea that such a transfer of emotional states occurs upon exposure
to fictional characters remains an article of faith among ordinary audience
members and professional critics alike. Both groups speak freely of *identifying*
with characters, by which they most often appear to mean that they suffer the
selfsame emotional states—the same joys and fears—that possess the relevant
fictional personae.

Furthermore, on this view, it may be suggested that a large part of the attraction of fiction is that it affords us the opportunity to experience vicariously

the emotional states of the characters in question—most notably the protagonists. This is what accounts putatively for our interest in such fictions. When this possibility is not available—when we are said to be unable to identify with the characters—that then is often given as a reason why the fiction has failed to grip us. How often has one heard the refrain "I could not identify with so-and-so (usually the hero or heroine)" offered as a reason for why some or another popular fiction failed?

The notion of identification is so commonplace that one readily forgets that it is a highly theoretical hypothesis with a long philosophical lineage. It is a piece of theory that has seeped into ordinary language where it evades close scrutiny. However, the idea, at least in its most blatant form, has little to recommend it. If identification were the characteristic mode of our emotional involvement with characters, we would expect audiences to be in the same emotional states as the characters to whom they are exposed. But more often than not, this is not the case.

A young couple in a TV drama blissfully walks down the garden path holding hands, while, unbeknownst to them, they are being stalked by a serial killer. Seeing this, we are consumed by fear for them, although from their point of view, things could not be better. Such scenes recur with numbing frequency in suspense fictions. The emotional frisson they engender cannot be explained in terms of identification, since the audience is in a radically different mental state than the protagonists. Likewise, when a Harold Lloyd type is embarrassed, we are apt to be comically amused, but he is disconsolate. And when Oedipus is wracked with guilt, we do not share his remorse but feel pity for him. Whereas the theory of identification predicts shared emotional states between characters and spectators, quite often—perhaps most often—our emotions go in different, and sometimes even opposite, directions.

Moreover, this is not only true with regard to protagonists. When the villain is frustrated ("foiled again!"), we are likely to feel joy, while, as he is gloating about his imminent triumph, our ire mounts. Whereas the notion of emotive identification would appear to presuppose symmetry between the emotional states of characters and audiences—why else would it be called "identification"—in a vast number of cases, the pertinent relationships are asymmetrical. So, at the very least, identification cannot provide us with a general account of our emotional relationship to characters.

Of course, one response to this observation might be that it is not our emotions that are the substance of identification here; rather, we are identifying with the character. But if we were identifying with the character—one of the aforesaid young lovers—and contemplating the situation as he or she understands it, then we would not be feeling consternation. We should be feeling bliss. But that is not the case. So there does not seem to be any theoretical gain in saying that it is the character with whom we identify—at least not if it is our intention to explain our emotional engagement in terms of identification.

Perhaps it will be granted that identification is not a comprehensive account of our emotional bonding with characters. There are all those cases of divergent reactions of the sort to which I've already alluded. Instead, it might be claimed that identification merely accounts for a great many instances of the emotional connection between characters and audiences. For example, when the protagonist is angry with his nemesis, so are we; when the heroine is disgusted by the monster, we are too. There are a great many cases like these. Are they not cases of identification?

Even if some may be, many clearly are not. I may be angry with the villain for the same reasons that the hero is. This no more implies that I identify with the hero than my dislike of a certain political candidate implies that I identify with everyone else in my party who shares this dislike with me. For we have all arrived at this appraisal through our own route. I have not become possessed by the feelings of some or another member of my political persuasion.[5] It is my own emotive appraisal. For a mental state to count as a case of emotive identification, we should not only share emotive states, but I should be in an emotive state like yours *because* you are in that state. It is in this respect that identification appears to be something akin to emotional contagion. But I may be angry with the villain because he acts wrongfully and be repulsed by the monster because it is disgusting, and *not* because the hero is angry or the heroine is disgusted. Sharing similar emotional states will not count as identification unless the state is not only similar but is a causal consequence of the character being in that state. And in an immense number of cases of converging emotional states, audiences are in the emotional states they are in because they appraise the fictional situations in the same way the characters do, and not because characters, in like states, have infected the audiences with their passions. To suppose the latter in most instances is to add an unnecessary bit of theoretical baggage, since the impurity of the monster and the evil of the antagonist respectively is enough to motivate the horror of the audience, on the one hand, and their anger, on the other.[6]

Another sort of evidence that might be mistakenly adduced in behalf of identification would be to note that quite often the emotional states of the audience appear to converge qualitatively with those of the relevant fictional characters. The characters suffer, and our hearts go out to them; we feel compassion. Our emotional states seem coordinated or synchronized with those of their fictional objects. This obviously happens. But, at the same time, it is not proof of emotional identification, since our emotional states, though compatible and even consilient, are not identical. Compassion is something that we feel toward the fictional characters, not something that they feel toward themselves. Indeed, with regard to your average popular melodrama, the emotive difference is even more pronounced, since we usually feel both pity *and* admiration for the victims of adversity, like Stella Dallas, whereas they evince neither of these emotions toward themselves. Indeed, would we so admire Stella Dallas for being self-sacrificing if she admired herself for being so?

This last example, moreover, illustrates the way in which the notion of identification frequently obscures the complexity of our emotional relations to fictional characters. Suppose we are confronted with a character plagued by the loss of a loved one; the character feels grief. The object of the character's emotional state is her loved one. We, in turn, are moved by the character's plight; let us say we feel sorrow. But our sorrow is not the same as the character's grief, since our sorrow has a different object. The object of our sorrow is the grief-stricken character; that the character is in anguish is part of the reason we feel sorrow for him. We are not grieving at our loss of a loved one but are saddened that the character's loss pains him. We are not in the same emotional state, since the object of our emotional state is different and more encompassing than the object of the character's emotional state; the object of the character's emotional state is only the loved one, whereas the object of our state is someone who has lost a loved one.[7] Inasmuch as it is generally the case (1) that the object of the audience's emotional state includes the character *and* the object of his state and (2) that the object of the audience's state is not reducible to the object of the character's emotional state, the claim that the audience's emotional state is identical to that of the character will be typically suspect. Talk of identification merely tends to flatten out our understanding of the emotional relationships of audiences to fictional characters rather than to acknowledge their complexity.

Of course, it is not only the case that the constituency of the objects of the audience's emotions differ significantly from those of fictional characters. It is also the case that there is an ontological difference here. Presumably, in the world of the fiction, the characters' emotions are grounded in their beliefs, whereas, given our metaphysical location, our emotional responses arise from simply entertaining or imagining certain thoughts about that world.[8] Furthermore, this probably contributes to yet another palpable difference between the emotional states of audiences and those of characters—namely, that the former are generally presumed to be felt less intensely, all things being equal, than the latter.[9] And, of course, another salient difference in this ontological neighborhood is that the emotions of fictional characters are still connected to the agent's action-behavior system, while the audience's emotions are disengaged, undoubtedly because of the way in which they have been decoupled from certain beliefs about the existence and urgency of the situations the fiction has invited us to imagine. All these differences should underscore that the relationship betwixt the emotional state of fictional characters and those of their audiences can rarely, if ever, be that of identity, thereby suggesting that the notion of identification is moot.[10]

But it may be argued that the idea of identification that I am criticizing is too simplistic. Identification, it might be said, is not something that happens to me as a result of what the character feels. It is something that, in part, I bring about. The fiction invites me to imagine that I am the character in certain circumstances and then to further imagine aspectually what I would feel so situated.[11] For example, I imagine I am the child of a farmer who has been bushwhacked, and then I imagine the desire for revenge that would overtake me, including the passion of hatred with which I would regard my father's murderers.

However, I distrust this more sophisticated version of identification on several counts. First, it is overly elaborate. What motivates postulating our imagining that we are the character? If our own sense of justice has been violated by the murder of the farmer, then that will account for our indignation toward his killers and our desire for their punishment. That is, we can find an explanation sufficient to our emotional reaction without adding identification—including aspectual identification—to the story. So why do so? It offends the principle of explanatory parsimony.

Second, I wonder whether it is even plausible to suggest that the fiction invites us to imagine being the character. How is it marked? For certainly it should be marked, since no one wishes to claim that we imagine being all the characters. How could we? When would we have the time? That is, there is the question—especially with respect to films, TV dramas, and plays—of how we would find the opportunity to indulge in these imaginings while still keeping up with the story as the production evolves rapidly in real time.

But maybe an even deeper problem with this version of identification is that it courts paradox. For if I really did imagine that I was the aggrieved child in search of revenge, shouldn't I resent the fact that the fictional character is beating me to the punch? Or, to see how extensive this problem is, suppose that I am imagining that I am the central character and that I am in love? Shouldn't I be jealous of that guy on the screen who is courting my baby? Or imagine that the character with whom I am identifying is bidding for a job. Wouldn't I resent the competition and find his hopefulness offensive? But none of these paradoxes arises. Why not? Presumably because I am not imagining that I am the character and/or that I have taken on his emotions, motives, and desires—not even aspectually.[12]

The emotional states of the audience may be coordinated with those of the characters in various ways. They may share the same emotive valence. For example, when the character is miserable and the audience feels pity, both are in dysphoric emotional states. These states converge vectorially—they both belong on the negative, distressful, or painful side of the scale of the emotions. Likewise, when the character is joyous and we are happy for her, our emotions converge vectorially on the euphoric side of the scale.[13] But though our emotions are similar in their valence, they are not identical. Thus, the fact that our emotions are often coordinated does not in any way support the notion of identification, unless that means nothing more than a somewhat similar feeling. But why invoke the notion of *identity* to describe that?

SIMULATION

We appear to be emotionally tied to popular fictions predominantly through our relations with certain characters, particularly those called protagonists. But what is the nature of that relationship—at least in the largest number of cases? We have just argued that the concept of identification does not seem to do it justice. Perhaps it is what is nowadays called "simulation."[14]

Simulation is a concept from the philosophy of mind that has recently been imported into aesthetics. In the philosophy of mind, the idea is that we understand and explain others, ascertain what they are feeling, identify their intentions and motivations, and predict their behavior by simulating them. That is, we input their beliefs and desires into our own off-line cognitive-conative system. Since, ex hypothesi, our cognitive-conative architecture is the same as theirs, if we run their belief-desire program on ourselves—their software on our hardware—then we should be able to derive a reasonable fix on that which people just like us (folk psychologically speaking) are likely to think, feel, plan, want, and so forth. That is, we put them into our shoes—or, equally metaphorically, we put their beliefs and desires into the black box that outputs our emotions, decisions, and behaviors—in order to project what they are likely to feel, think, or do.[15] This, moreover, is done on the presupposition that with respect to processing beliefs and desires into emotions and deliberations, we are structurally the same.

This theory—called simulation theory—is counterposed to another view in the philosophy of mind of the way in which we go about understanding others—which alternative view is called the theory theory, that is, the *theory* that we understand what others are about by applying something like a scientific *theory* to their behavior. Simulation is thought to have several advantages over the theory theory when it comes to reading the minds of others, because, on the one hand, the theoretical framework ostensibly presupposed by the theory theory would be monumentally complex—too complex, indeed, to postulate with great confidence—and, on the other hand, even if there were such a theory, it would take an immense amount of time to deploy in real time to particular cases, whereas we frequently size up people's emotional states and intentions in the blink of an eye.

But what does all this have to do with aesthetics—specifically with the question of our emotional relationship to the protagonists in popular fictions? Putatively, our relationship with fictional characters is generally like the relationships we have with other people in the world outside of fiction. The fiction invites us to understand them, to apprehend what they are feeling and intending, to speculate about what they will do next, and so forth, just as we must mind read our conspecifics in everyday life. In order to do so—in order to follow the fiction (the unfolding of the intentions and feelings of fictional characters)—we simulate them, or at least the leading ones, notably the protagonists.

We input their beliefs and desires into our cognitive-conative architecture and discover what they are thinking and feeling by coming to think and feel broadly similar things, as our own system runs through its paces on their steam. Consequently, on this view, we are engaged emotively with the fiction by being immersed in a virtually continuous process of replicating the emotions and desires of (especially) the protagonists.

Unlike the proponent of identification, the simulation theorist does not claim that the emotions allegedly reproduced in us are identical, either thoroughly or aspectually, with those attributed to the protagonist. At best, they are only approximately similar. However, this still leaves the simulation theorist open to one objection that was leveled at the friends of identification—namely, the charge that simulation theory can be nothing near to a comprehensive theory of our emotional relationship to fictional characters because of the staggeringly vast number of cases where the emotions of the audience are different from and even opposed to those suffered by the fictional characters. When the protagonist rushes home joyously to tell her spouse that she's been promoted at the same time that we know she will find her family massacred, our despondent emotive state is nothing at all like hers. Moreover, if we were simulating her psychology, we would not be following the story appropriately. Furthermore, since similar asymmetries are so often the rule in popular fictions, simulation cannot be anything like a comprehensive account of our emotive engagement with characters.

Of course, sometimes the emotions of the audience and the characters do converge. Perhaps simulation explains those cases. However, this seems unlikely. Fictions, especially audiovisual ones, proceed at a pace that would seem to be uncongenial for simulation. Supposedly one advantage of simulation theory over the theory theory is that it is more suited temporally to sussing out the emotive states of conspecifics. But be that as it may, simulation takes time too, and one wonders whether one typically has sufficient breathing space to simulate in reaction to a spritely edited audiovisual array.[16]

Yet even deeper than the question of how simulation can occur in these cases is whether or how often it does occur. Simulation theory in the philosophy of mind is advanced as a view of how we go about determining what our conspecifics are feeling and thinking—a way of understanding and predicting their not transparently fathomable behavior. But popular fictions are not like everyday life. They are designed to be understood; indeed, they are designed to be understood quickly and clearly by untutored audiences.[17]

Moreover, that aspiration extends to the way in which the fictional characters are constructed. Perhaps in our ordinary experience our conspecifics strike us as opaque in a way that calls for simulation. I would not say this never happens, though I am not convinced that it is happening all the time. Nevertheless, I will argue that the kinds of situations that call for simulation occur rarely with respect to fictional characters, especially those who inhabit popular fictions, because those characters are expressly contrived in such a way that they wear their feelings and their thoughts on their sleeves. Thus, there is little or no need to hypothesize the operation of simulation in response to popular fiction, since we usually know exactly what the fictional characters are feeling and thinking faster than it would take to simulate these fictional beings.

This is most evident with respect to literary fictions. Most popular fictions employ the device of free, indirect discourse, which means that the author can narrate what the character is thinking and feeling from both the outside and the inside. We have his or her context described for us, often in emotionally suggestive terms; her physical state is delineated; and then we are also made privy to her thoughts. In such situations, there is no call for simulation. We are just told what the character is feeling and thinking. Perhaps some readers use the text as a script for attempting to raise similar emotions in themselves. I don't, but I wouldn't claim that others are like me in this respect. Nevertheless, it should be clear that there is no pressure to mobilize simulation theory in cases like this to explain how we come to understand the feelings and thoughts of the protagonists. We are told them outright.

Of course, this feature of literary fictions is not as common in audiovisual fictions. We do not as frequently enter the mind of the protagonist in films and TV dramas. But it is true that quite often they do tell us how they are feeling and what they are thinking, frequently by way of dialogue with interlocutors. And even in those cases where the characters do not explicitly articulate their states of mind, I would still contend that the characters in those fictions manifest their feelings and thoughts so openly that simulation is effectively beside the point.

How is this possible? Perhaps one way to get at this is to ask whether, with respect to everyday experience, simulation and the theory theory exhaust our ways of gaining access to the feelings and thoughts of others. Arguably, they do not. Often—indeed, probably most often—we impute thoughts and feelings to others on the basis of schemas, scripts, prototypes, contextual cues, and heuristics, rather than on the basis of a theory, which stratagems, in turn, enable us to infer the inner states of others.

Confronted with a coworker who has just been fired or a friend who has lost a loved one, we infer, all things being equal, that they are down. If their shoulders are slouched and their eyelids heavy, we recognize these as signs of distress. We have no need to perform a simulation, because, through experience, we have amassed a repertoire of schemas, heuristics, and contextual and recognitional cues to alert us to the inner states of conspecifics.[18]

When we hear that a relative has secured a long-sought-after job, all things being equal, we suppose that the relative is happy, and we rejoice for her. There is no need for simulation. We have access to a body of prototypes regarding emotional responses in certain contexts, as well as recognitional cues, such as facial expressions and postures, that enable us to assess the emotional states of others. These are not theories, and they are not applied by subsuming particular situations under nomological generalizations, as the theory theory might have it, but they are prototypes—schemas, heuristics, and recognitional cues—employed by *analogy*. Such is a reasonably reliable means for tracking the emotional states and thoughts of conspecifics, and I am confident that we depend on it in everyday life far more than we do on simulation. For, quite frequently, simulation would just be too time consuming.

Moreover, this has important ramifications for popular fictions. Inasmuch as popular fictions are designed to maximize accessibility, they gravitate naturally toward the use of the schemas, heuristics, and contextual and/or recognitional cues that abound in the cultures of their target audiences. Indeed, it is part of the art of designing a character for the purposes of popular fiction that one be able to streamline the details of the character's persona so that it calls forth the schemas, heuristics, and cues that fit it almost automatically.

In the situation comedy *Sex and the City*, the character of Samantha snugly fits the schema of the carnal woman—the sensual woman who loves sex (e.g., the Wife of Bath). When her eyes open wide as a handsome swain glides by, we do not need to simulate Samantha in order to determine her internal state. We can infer it based on our prototype for Samantha and the recognitional cues she supplies. Moreover, with respect to this particular TV series, our surmise will almost always be confirmed when Samantha slyly, albeit redundantly,[19] confides her desires to her friends, Carrie, Miranda, and Charlotte. Nor does this seem to me to be a peculiar example of the way in which the characters in popular fictions function.

But if this is a fair observation, then there appears to be little urge to hypothesize the operation of simulation in response to the characters in popular fiction. The problem that simulation is supposed to solve with respect to understanding the feelings and thoughts of others in everyday life does not generally arise with regard to popular fictions because popular fictions intensively exploit the schemas, heuristics, and contextual and recognitional cues that constitute our prototypes for discerning the inner lives of others.

Popular fictioneers build characters, economically sculpting their features, precisely to trigger quickly and effortlessly the mobilization of those prototypes by audiences. Thus, the need to postulate the operation of simulation as the means by which we apprehend the emotions and thoughts of the characters in popular fictions is largely otiose. But if we are not simulating the emotions of said characters, then it is not the case that we are emotionally bound to them by a continuous process of sharing congruent feelings.

SYMPATHY[20]

We are emotionally tied to popular fictions generally due to our relationship with characters, especially the protagonists. Neither the notion of identification nor that of simulation appears to explain the usual structure of this relationship satisfactorily. Whether or not identification or simulation ever occurs, they occur far more rarely than is often supposed, and therefore neither can afford a relatively comprehensive account of the emotive address of popular fiction. One thing that both identification and simulation have in common is that they postulate more-than-less closely shared emotional states between audiences and fictional characters. Moreover, it is the unlikelihood that such states are the norm that calls into question the adequacy of these accounts respectively. So maybe the way to go is to look for an emotional bond where the audience's emotional state is categorically different from those of the fictional characters.

One obvious candidate is sympathy. Sympathy is not an emotional state that persons bear toward themselves. It is, by definition, directed at others. For our purposes, we will construe sympathy roughly as nonfleeting care and concern, or, more broadly, as a nonpassing pro-attitude, toward another person (or a fictional character). Sympathy is a supportive response. Sympathy, conceived as an emotion, involves visceral feelings of distress when the interests of the objects of our pro-attitude are endangered, and feelings of elation, closure, or satisfaction when their welfare is achieved. The emotion in question has as a component the enduring desire for the well-being of its object—a desire that things will work out well for her. In order to be the object of this pro-attitude, the person in question must be thought to be worthy of our benevolence as a result of our interests, projects, values, loyalties, allegiances, or moral commitments. When X is appraised to be worthy of our nonpassing desire that things work out well for her, and this is linked to positive feeling tones when gratified and negative ones when frustrated, then we are in the emotional state that I am calling sympathy. If *sympathy* strikes you as having connotations of being too saccharin, you are welcome to refer to this emotive state merely as a pro-attitude.

The suggestion that sympathy plays a role in our emotional involvement with characters is surely unobjectionable. However, I am claiming more for it than that. I want to argue that it, along with antipathy (about which I will have little to say in this chapter), constitutes the major emotive cement between audiences and popular fictions. This, of course, requires me to say why I believe that sympathy holds this place of privilege and also how it is able to do so.

Obviously, in the course of a popular fiction, one undergoes many emotional states. One is angry for a while, then sad, then happy, then gripped by suspense, and then happy again. Sometimes sympathy for the protagonist is so strong that you can feel it. At other times, it appears to take the backseat for an interlude of comic amusement. Why select out sympathy as the most crucial lever for moving the audience's emotions with regard to popular fictions?

The first reason might be called its breadth. Sympathy for the protagonist is the most pervasive emotion from beginning to end of a popular fiction. As soon as sympathy is secured, unless it is later intentionally neutralized by the creator of the fiction, it stays on the alert, tracking the protagonist's fortunes, registering distress as her fortunes waver and pleasure as they rise. Sympathy, once enlisted, is constantly on call throughout the fiction. Generally, no other emotive stance—save antipathy for the antagonist—is as long lasting. The indignation we feel toward the surly guard who cuffs the hero comes and goes, but our sympathy for the protagonist endures. It provides the emotive optic through which we survey the narrative from one end to the other. Each event in the story is weighed in light of our sympathy for the protagonist; of every event, it is pertinent to ask whether it advances or deters her fortunes, even if the answer in some cases is neither.

The protagonists in popular fictions have goals and interests that are hard to miss. The narrative trajectory usually involves the accomplishment of those goals and the satisfaction of those interests in the face of various obstacles. We follow this quest from the perspective of sympathy, cheering the protagonists on as they advance and feeling consternation as they falter. Of course, sometimes our sympathy for the characters puts us out of sync with them—when we believe a character is falling for the wrong guy, for example. But still we track the unfolding narrative from a sympathetic viewpoint, one that disposes us to care about her best interests rather than her subjective assessment of them.

Sympathy is the most persistent emotional bond that we have with respect to the fictional protagonist; in this sense, it generally has more breadth than other emotions elicited by popular fictions. Furthermore, sympathy also has what might be called depth. It is our sympathy toward the protagonist that shapes our overall reception of the fiction. When we are angered by the way in which the heroine is mistreated, that anger itself is subsidiary to the sympathy we bear toward her. It underlies and reinforces our anger. It is our sympathy for the character that disposes us to regard her as inside our network of concern and, therefore, to assess an injustice done to her as something perpetrated against one of "our own." The negative emotions we muster in response to the protagonist's setbacks are a function of our sympathy for her. Sympathy is the foundation here. That is why we say it has depth.

Two reasons, then, suggest that sympathy is the major emotional bond between audiences and leading fictional characters, namely that sympathy appears to have greater breadth and depth than any other emotion we undergo while consuming a popular narrative. The obvious exception here may be the antipathy, distaste, and hatred that we often bear toward the antagonists in popular fictions. However, since this antipathy is generally the reverse side of—and indeed a function of—the sympathy we bear toward their rival protagonists, this case seems less of a counterexample to our conjecture than a corollary.

Admittedly, sometimes the influence goes in the opposite direction; there are cases—involving the enemy-of-my-enemy-is-my-friend syndrome—where sympathy may be a function of antipathy. Yet, in the main, in popular fictions, I would guess as a matter of empirical speculation that antipathy is usually an offshoot of sympathy. Nevertheless, in any event, the two are always connected so as to permit us to adjust our hypothesis and to propose that sympathy-cum-antipathy is the fundamental axis of the emotional address of popular fiction. Moreover, since it is neither the case that protagonists sympathize with themselves nor that antagonists hate themselves, pace both the notions of identification and simulation, our major emotional bond with popular fictions is, on this account, not a matter of our sharing the same or closely similar emotions with fictional characters.

If sympathy—or, more cumbersomely, sympathy-cum-antipathy—is the crux of our relationship to characters in popular fictions, there remains the question of how it is mobilized. In everyday life, we extend our sympathies to those with whom we share interests or projects or loyalties, or those who exemplify values of which we approve, or those who fall under the protection of certain moral principles. Of course, most of the interests, projects, and loyalties that we base many of our quotidian sympathies upon are highly specific to us. Needless to say, the creator of popular fictions cannot hope to activate the individualized interests of every member of the audience on behalf of her protagonists. Consequently, she must aim at engaging the audience at a fairly generic level of interests, projects, and loyalties. She must try to find some common ground amongst the diverse audience membership which will encourage us to find the protagonists to be worthy of our goodwill.

This is a design problem for the popular fictioneer; he must find some way to elicit from a variegated audience the converging desire that the protagonists do well—that is, our conviction that it would be good for them to do well, or that they deserve to do well. Moreover, as an empirical generalization, I hypothesize that the most common solution to this problem is to create protagonists who command the audience's moral endorsement. That is, morality provides the popular fictioneer with an interest, or project, or loyalty upon which target audiences from the same cultural background are likely to converge, at least broadly speaking.[21] Thus, by presenting protagonists who are morally appealing, the creator of popular fictions secures the criterial wherewithal to garner the sympathy that is required for her intended audiences to be emotionally absorbed by the story. That is, said protagonists meet the criterion of being deserving of our benevolence because they are morally deserving. It is no accident that the protagonists in popular fictions are good guys. Good guys are precisely what are likely to engender a pro-attitude from heterogeneous audiences of otherwise varied and often conflicting interests and loyalties. Morality, of the fairly generic sort found in popular fictions, is something that people from different backgrounds are apt to agree upon, at least roughly. Few, for instance, would disagree that Maximus was wronged when his family was slaughtered in *Gladiator*.

Characters in popular fictions are presented as morally right. This is obviously so in the greatest number of cases. But even so-called antiheros usually oppose some form of conventional/corrupt moral order in the name of some deeper sense of justice. Hard-boiled detectives always discover that society is even more rotten than they are. Alienated gunslingers protect the little folk against greedy cattle barons and bullying railroad magnates. Disaffected teenagers really care about problems that adult society culpably neglects or misunderstands. And so on. No matter how antisocial the protagonist appears at first glance, he or she is quickly seen to be prosocial at heart. Moreover, this is how it should be if sympathy is to take hold across a diverse audience whose likeliest point of convergence is apt to be morality very broadly construed.

By "broadly construed," I do not simply mean that the audience shares some rough and ready principles, but also a sense of what counts as virtuous. Protagonists enlist our moral approval, and thence our sympathy, because they are portrayed as persons of a variety of virtues, including a sense of fairness, justice, respect for others, loyalty, honor, honesty, and dignity; respect for the family; and concern for the weak, the lame, the halt, the elderly, and children, as well as less morally charged and more pagan virtues such as strength, cunning, and wit. These virtues, in turn, engender in audiences the palpable desire that the protagonists do well and that their rivals do badly.

Often in popular fictions, it is not the case that the protagonists are what we would call morally upright, and yet they still win our sympathy. Consider, for example, caper films. However, when one examines the structure of these exercises, one notices that the fictional universe has been constructed in such a way that the characters we might normally upbraid as criminals are presented in such a way that they are the most virtuous characters in evidence.[22] The forces of everyday society are either kept offscreen so that their countervailing claims never impinge on our sympathies, or they are shown to be venal and/or culpably stupid.[23]

In short, mobilizing sympathy for the protagonists—and the corresponding ill will toward the antagonists—in popular fictions generally relies on establishing that the protagonists are representatives of a value—generally a moral value—widely shared among the mass audience for popular fictions. This approval, then, is what grounds the audience's sympathy for the protagonist, which sympathy, in turn, binds the audience emotionally to the fiction. For example, it is undoubtedly the shared conviction in the moral rightness of the survival of humanity that makes science-fiction films—like *Independence Day* and *Jurassic Park*—such international blockbusters, since a pro-attitude toward humanity's continued existence is at least one thing upon which most members of the worldwide audience can agree. Perhaps this is the reason that science fiction (and, for related reasons, fantasy) can lay claim to being among the presiding popular genres of globalization.

MIRROR REFLEXES

Thus far, I have been stressing that the most important affective bonds between popular audiences and their fictions involve us in marshaling emotional responses to characters, which emotional states are categorically quite different from the states undergone by the relevant fictional beings. And though I think that this hypothesis is generally accurate when it comes to describing the *emotional* relationships between audiences and characters, it is not a complete account of our *affective* engagement with popular fictions, especially audiovisual ones. For there is a stratum of affective communion that involves charged visceral feelings, which, though not exactly full-fledged emotions, nevertheless resonate congruently in the breasts of audience members and protagonists alike. What I have in mind may be called mirror reflexes.

Occasionally, when speaking to another person, we suddenly realize that we have adopted her facial expressions. She is frowning; we start to frown. Or she is smiling, and we find ourselves smiling. The same is true of gestures and postures. We watch the outfielder reach for a fly ball, and the muscles in our arm tug slightly in that direction. If our informant bends to us, we bend toward him. And so on. We have an involuntary tendency to mirror automatically the behavior, especially the expressive behavior, of our conspecifics.[24]

Putatively, we do this in order to gain some sense of what they are feeling. By configuring our own facial expression after the fashion of our interlocutor's—smiling, for example, when she is smiling—we gain an inkling of her inner state. The feedback from the disposition of our facial muscles buzzes our autonomic system in a way that is presumably isomorphic to what is going on in her system, if she is not dissembling. This does not give us full access to her emotional state, but it provides an important clue, since it yields something like a facsimile of the bodily feeling component of her overall state. Similarly, gestures and postures are often mimicked—though usually only in a highly truncated manner—in order to gather information about what is percolating inside our conspecifics. Moreover, this mimicry is predominantly automatic, not intentional. It is, in all probability, part of our biological endowment.

Children on their caregiver's knee evince mirror reflexes in abundance.[25] Clearly this behavior is a boon in learning the emotional repertoire—and much else—of one's culture, for it enables the child to discern the situations the caregiver associates with feelings of distress or elation. Among adults, mirror reflexes are also highly adaptive, since they facilitate social coordination.[26] Albeit subliminally, one can gauge—at least very broadly—the temperament of a room or the disposition of one's spouse by using your body as a detector of the kind of internal sensations that are apt to be associated with the manifest expressions of others.[27] The human capacity for mirror reflexes is, in all likelihood, an asset from the perspective of natural selection, since they are a means for both gaining information about conspecifics and for synchronizing our moods in joint ventures, from face-to-face conversations to cheerleading.

Aestheticians have been aware of the phenomenon of mirror reflexes at least since the work of Theodor Lipps.[28] And Sergei Eisenstein attempted to exploit Lipps's insights explicitly in his theory of filmmaking.[29] Though neither he nor Lipps used the terminology of mirror reflexes, Eisenstein included close-ups of stereotypical facial expressions and of body parts, such as clenched fists, in his films, in the hope of inspiring the sort of mimicry in audiences that would prepare them viscerally for the kinds of emotional states that he wished to arouse in them.[30] Less theoretically inclined filmmakers also discovered the importance of such affective modeling intuitively, and it has been a staple of popular cinema since the twenties. This is a legacy, furthermore, that movies have bequeathed to TV. Undoubtedly, a significant amount of the affect stirred up by audiovisual entertainments is connected to the way in which they educe muscular mimicry in their audiences.

Watching a videotape of *Riverdance*, the audience taps its feet, accessing a simulacrum of the spirited pulse of the dancers. As Bruno in Hitchcock's *Strangers on a Train* reaches for the lighter he has dropped into the sewer, our arm muscles flex, within the abbreviated ambit of our theater seat, in a manner like his in order to help us feel his intention with our body. And even before we see the monster onscreen, the screaming visage of the victim, etched in horror, prompts us to tense our face analogously in a way that sends a signal through our muscles that things are about to get unpleasant.[31] The activity onscreen primes mimicry of a limited and circumscribed variety which may deliver information about the internal states of characters which we sample in terms of similar sensations in ourselves. Though not full-scale emotions—but only feelings sans objects—these sensations may be nevertheless a serviceable source of the affective grip that such spectacles have on us in at least two ways.

First, they contribute to keeping the excitement level in our body elevated, thereby realizing one of the promises of popular audiovisual fictions. And second, they may make available information that we can integrate into our more encompassing emotional responses to the characters. The bodily feeling of distress the protagonist feels that is imprinted on his twisted features is relayed into us by our selective imitation of his expression so that we can use the dysphoric taste of that sensation as a recognitional cue for the kind of emotion he is undergoing and as an indicator of the kind of vectorially convergent emotion that is appropriate in his behalf—as, for example, sorrow would be apt if he is feeling some sort of pain. That is, mirror reflexes may function as subroutines in the formation of our emotional responses to fictional characters, not only alerting us to the general valence—whether positive or negative—of their mental state but also calibrating the kind of passion we need to send back their way.

Mirror reflexes are not examples of emotional identification, since they do not involve the replication of complete emotional states but only feelings, which need not be the same feeling states but only similar ones. They are not simulations of emotions either, since they do not involve beliefs and desires, and they do not appear to require going off-line, if I understand that metaphor correctly. On the other hand, they are important elements in the affective address of audiovisual popular fictions like movies and TV. They can make our bodies vibrate with feeling in the presence of certain characters, and, even more importantly, they can facilitate our recognition of character emotion and modulate our own emotional response to it. In this regard, it would appear that audiovisual popular fictions have resources for exciting the affective reactions of audiences that popular literary fictions lack.

SUMMARY

In this chapter, I have attempted to explore the affective address of popular fictions by focusing on the way they structure the audience's relationships to characters. I began by exploring two models for characterizing this subject—identification and simulation.[32] These approaches have in common the hunch that the nature of the audience's relationships to fictional characters, especially protagonists, involves sharing the selfsame or nearly the same emotions that the characters suffer. I have argued that this seems to be rarely if ever the case. Alternatively, I maintain that a better view of our emotional response to the characters in popular fictions is that it generally comprises a pro-attitude; it is a matter of care, concern, or sympathy—an emotional state that we have for and not with the characters in question. However, even if this is the dominant form of our emotional relation with characters, it is not the only affective relationship that is important in our commerce with popular fictions, especially audiovisual ones. There are also mirror reflexes. These responses engender in us something like an echo of the *feelings* that fictional characters are represented as undergoing by virtue of their expressive behavior. No account of our affective bond to such fictions would be complete without acknowledging these responses. Moreover, it is probably mirror reflexes that give rise to the claim that audiences emotionally identify with characters, whereas it might be more accurate to say that said reflexes enable us to sample something like the bodily feelings of fictional personae on our way to responding emotionally to them.

NOTES

1. See Noël Carroll, *Philosophy of Mass Art* (Oxford: Oxford University Press, 1998).

2. It is important to note that I use the concept of affect to include not only emotions but also moods, phobias, and reflex responses such as the startle response and what, in this essay, are later called mirror reflexes. For me, the notion of the emotions, properly so called, refers narrowly to mental states that take objects and that have at least a cognitive component as well as a feeling component. Other affective states may differ from emotions in the sense that they lack objects and/or cognitive components. In this essay, mirror reflexes are singled out as an important type of affect found in audiovisual popular fictions which are different from emotions. Though not discussed in this essay, startle reflexes are also a significant form of affect available to audiovisual popular fictions which are not emotions.

Startle responses, however, are not discussed herein, since they need not involve the audience's connection to fictional characters, whereas mirror reflexes do.

3. Though in a recent article, Amy Coplan does not list me as a pluralist in this regard, I have always been so. See, for example, my "Film, Emotion, and Genre," in *Passionate Views: Film, Cognition, and Emotion*, ed. Carl Plantinga and Greg Smith (Baltimore, MD: Johns Hopkins Press, 1999), 21–47. See also Amy Coplan, "Empathic Engagement with Narrative Fictions," in *The Journal of Aesthetics and Art Criticism*, 52 (2004): 141–52.

4. I stress that my concern here is with the extent to which audiences deploy simulation in response to the characters in popular narrative fictions. I am neutral about the degree to which simulation is employed in everyday life and even somewhat agnostic about whether it is employed at all (though, on most days, I lean in the direction that it is, at least to some degree). In any event, I leave the latter two issues to philosophers of mind to adjudicate.

5. And, in any event, wouldn't there be too many other people for me to identify with—many of whom I have no knowledge?

6. This argument from explanatory parsimony has often been overlooked by my critics. Amy Coplan, for example, invites us to imagine a case where we witness a student being humiliated by a professor and then "share" the student's anger at the professor. I agree that mutual anger at the professor is readily conceivable in such a situation. But I do not see why we need to postulate an intervening stage in which I share the student's humiliation (though I concede we may feel pain or distress on his behalf). Why doesn't the professor's boorishness and insensitivity suffice to explain our anger? What—once our reaction to that is taken into account—remains to be elucidated?

Consider, for example, the construction of the entrance scene of the monster in a horror film. Here are two possible ways of doing it. First, the monster, oozing with slime, rises from his hoary gravesite and stalks toward the camera. No other character sees him. Yet we are horrified by its appearance. Alternatively, a gravedigger sees the monster, and this is interpolated into the scene by means of several point-of-view shots. Again, we are horrified. *But,* why suppose in the second case that our horror has been channeled, so to speak, through the gravedigger? That is, why imagine that we have identified with the gravedigger and, in consequence, have "caught" his horror?

For there is no need to suppose that our horrified response to the first scene is any different than to the second scene. But if we can explain our emotional responses to the first scene in terms of the way in which it has criterially prefocused our attention and kick-started our own emotional processing (sans any link to some human character in the fiction), then why must we add an identificatory epicycle to explain the way in which we arrive at the same emotional state in the second instance?

See Amy Coplan, "Empathetic Engagement with Narrative Fictions."

7. That is, the object of the audience's emotional state is typically the character's situation, which includes the object of his emotion. Standardly, the object of the audience's emotional state is not simply identical to the object of the character's state.

8. That is, a fiction mandates that we suppose or imagine its propositional content, not that we believe it.

9. Discussing empathy apart from the case of fiction, Edith Stein remarks on these phenomenological differences, "The subject of the empathized experience, however, is not the subject empathizing, but another. . . . [W]hile I am living in the other's joy, I do not feel primordial joy. It does not issue from my 'I.' Neither does it have the character of once having lived like remembered joy." See Edith Stein, *On the Problem of Empathy* (Washington, DC: ICS Publishers, 1989), 11–12.

10. Though I am very dubious about the idea that identification ever occurs, I am not claiming that I know that it does not. Rather, I am arguing that it is not a particularly comprehensive model of our emotional interaction with narrative fictions, a claim that most friends of identification have advanced. Since my argument concerns the generality of the notion of identification, it is not to the point to respond to my objections, as some have, by observing that I have not shown that it is self-contradictory to assert that spectators might identify with characters or that identification is in any other way, in principle, precluded. That may be so; however, that is not incompatible with my central allegation which is that we have little to gain by adverting to identification to account for our emotional responses to fictional characters in the largest number of cases.

Philosophical debates often follow a predictable trajectory. One side begins with a bold claim—like: everything is really mind. After a series of objections, the position gets refined drastically down to "it has not been shown that it is logically impossible that everything is mind" or "it has not been shown that there is not some evidence of the existence of mind."

At one time, it was believed that identification was the whole story or, at least, a major part of it, with respect to our emotional responses to narrative fictions. Perhaps for some, this conviction is still firm. It is this view that I am denying.

Whether identification might be logically possible in some circumstances or whether it actually obtains on rare occasions is not an option that I claim to have foreclosed categorically. What I have argued is that identification, as it is usually understood, is extremely unlikely.

11. This approach is defended by Berys Gaut in his interesting article, "Identification and Emotion in Narrative Film," in *Passionate Views: Film, Cognition, and Emotion,* ed. Carl Plantinga and Gregg M. Smith (Baltimore, MD: Johns Hopkins University Press, 1999), 200–216. For criticism of this view, see Noël Carroll, "Sympathy for the Devil," in *The Sopranos and Philosophy,* ed. Richard Greene and Peter Vernezze (Chicago: Open Court, 2004), 121–36.

12. Amy Coplan appears to think that identification, which she calls "empathy," in cases like these involves suffering the self-same emotion type while, at the same time, differentiating oneself from the character. This is certainly logically possible. However, it would be a rather ad hoc solution to the paradox I've imagined, since it is more economical to suppose that the problem does not arise to begin with because we are not identifying with the character than it is to posit that we are identifying with the character while simultaneously we are also *differentiating* ourselves from the character. Unless something motivates postulating identification in the first place, there is no reason to conjecture differentiation in the second place. But as I have argued earlier, identification is not a wheel we need to add to this mechanism, since the operation of our own emotive apparatus—with no assistance from character contagion—can explain our feelings toward the protagonists.

13. Similarly, it should be noted that not only do our emotional states vis-à-vis characters vary systematically in terms of convergence. There are also systematic relationships in the way they diverge. For example, when the villain is frustrated, the audience is apt to feel joy, whereas when he is happy, we are likely to feel anger—as when he strokes the fair heroine's cheek with his clammy fingers. That is, sometimes when certain characters are in euphoric states, our emotions diverge vectorially toward an opposing dysphoric state, and vice versa.

14. The locus classicus of the application of simulation theory to fiction is Gregory Currie's "The Moral Psychology of Fiction," *Australasian Journal of Philosophy,* 73 (1995): 250–59. This article is criticized in Carroll, *Philosophy of Mass Art,* 342–56.

15. Though the proponents of simulation seem to think that insulating our target's beliefs and desires from our own is not a problem, I suspect that when we put others in our shoes (or, ourselves in their shoes), it is probably very unlikely that we can prevent seepage from our own character, beliefs, desires, and so forth from

contaminating the outcome. Thus, the *similarity* that is supposed to obtain between our emotional responses and our targets may be exceedingly rough.

16. Though he does not discuss the case of popular fictions, Jose Luis Bermudez points out that there may be real-time problems with respect to simulation theory. See Jose Luis Bermudez, "The Domain of Folk Psychology," in *Mind and Persons* (Cambridge: Cambridge University Press, forthcoming).

17. Indeed, such accessibility is arguably a necessary condition for mass art. See my *Philosophy of Mass Art.*

18. Likewise, we generally rely on heuristics rather than simulations or theories when we design our behavioral responses to conspecifics. As Bermudez points out, if we are engaged in iterated negotiations with others, we typically adopt a tit-for-tat heuristic, sans simulation.

19. Redundancy is a feature of all effective communication, but it is especially crucial in mass fictions where a premium is necessarily placed upon accessibility.

20. Though I do not agree with his conclusions, especially regarding empathy, this section has been influenced by Stephen Darwall's thinking about sympathy and caring. See Stephen Darwall, "Empathy, Sympathy, and Care," *Philosophical Studies* 89 (1998): 261–82.

21. The importance of morality for engendering audience allegiance to fictional characters is defended in my "Toward a Theory of Film Suspense," in *Theorizing the Moving Image* (Cambridge: Cambridge University Press, 1996); and "The Paradox of Suspense" in my *Beyond Aesthetics* (Cambridge: Cambridge University Press, 2000).

22. Since, for example, the recent remake of *Ocean's Eleven.*

23. Sometimes the moral standing of the protagonists relies on his being lesser than the evils that surround him. See my "Sympathy for the Devil," which attempts to explicate our sympathy for Tony as grounded in our apprehension of him as the least vicious of the prominent denizens in the fictional world of *The Sopranos.*

24. Elaine Hatfield, John T. Cacioppo, and Richard L. Rapson, *Emotional Contagion* (Cambridge: Cambridge University Press, 1994), especially chap. 2.

25. This begins quite early on. Twelve-to-twenty-one-day-old infants show evidence of mimicry. See A. N. Meltzoff and A. K. Moore, "Imitation of Facial and Manual Gestures by Human Neonates," *Science* 198 (1977): 75–78.

26. See Hatfield, Cacioppo, and Rapson, *Emotional Contagion.*

27. Of course, if through mimicry we detect that our spouse is "hot under the collar," that need not suck us into a comparable emotional state of anger. Instead, we may use that affective information to be wary—to be on guard lest we trigger the wrath of our antecedently upset mate.

28. Theodor Lipps, "Empathy and Aesthetic Pleasure," in *Aesthetic Theories: Studies in the Philosophy of Art*, ed. Karl Aschenbrenner and Arnold Isenberg (Englewood Cliffs, NJ: Prentice Hall, 1965), 403–14.

29. David Bordwell, *The Cinema of Eisenstein* (Cambridge, MA: Harvard University Press, 1993), 116.

30. Though it is probably by osmosis that most filmmakers pick up on the efficacy of mirror reflexes for modulating audiences affectively, Eisenstein's writings have figured in film pedagogy in many countries and possibly may have alerted at least some fledgling filmmakers to the existence of this resource.

31. Since the appearance of the monster onscreen should, all things being equal, be sufficient to raise horror in audiences, a question may arise about why affective cues like the reaction of the character to the monster is included at all. One reason is that it is an added, although redundant, means of clarifying exactly how the spectator should take what is happening in the film. Redundancy, of course, is an indispensable in popular entertainments, given their commitment to utter accessibility. And perhaps there is also another consideration. Like laughter and crying, screaming itself tends to be infectious. Thus, the way to set the viewers off on a screaming jag is to start it up from inside the film. As football games have cheerleaders, horror films have scream leaders—characters, like the one played by Faye Wray in *King Kong*, whose job it is to get the audience worked up. In such cases, the filmmakers hope that abundant screaming echoing throughout the theater will convince the viewers that the movie is scary enough to recommend to their friends.

32. When this chapter was originally presented as a talk at the State University of New York at Buffalo, members of the audience asked me why I did not discuss empathy. The reason is that I have found this notion to be exceedingly ambiguous and ultimately too confusing. It means many different things to different theorists. Some of these views I find unobjectionable. In other cases, the notion of empathy is pretty close to what I call identification in this essay. I have not addressed the identification view of empathy at length in the text, since I feel what I have said about identification does not need to be repeated.

  In his *The Nature of Sympathy* (London: Routledge and Kegan Paul, 1954), Max Scheler thinks of empathy as a sort of pathological identification, as occurs in schizophrenia. Since this does not seem to be a conception of empathy that most aestheticians have in mind when they invoke the concept, I do not think that I need to address it here.

On the other hand, in a less idiosyncratic vein, by *empathy*, some simply have in mind that I understand another's point of view. But since I may understand the plight of another—may comprehend where she's "coming from"—without feeling precisely what she feels, I have no qualms about this variant of *empathy*. I can *hear* you, without feeling your pain.

To "empathize" with someone else often means to acknowledge that her feelings are warranted. Insofar as this does not require exactly parallel emotions, I have no problems with this construal either.

Empathy may refer to *sensing* the emotions of others. But I can sense that my chairman is dispirited without being unhappy myself. My own emotional state may be contrary to his. Sensing that he is down may make my day. So this notion of empathy is acceptable in principle from my viewpoint. Even if, instead, my response is complementary to my chairman's mental state—that is, for example, sensing his dolors induces a feeling of troubled concern for him in me—this does not involve identification, since our emotions, though suited to each other, are not the same.

Indeed, if empathy only involves broadly congruent—that is, vectorially converging—emotive states, I am happy to agree that it occurs quite often in response to narrative fictions. I only draw the line when theorists use the label *empathy* to mark what I have challenged under the rubric of identification. I concede that this is how many, though far from all, use the term *empathy*. Of them, I ask that they consider my objections to identification.

Amy Coplan contends that my acceptance of empathy as involving nothing more than broadly congruent emotional states between fictional characters and audiences belies my confusion of empathy with sympathy. Empathy, she contends, involves sharing the same emotions but not necessarily in a way that elicits care for the other. But, she points out, in one of my examples of vectorially convergent empathy— where the character feels sorrow and I feel pity—my state does involve concern for the character, and, therefore, is a state of sympathy. Nevertheless, I would respond that it is not the case that empathy in my sense always collapses into sympathy, even if it does in the preceding example.

Given the difference in the information available to us, a fictional character may feel fear due to his superior knowledge, whereas the audience feels, at most, disquiet or unease: let us imagine that he is an experienced tracker, savvy in the signs of the jungle, whereas we, unlike him, do not know exactly what and how dangerous that which is headed toward us really is. This would be an example of the broadly congruent sense of empathy that would not be reducible to a case of sympathy. I think that cases like this obtain in narrative fictions, so the distinction between empathy and sympathy that Coplan respects can be made out on my view, though I agree that empathy of this sort is often mixed with sympathy. On the other hand, even Coplan would have to acknowledge that empathy and sympathy—in either her sense or mine—often overlap and are continuous.

Amy Coplan's carefully argued article against my position only reached my desk as I was struggling to meet the deadline for this article. Thus I have not had the opportunity to give it the close attention it merits. However, it is my general impression that she takes empathy to be what I treat as identification and that she fails to grapple with my argument from explanatory parsimony, which is one of my leading objections to the identification hypothesis.

Of course, Amy Coplan is not the only philosopher to equate empathy with identification. I suspect this also occurs in Douglas Chismar, "Empathy and Sympathy: The Important Difference," in *Journal of Value Enquiry* 22 (1988): 257–66.

For a discussion of empathy in relation to film, see Carl Plantinga, "The Scene of Empathy and the Human Face," in *Passionate Views*, 238–55.

6

Liking What's Good: Why Should We?

Ted Cohen

INTRODUCTION

If we are to compare popular art with high, fine art, then we will need something they have in common in order to locate a kind of scale along which their relative standing might be plotted. Almost all of this chapter is an attempt to do that by way of a description of art, along with other things, as consisting of objects around each of which is gathered what I call "a community of appreciation." With that in hand, it is possible for me to offer a very brief, highly tentative guess about what difference it might make whether such an object were an instance of popular art or of something more "refined."

THE MAIN PART

When you like something, does it matter how good that thing is? Augustine thought so, at least with regard to political communities. He thought that the ancient Romans were a *people*, as he thought of a people, because they loved something in common, but that they were less than a very good people because the things they loved in common were not such good things (they did not love God).[1]

Let us think, not of political communities, but of what might be called "aesthetic communities," and ask about how they are constituted. For some years, in a few papers and one small book, I have argued that when a number of people care for the same thing, they therein constitute a community exhibiting at least some mutuality. Here, too, it has been thought that it is better to like better things. As an example of this sentiment, you might consider an admonitory remark printed in 1897 in one of Chicago's cultural magazines, the *Dial*. That magazine was admonishing audiences of the Chicago Orchestra not to resist difficult works of European "classical" music, and it said this:

> This masterpiece deserves your attention . . . for it has the power to raise you to a higher spiritual level. If you do not like it now, pray that you may learn to like it, for the defect is yours.[2]

These aesthetic communities, as I have conceived them, are constituted in innumerable ways, are grouped around an enormous variety of objects, and are sometimes characterized by their comparative preferences. For instance, there are those who laugh at the same joke, those who prefer Glenn Gould's early performance of *The Goldberg Variations* to other performances, those who like their meat cooked rare, those who would rather see the performance of a play than watch a movie, and so on.

Here are three extreme examples: those readers who are devoted to *Don Quixote*, those viewers who regularly watch *The Simpsons*, and those jokers who like ethnic jokes. I have no idea whatever how to compare this novel, this television series, and these jokes with one another, but I will just assume that intellectuals in general, and academic intellectuals in particular, will think that Cervantes's book is, in some sense, better than the television cartoon, and certainly better than any Polish joke. And I will overlook—but only temporarily—the fact that a single person might belong to all these groups, as in fact I do, being a fan of the adventures of the man of La Mancha, Homer Simpson's foibles, and the joke about this year's Polish science prizes.

Now there are plainly two immediate problems besetting the assertion that it is better to like better things. The first is, simply, that it is utterly unclear what argument would lead from "X is better than Y" to "It is better to like X than it is to like Y." I think it seems to many thinkers that it is *obvious* that it is better to like the better thing, but not only is it not obvious, but, as a few minutes' reflection shows, it is not at all clear that it is even true. Let us have a mundane example and not yet become entangled in the question of what makes one thing better than another. That tangle awaits us, but for a moment, let us just suppose it given that, say, a meal prepared with care by a four-star chef is better than a burger and fries at McDonald's. (Make it a complete meal, say that American curiosity, the Big Mac, with extra fries along with a Diet Coke—the choice of a *Diet* Coke being for health reasons.) Is it better, all things being equal, as the saying goes, to prefer the chef's offering to the grease combo? Well, we might say, at least the preference shows better taste on the part of the diner. Let's say that. We aren't giving much away, as I see it, for now we run up against this question, which, as I have argued elsewhere, I consider highly unlikely to be answerable: "Why is it better to have better taste?"[3] An instinctive reply is, well, then you will like better things, but that runs right into another question which is not really *another* question, for it is the same old question: "Why is it better to like better things?"

Perhaps I don't convince you about this, and maybe I shouldn't. If you can provide answers to these questions, I will be delighted to hear them. Until then, we have this problem: we have no reason to think it is better to like better things. That is the first immediate problem.

The second problem, of course, is just this (and in fact it was probably the first problem): what could possibly establish that X is better than Y, whether X and Y are meals, wine vintages, or works of art? If X and Y are meant to serve some purpose, or are intended to answer to some special consideration, then there may be answers. For instance, if X and Y are automobiles, and I need my car to carry my wife's unbelievably difficult-to-carry gardening paraphernalia, then if X is a five-door hatchback Saab while Y is a Miata two seater, then X is better than Y. And if X is an all-organic, low-calorie, no-fat meal, while Y is that McDonald's grease mélange, and if I am trying to lose weight, then X is a better choice.

But, and pace Aristotle and his fans, I see no way to construe works of art in this way as long as they are considered as works of art. Considered otherwise, there may be a way to make comparisons. If you're trying to learn German, it may be better to attend a performance of Mozart's *Magic Flute* than to listen to his *Marriage of Figaro*, and if you'd like to gain a sense of Victorian England, you might better read Dickens than Mark Twain. We are not considering them otherwise, however, and the question is, what could establish that *The Marriage of Figaro* is better than *The Magic Flute*, or that *Huckleberry Finn* is better than anything by Dickens, even *David Copperfield*?

It is not that no one has tried to show such things. Indeed, the history of the philosophy of art, as well as all of art criticism, music criticism, and the rest, are full of these attempts, and they are often worth reading. It is just that they do not succeed. Adorno might have produced ten times as much blather as he managed, and he would still not have moved one step closer to showing that Beethoven's *Ninth Symphony* is less good than other works by Beethoven, much less that American jazz is inferior to Adorno's prized European art music.

And why don't these attempts succeed? Well, now I come clean, and if you wind up thinking I'm a so-called positivist and you want to ride me out of Buffalo on a rail, then I will live with that. (Did you know that Abraham Lincoln once compared a disagreeable occurrence with being ridden out of town on a rail, and noted that if it weren't for the glory of it, he would just as soon skip it?)

Thus I come clean and say, any reason that could be given for claiming X better than Y will be unacceptable.[4] And it will be unacceptable even to the critic who thinks to give it as a reason, just as soon as he realizes the implications of taking it as a genuine *reason*. It will force him to denigrate things he thinks good, and, even more unacceptably, it will force him to praise things he thinks poor. Here is one example, to stand for the general point:

A common reason cited for preferring one thing to another is the greater "complexity" of the one. You can see as well as I that it is going to be impossible to unpack the idea of complexity successfully, especially given the results one needs to arrive at. But even without that worry, how about this? "I prefer much of the music of the standard Western art tradition, say, to rock and roll, because the music I prefer is more complex. Bach, for instance, or Beethoven, especially in the late string quartets, is far more complex harmonically and even melodically than any music by Elvis Presley." Fine, and so far so good— but only so far. Among composers of the mid- and late twentieth century, we find music of complexity equal to or greater than that of things by Bach or Beethoven. Some of that music—say, some things by Milton Babbit or various late twelve-tone composers—is so complex that virtually no one can *hear* the music's internal relations. I have, finally, learned to do that, at least a little. Recall that I am one who prefers Bach to Elvis on account of Bach's greater complexity.

Now this is a subtle point, one whose subtlety escaped me for quite some time. It may well be true that my preference for Bach over Elvis is in fact due to the greater complexity of, say, *The Goldberg Variations* when compared with, say, *Heartbreak Hotel*. But it cannot be true *in general* that I prefer the more complex to the less complex, because, among other things, I do not prefer anything by Milton Babbit to *The Goldberg Variations*. And this means that it cannot be true, even for me, that in general X is better than Y whenever X is more complex than Y.

I am not advancing a confusion between liking something and thinking that the thing is good, at least not as yet, because I not only like Bach more than I like Babbit, but I think Bach is better than Babbit.

So what are we to say about the kinds of art one likes, and about one's preferences for one work over another? Before *I* try saying something, I will back away from these questions about art for a moment and go back to what seem to be questions of morality and politics, just as a way of helping us to loosen up a bit when thinking about these things.

Let us ask, when one person is morally superior to another, is it better of us to like that better man more than we like the other? To help in thinking about that, I give you two examples from my own affective life. The first concerns a man who was once in charge of the editorial page of an important newspaper but who was forced to leave his position when he committed journalistic plagiarism. The other concerns a man who was once a leading figure in city government but was sent to jail after being charged with using his office to solicit bribes.

Both these men were my friends. The day I read the news of the journalist's disgrace, I spent a very long time wondering not only what to do but how to feel. Finally I had an epiphany of a kind, and I took out my stationery and wrote him a note saying I'd read of his trouble and was sorry. When the former alderman had done his jail time, I came across him walking down the street. My earlier experience with the journalist made it easier for me this time, and I simply shook the man's hand, expressed sympathy, and welcomed him home.

In a phrase, these men not only *were* my friends, but they still are my friends. Do you think I have made a mistake? A moral error? Should I shun these people, or at least moderate my affection for them? If you think so, then you may be right, but I consider you a kind of fanatic, someone whose view of life, and whose sensibility, are far too simple for the subtleties and difficulties of human existence.

Now that I've confessed to my own opinion as to whether it is better to like morally better things, I will get back to the similar question, namely whether it is better to like aesthetically better things. I begin by noting that among the bromides, chestnuts, and many offhand remarks made about works of art are two that seem to be at odds with one another. One is the one that lurks in the background throughout this volume, namely that the most elevated, rarefied, and refined works of art are appreciated by only a few, the true connoisseurs. But the other is the idea that art is "universal," that it is the peculiar and redeeming fact about art that it reaches right through people's differences, which is to say, in a word, that it has the capacity to be "popular."

A few years ago, I made the probably unwise decision to teach a little Shakespeare. Feeling inadequate, I decided to dip into the Shakespeare literature. I came away from that excursion stupefied by the incredible volume of material published about Shakespeare, and so I asked for some guidance from my Shakespeare-expert friends. But before I did that, I ran across an interesting assertion. I have no idea how well this assertion is supported, but genuine Shakespeare scholars have made it more than once, and I give it to you: measured in terms of the frequency of their performance, Shakespeare's two most popular plays are *Hamlet* and *The Merchant of Venice*.

I found that surprising. I still do. On the one hand, *Hamlet* seems to me a stupendously great work of art, a creation of unfathomable depth, something to be engaged with for all one's life. On the other hand, *The Merchant of Venice* surely is not even one of Shakespeare's better plays. I think there may be more in this play than many have found, but it is, simply, on an entirely different level from *Hamlet*.

How can this be? How can *The Merchant of Venice* have snuck into one of the two top places, outdistancing, say, *King Lear* and *Othello*? Those two tragedies have their own great depths, their mysteries, their perpetual attraction, and for some very keen Shakespeare lovers, *King Lear* outranks *Hamlet*. The reason seems to be that *Hamlet* has succeeded for hundreds of years in lands all over the world just because it is what great art is said to be—universal, with themes and attractions that can reach us all. *The Merchant of Venice*, on the other hand, seems to owe its popularity to something else. I say "seems." I am not sure. But what would that something else be? Perhaps it is this: the mark of popular art is supposed to be that it is somehow "easy" and therefore widely accessible. *The Merchant of Venice*, despite its unignorable anti-Semitism, is fun, in its way. A Jewish man bests the best that Christian manhood can offer, and Christian manhood is so benighted about its own powers that it is only by pretending to be a man that the one person who can stand up to Shylock is given a chance. Portia overcomes them all, prevailing even over Bassanio by forcing him to break his word and then forgiving him.

Then it would seem that *Hamlet* reaches all of us in our depth, while *The Merchant of Venice* does what—reaches us on our surface?

Oddly enough, despite the fact that, virtually by definition, popular art is more popular than "high" art, popular art may be likelier to offer you the opportunity for discovery. When you are first taken with Mozart's *Marriage of Figaro*, you are not in the least surprised to find others who feel as you do, including listeners completely devoted to Mozart operas who can tell you many things about them and their performances. But when you stumble upon a pedestrian work, especially if the work is not yet known to you nor even heard of by you, and you are taken with it, it will be a special, extra treat to find others who care for it.

This is not a paradox, nor even more than mildly ironic, but it is interesting that in some cases it is the "popular" that is rare or novel. It is, one might say, "standard" that one like Mozart, and in that sense it is "popular" to like Mozart. Now, with regard to the popular arts, some things are standard and some are not. Elaine May's failure *Ishtar* is, to the degree that movies are a popular art, popular, but in another sense of *popular*, the movie was not at all popular, and I am nearly alone in my good opinion of it.

And then there are subtleties and refinements within the popular arts. Here is an example. In one episode of the television series *The West Wing*, which is a popular program, this happens: At the beginning of the episode, we see a very peculiar event, shown, as I remember it, in black and white. Three orthodox Jews are sitting in a car, two in the front seat, one in the back. There is some conversation (not remembered well by me), during which the man in the back, the youngest of the three, tells the others about Cole Porter, mentioning that he was at Yale where they have a curious singing group called "the Whiffenpoofs." Then their conversation shifts, and one of the men in the front seat tells the other that the backseat man has just become a father. The baby is named Tobias.

Next, the two front-seat men leave the car, go down the street, and after the sound of a gunshot, one of them returns. At this point, the episode shifts and becomes the familiar scene, in color, in Washington. As the episode progresses, Toby is visited by his father, and, oddly, Toby is not at all happy to see him and virtually ignores him. When someone inquires of Toby, he tells the questioner that his father is recently retired from the garment business, and that before that he was in prison because he'd been a member of Murder Incorporated.

Toby plainly disapproves of his father and resists the old man's attempts at friendship. Eventually, another regular character speaks to Toby about his father and tells Toby that his father was an immigrant trying to support a family with no other work to do, and, besides, the people assassinated by Murder Incorporated were pretty bad guys. Toby is unrelenting.

But by the end of the episode, Toby makes an overture to his father, who has been waiting, alone, in Toby's office, and invites the old man to stay in his apartment. As they are leaving the building, they stop to listen to a visiting chorus that has come to sing during the Christmas season. The old man asks who they are, and he is told that they are the Whiffenpoofs from Yale.

I do not always see *The West Wing*, but surely this is one of the most thoroughly crafted episodes in the series, especially because this development in the relationship between Toby and his formerly murderous father plays out against the background of what's been happening in the White House, where, as it happens, the president has authorized the assassination of a foreign bad guy.

The complexity of my liking for this particular episode of *The West Wing*, which clearly is a function of the complexity of the episode itself, might easily be compared with the complexity of my liking for Mozart's *Don Giovanni*. But in developing my affection for that television episode, I was much more on my own than in coming to love *Don Giovanni*, and this is not only because *Don Giovanni* has been around so much longer. It is partly because television episodes do not come to me already surrounded by a canonical appreciation.

By now, whether or not you agree with me, you can see, surely, (1) that I don't believe in any compelling argument to the effect that one thing is (aesthetically) better than another, and (2) that I don't believe it possible to show that it is better to like better things. Where does that leave me? Nowhere, you might say, but I prefer to think that I've been freed to start again, to try to understand what to make of the communities of people who care for the things they care for. I start, characteristically for me, I suppose, with a little autobiography.

Not long ago, my wife and I were in Memphis, and after completing family obligations, we spent an evening on Beale Street. While having dinner in B. B. King's, listening to an amplified blues band, I was almost mesmerized by twelve other members of the audience. They were in two groups of six. The first were a half dozen young Japanese women who had preceded my wife and me waiting to pay the club's cover charge. I'm not good at estimating ages, but I judged these young women to be in their twenties. They were dressed casually but neatly, and they sat at a round table between us and the stage, eating their dinner of ribs, rice, beans, and so on.

⌐ The other group I did not notice until after the music had begun. They must have been seated before we came in. They were six elderly black women whom I estimated to be, on average, about forty years older than the Japanese. They were very well dressed, almost as if they'd come from church, and they all wore hats as they sat slowly drinking their beer straight from the bottle.

A great feeling of well-being came over me, augmented, perhaps, by the two large glasses of beer I was drinking and the presence of my beautiful, great-spirited wife, herself captivated by the music. Everyone was swaying to the blues, and a couple was dancing in the small area in front of the stage. When the band temporarily abandoned the blues and dug into a rendition of "Mustang Sally," they encouraged sections of the audience to sing the refrain, "Ride, Sally, ride." Having just seen Bill Murray in *Lost in Translation* mistake a Japanese lady's request to rip her stockings for a plea to "lip my stockings," I was desperate to get close enough to the Japanese to hear whether they were singing "Lide, Sally, lide," but I behaved myself, and I can tell you only that the young Japanese women sang with gusto.

That evening, in Memphis at B. B. King's, I may have been mellowing out to the point of being sappy, but I thought, by God, this is it; this is the so-called universality of art. This is how art joins people one to another; this is how it unites, if only in certain aspects, people who may otherwise have nothing to do with one another and, apparently, very little in common. They have this in common, this music, right now.

But of course this is not real "universality," not in Kant's sense. The music doesn't get to *everyone*, and, at least so I think, Kant was wrong to think that such universality had to be the property of genuine judgments of beauty and art. But, whatever Kant may have thought, this doesn't diminish the importance of those less-than-universal groups that are gathered around specific works. It seems to me important to ask about those groups, how are they constituted and how are they related to one another?

In fact, we have two different points from which to begin. We might take a specific work, say Beethoven's *Waldstein* sonata or Hitchcock's *North by Northwest* or Gary Trudeau's *Doonesbury*, and then look to the audience the work has earned. Or we might take a specific person, say you or me, and look into the various works that person cares for.

What we have, I think, is a wonderfully intricate array of circles, all of them organized around two different foci. Despite my contempt for PowerPoint and my aversion to slide shows, I would have drawn this configuration for you, but I am not up to that, and you'll have to imagine it, either visually or otherwise.

First we have works of art, and other objects of appreciation, and around each of them is the intimate circle of those who care for these things. But the auditors themselves are foci, each of them in turn, and each of them belongs to the circles of many objects. So we would have to make both the works and the appreciators centers of circles, and these circles will be overlapping, sometimes entirely within one another, sometimes completely separate from one another, and there will be lenses and lunes galore.

This may look to you like the result of a sociological survey, but I don't mind; I'm not one of those riding a keen distinction between philosophy and other things, and there is at least a little of what seems to be philosophy on the way.

Let us have a slight, very brief and partial illustration. Take as the work Mozart's *Marriage of Figaro*. In its circle, you will find me, my wife, many of my friends, certainly the musicologist Joseph Kerman, and many, many others, but you will not find the late Alan Tormey, for instance, nor many people with no taste for Mozart, nor many of those who do not care for opera at all. Now take me. I'm already in the *Marriage of Figaro* circle, but I am myself the center of a circle, and within that circle, the one defined by me, are at least five Mozart operas, Alfred Hitchcock's *North by Northwest*, piano trios by Schubert, Clint Eastwood's *Unforgiven*, Leon Redbone's *Walking Stick*, many poems by Robert Pinsky, two books by Imre Kertsz, and many, many other things.

One wants to know—at least I want to know—what characterizes the things inside these circles, or, to put it in a good, old-fashioned way, (1) what do all those who love the *Marriage of Figaro* have in common, and (2) what do all the works I love have in common?

I think I know the answers to these questions, and I think I know an absolutely essential corollary to the answers.

The first answers are—and I'm sure Nelson Goodman would be glad to hear this—*nothing*. The only thing you're going to find that we Mozart lovers have in common is that we love Mozart. And the only thing you will find in common when you look over all that I love is that I love it all. Nominalism, I guess.

I am not going to argue for these answers here. I have previously given a sketch of an argument for the proposition that each of us has what I call "an aesthetic personality" that exhibits no essential characteristic.[5] My idea was, and is, that whatever reason you or I may have for our attraction to some work, some other work with exactly the same characteristic may well fail to attract us.

My idea about the other circles is similar. If you take all those who care for some work, you will not find that they care for it in just the same way and for just the same reasons. Thus your attraction to the *Marriage of Figaro* or *Don Quixote* may be anchored differently from mine. A likely example is Hitchcock's *North by Northwest*. Perhaps you like that movie as much as I, but chances are you do not find in that movie an extended meditation on what it means to be an American, the very thing that most attracts me to the movie. So then we are both in the movie's circle, but we are held there quite differently.

If I am right about this, or even most of it, we find ourselves and our art— the popular art, the high art, and all the rest—linked to one another and separated from one another, and there seem to be no underlying "principles" to explain these groupings.

These circles of appreciation are defined by an enormous number of objects and activities. Some of us like stock-car racing, some like to play pool, some love baseball, some are bored by baseball (they are mistaken), some like to watch bullfighting, some can't stand even the thought of bullfighting, and so on and on.

We can draw my circles with regard to any and all of these things. My personal circle includes watching baseball, listening to Schubert, playing pool, telling jokes, listening to jokes, listening to jazz, playing drums, and on and on, and it excludes bullfighting, music by Andrew Lloyd Weber, playing football (but not watching football), and on and on.

Some of the items inside my circle, and some outside it, and surely things inside and outside your circles, are art, or things like art, and some are not. Please don't think for a moment that I'm going to offer any "definition" of *art*, or accept anyone else's, but I am going to suppose we know what we're talking about when we talk about art and things that seem pretty much like art but about which we're not so sure. In these circles—and, more to the point, in the relations between us and our favorites—what does it matter that some of them are art? If I am known for much of anything in contemporary aesthetics, I think it is that I am customarily, inveterately, obstinately, and even nastily opposed to *theories*, but I do indeed think that those bromides, chestnuts, and the rest that I spoke of much earlier contain some pretty good thoughts. One long-standing thought about art is that it is a medium through which human beings reach one another, and there is an ancillary thought, a favorite of mine, that our relations to the works of art themselves are strikingly like our relationships to people.

The dimensions of your humanity are exhibited in the tangents, radii, and intersections appearing in your circle array, but I think that there is a special significance, a depth, in those dimensions along which you are connected to other people.

The works of art are not different from any of the other things we like, or don't, with regard to whether there are principles to be found that would explain how these things and their audiences are constituted. There are no such principles.

But then my corollary to this is unexpected. I suppose it is not a genuine corollary, but rather an injunction, a kind of desperate imperative. I think we must *look* for the samenesses, the similarities, the essential links in full knowledge that we will not find them. And why is that? It is time for the unabashed, romantic declaration: each work, each object of appreciation and affection is unique, and equally unique are those of us who are the appreciators, and, in addition, those bonds that link us to our loves may also be unique, or nearly. It is critical to appreciate this uniqueness, and the way to do this is to do away with, one by one, all the temptations to think we are not unique, that we are just like one another. In doing this, we have a chance to discover two things we absolutely need to know, namely just how much we are indeed like one another, and how much we are not. I doubt that we will ever know these things, but we must try.

HIGHLY TENTATIVE CONCLUSION

The community of appreciation grouped around something can be thought of no matter what kind of thing it is that is appreciated. It might be a game, say, or the playing of a game, or a mountain view, but presumably things are at least somewhat different if the object of appreciation is a work of art, and I think that this is so because in the appreciation of a work of art, one is also somehow in touch with the maker—the artist. The community created by Melville's *Billy Budd*, for instance, in addition to those readers who care for the novel, also includes Melville, whose palpable sensibility lies behind—and, one might say, is in—the book.

This seems to me a difference between the appreciation of made objects and objects that do not embody the sense of any creator, but that is not a difference marked between works of fine art and works of any other kind of art. If there is a difference here, it will be a reflection of some difference between the creator of a work of fine art and the creator of something else, say the kind of work of "entertainment" commonly regarded (at least by academic and other intellectuals) as trivial. The community of appreciation of a "serious" work will include the robust presence of a serious artist, and the community that appreciates an object of popular, mass art presumably will not. One has a relationship with a work of art, and thereby a relationship with the work's creator, and perhaps this relationship has more depth and texture when the work is wonderful and wonderfully serious. Perhaps. If so, then this difference remains to be explained, and I am unable to do that; at least I am unable to do it yet.

And then, even if that difference can be formulated persuasively, there will remain the question of whether it is in any way better to join company with a fine, serious artist than with an entertainer; and, to paraphrase Hume, with a difference, this question is embarrassing and throws us back into the uncertainty with which we began. My apologies, I have nowhere else to go.

NOTES

1. See Augustine, *The City of God Against the Pagans*, bk. 19, chap. 24.

2. "The Chicago Orchestra," *Dial* 22 (May 1, 1897): 269–71, quoted by Lawrence W. Levine in *Highbrow/Lowbrow* (Cambridge, MA: Harvard University Press, 1988).

3. "The Philosophy of Taste: Thoughts on the Idea," in *The Blackwell Guide to Aesthetics*, ed. Peter Kivy (Oxford: Blackwell, 2004).

4. I have tried to give a generalized argument for this in "On Consistency in One's Personal Aesthetics," in *Aesthetics and Ethics: Essays at the Intersection*, ed. Jerrold Levinson (Cambridge: Cambridge University Press, 1998).

5. Cohen, "On Consistency in One's Personal Aesthetics."

7

Popular Art and Entertainment Value

Richard Shusterman

PROBLEMS, PREMISES, AND METHODS

Among philosophers and cultural critics, the value of popular art has been hotly contested. Denouncing it for lacking artistic or aesthetic value, critics have also condemned it for having noxious social and cultural consequences, while defenders have often tried to mitigate the critique by pointing to the genuine democratic need for the expression of popular tastes and to the consequent social, political, and cultural value of ensuring that this expressive need is satisfied. Such social apologies for popular art, I have argued, prove inadequate, because they leave untouched the question of artistic value that lies at the core of the critique, since even the sociocultural charges against popular art (for instance, that it waters down high culture, inspires unthinking conformism, and corrupts taste) all can be shown to rest on the presumption that it is aesthetically inferior.[1]

Moreover, preoccupation with such "external" justifications of popular art in terms of its social or political instrumentality only serves to cast darker doubt on its intrinsic value of aesthetic worth. The commonly made contrast between instrumental and intrinsic value, together with the presumptions that popular art is distinctively functional and that aesthetic value is essentially intrinsic, makes the assertion of popular art's aesthetic value seem especially problematic. One of the aims of this paper is to alleviate this difficulty through a more careful analysis of value that tries to reconcile the conflict between the intrinsic and the instrumental. This aim is nested in my continuing advocacy of a pragmatist position on popular art that I call meliorism, which recognizes popular culture's flaws and abuses but also its merit and potential. Meliorism holds that popular art needs improvement because of its many failings, but that it can be improved because it can and often does achieve real aesthetic merit and serve worthy social ends.[2]

Scholars often seem more comfortable speaking about popular culture rather than popular art because the concept of "art" is so often regarded as honorific and as tightly linked to modernity's high-art tradition which typically defined itself against popular taste (though actually nourishing itself in large part from popular experience and artistic expression). In contrast, the term *culture* has a more value-neutral, anthropological meaning of "way of life," but it also has a distinctively evaluative sense of excellence in the arts and humanities, thus connoting high culture. Because of such honorific connotations, Pierre Bourdieu describes "popular culture" (like "popular art") as a contradiction in terms,[3] while some French politicians have refused to recognize hip-hop as even being popular culture (let alone real music), branding it instead as a "social" (rather than cultural) phenomenon. More often, cultural elitists who wish to categorize the popular arts without using the honorific categories of art and culture resort to the concept of entertainment. When popular art is aesthetically disparaged for being concerned with functionality rather than form, the prime function intended is entertainment, and the consequent charge is that we are being amused into lazy, autistic, fun-loving, irresponsible idiocy. Is "entertainment value," then, something that precludes aesthetic value in popular art, or can it indeed contribute to aesthetic value in all the arts?

Entertainment is obviously central to popular art and popular culture, and I believe this concept underlies the high-culture/popular-culture debate, which can be seen as largely structured on the contrast of art versus entertainment.[4] Moreover, the concept of entertainment is significantly older than the concepts of popular art and popular culture, whose use (at least in English) seems to go back only to the nineteenth century.[5] Long before philosophers were denigrating popular art, and even before our modern concept of art had been established, we find deprecations of drama, poetry, and other arts for being mere entertainment and thus inferior, trivial pursuits that were negatively contrasted to the nobility of serious learning and action. So I think a philosophical understanding of the cultural logic and status of popular art can be well served by exploring the concept and values of entertainment. Moreover, since art has not only been contrasted to entertainment but is also sometimes regarded (for better and for worse) as a form of entertainment, such exploration could also enhance our understanding of the general concept of art.

The philosophical framework of my exploration is pragmatism. Because of its appreciation of instrumentalities, relations, and contextuality, pragmatism is often (but falsely) accused for denying intrinsic values. That is one reason I am sensitive to the need to maintain a notion of intrinsic value that will permit instrumentality. If there were only instrumental values, so that everything was valued only as a means to something else, there would seem to be nothing valuable for itself that could ultimately justify or ground the value of these instrumentalities. Our whole structure of values would seem to be an empty circle of mere means with nothing valuable to make them worth using as means.

Pragmatism is a forward-looking philosophy that judges ideas by their consequences, not their pedigree. But it recognizes that philosophical problems and concepts emerge through historical contexts and can therefore be properly understood only through recognition of that history. My analysis of entertainment therefore begins with some etymological study of the cluster of terms that denote this concept, followed by a brief genealogy of its philosophical deployment, through which its complexity of value and disvalue can be discerned. One point to emerge is that the art/entertainment contrast seems sustained by an opposition of knowledge versus pleasure that needs to be questioned. Invoking examples from hip-hop that insist on the fruitful unity of popular art that is both enjoyable and cognitively edifying, I will argue that pleasure need not be globally condemned as trivial and narrowly personal. It moreover seems to combine a sense of intrinsic value with the instrumental value of serving life. Aesthetically motivated criticism of entertainment's (and popular culture's) service to life will then be refuted, and the chapter concludes by refuting the incompatibility of intrinsic and instrumental value.

Before launching my analysis of entertainment, I should make two prefatory remarks about the cultural forces shaping our understanding of this concept. First, these forces are typically hierarchical and competitive in the struggle over culture. Like popular art, entertainment has been largely defined by its deprecatory contrast with what philosophy considered higher forms of culture, whether the contrast was with philosophy itself or (at a later stage) with forms of high art. Secondly, since the cultural forces shaping the concepts of entertainment and popular art are historically changing, so is the extension of these concepts and the boundary drawn between them and serious art. The popular entertainments of one culture (such as Greek or Elizabethan drama) often become the high-art classics of a subsequent age. Novels by the Brontës and Charles Dickens were initially received as light popular fiction, not as the masterpieces of great literature we regard them as today. Movies have undergone similar evolution of status. Indeed, even within the very same cultural period, a given work can function either as popular entertainment or as high art depending on how it is presented or interpreted and how it is appreciated by its public. In nineteenth-century America, Shakespeare's plays served as both high theater and vulgar vaudeville.[6] Thus, the precise meaning of entertainment is highly contextual, depending on what it is being contrasted to. Increasingly in modern times, the contrast term has become serious art. But in earlier times, entertainment or amusement was contrasted to philosophy, religion, and the serious business of life, while the fine arts as a whole were regarded as having the lower status of entertainment (even if one then still distinguished between higher and lower entertainments).

ENTERTAINMENT: TERMINOLOGY AND GENEALOGY

During its long philosophical history in the West, the concept of entertainment has been expressed through a variety of terms with slightly different but overlapping meanings. Other English words used to express this concept include *amusement, pastime, distraction, divertissement,* and *recreation,* and sometimes *play* and *game.* The French mainly employ such terms as *amusement, divertissement,* and *distraction,* but they also use such terms as *rejouissance* and *passetemps.* In German, *Unterhaltung* is the most common term for entertainment, but the terms *Zerstreuung, Zeitvertreib,* and *Belustigung* are also used. The English term *entertainment* derives ultimately from the Latin *inter + tenere,* which would mean "to hold together," "to maintain," or "to uphold." Its earliest uses, in the sixteenth century, were devoted to this sense of maintaining or sustaining, particularly the maintenance of persons. Another early usage of *entertainment,* found in Shakespeare's *Love's Labors Lost,* is an "occupation" or "spending of time." From these earlier meanings, the principal aesthetic meaning of *entertainment*—"the action of occupying (a person's) attention agreeably," "that which affords interest or amusement," "a public performance or exhibition intended to interest or amuse"—seems to have derived. The German term *Unterhaltung* clearly parallels the English, moving from connotations of support or sustenance to the idea of occupying one's time pleasantly. The straightforward philosophical lesson implied by this etymology is that entertainment helps maintain the self by occupying oneself pleasurably and with interest. The same idea is expressed in the term "recreation," where one sustains oneself by reviving or recreating one's energy through pleasurable activity.

The philosophical lesson is more complex when we consider the English and French terms of *amusement, divertissement,* and *distraction.* Here, instead of emphasizing the maintenance of one's self or one's guests, the focus is distracted to some other, presumably far less important matter that captures our attention. The English term *amusement* derives from the verb *to muse,* whose early meanings are "to be absorbed in thought," "to wonder," and "to be astonished or puzzled." But both English terms stem back to the French *muser,* meaning to waste time or trifle by idly attending to light matters. Amusements thus prompt us to stop the serious business of maintaining ourselves and others and instead lure us to meditate on other things. The terms *distraction, diversion,* and *divertissement* all suggest, through their root meaning of "tearing away" or "turning aside," that we are turned away from our habitual focus of attention and instead directed to something else. The German *Zerstreuung* likewise suggests that in entertainment the attentive subject is dispersed or scattered in contrast to the concentration of the self that high art demands and which Walter Benjamin denotes as *Sammlung*—a term that conveys the notion of collecting oneself or self-composure.

The philosophical lesson emerging from this etymology of distraction is more paradoxical: To maintain the self, one needs also to forget it and look elsewhere. To sustain, refresh, and even deepen concentration, one also needs to distract it; otherwise concentration fatigues itself and gets dulled through monotony. The paradoxical structure of entertainment—which binds, in a productive dialectic, the seeming opposites of focused attention and diversion, concentration and distraction, serious maintenance and playful amusement—also finds potent expression in various moments of the concept's history of philosophical use. I shall note only some crucial chapters of that history to emphasize a few keys lines of argument.

We can begin with Plato's *Phaedrus* (276a–77a), where Socrates, in arguing against the idea of writing philosophy, draws a sharp contrast between philosophy and entertainment. Written speeches, even of philosophy, are only valuable "for the sake of amusement" in contrast to the truly "serious" philosophical "art of dialectic" through oral dialogue, which actively inseminates the mind "and renders the man who has it as happy as any human can be." Philosophy is thus superior to amusement not only in its education but in its pleasures. The Greek term used here for "amusement" is *paidia*, which is strikingly close to the Greek word for education, *paideia*, since they both have the common root related to children, a point that Plato deploys in *Laws*, book 2. Trivialized as childish "kidding around" or playing, entertainment is contrasted with true education, which should be serious and controlled. The mimetic arts, with their strong entertainment function, are for Plato not only a childish diversion from the truth but a deceptive distortion of it and a corruption of the soul. Hence his *Republic* strongly condemns them, even to the point of urging their banishment in book 10.

Although Aristotle's *Poetics* introduced some independent criteria for assessing the aesthetic value of tragedies—the pleasures of formalist unity and cathartic release—his defense of the artistic entertainments of his time still depended on philosophy's high value of truth. Hence, art's mimetic pleasures are defined as lower versions of philosophy's higher cognitive joys, and Aristotle chooses to praise poetry for being "more philosophic and of graver import than history" because it describes not the mere contingent particulars of the past but rather "a kind of thing that might happen, i.e., what is possible as being probable or necessary"; hence, though poetry uses proper names of particulars, "its statements are of the nature rather of universals, whereas those of history are singulars."[7] The Latin word for entertainment, *oblectatio*, which has the primary sense of an alluring diversion or distraction, also has connotations of the childish, since it is derived from the verb *lacto*, which means both to allure and to take milk from the breast. The mother's breast provides the child with entertainment both in the sense of sustenance and in the sense of pleasurable comforting distraction from unpleasant feelings or anxieties. The mother's breast is probably one's first entertainment in both these vital senses. Could philosophy's haughty devaluation of entertainment be partly an unconscious rejection of man's "childish" dependence on mothers and on women more generally?

At the dawn of modern thought, Michel de Montaigne still observes the ancient distinction between entertainment and serious philosophical wisdom in his discussion of reading. However, he skeptically challenges the traditional hierarchy of serious thought and playful amusement by proudly affirming that he now reads primarily for pleasure.[8] Anticipating critique of this love of amusement, Montaigne counters, "If anyone tells me that it is degrading the Muses to use them only as a plaything and a pastime, he does not know as I do the value of pleasure, play, and pastime. I would almost say that any other aim is ridiculous" (3.3.629).

Montaigne was, of course, a passionately serious thinker, as the intensely demanding and scholarly self-study that constitutes his massive *Essays* makes clear. This meditative activity "of entertaining one's own thoughts," he insisted, was a form of entertainment that, in a strong mind, could rival all other activities in both intellectual exertion and pleasure. Feeling, however, that prolonged, vigorous self-meditation could be dangerously exhausting and unsettling, Montaigne recognized his mind's need to divert itself with other pleasures in order to "settle down and rest."

Montaigne's account of entertainment contains three crucial points. First, entertainment can take demanding, meditative forms that involve not merely pleasure but also the superior exercise of the mind, and hence the pursuit of entertainment, pleasure, and serious intellectual activity should not be seen as inconsistent. Second, since pleasure, more generally, is not a trivial value, entertainment's deep connection with pleasure should not demean but rather elevate it. Third, entertainment's diversion of the mind is not a necessarily negative feature that diminishes the mind by distracting its attention, but rather, in dialectical fashion, it strengthens the mind's powers by providing it with both relief and alternative exercise in changing the focus and style of its activity.

In the eighteenth century, the notion of entertainment begins to be contrasted not simply with the serious praxis of life and thought but with more serious forms of art. Thus Samuel Johnson, the key critical figure of eighteenth-century English neoclassicism, attributes to *entertainment* a specific application to "the lower comedy" and notes its growing use for denoting "an assemblage of performances of varied character, as when music is intermixed with recitations, feats of skill, etc."[9] In Immanuel Kant's *Critique of Judgment*, the notion of entertainment is used with both "low" and "high" connotations. Though applied to the sensual, "interested" pleasures that distinguish the agreeable from the beautiful (book 1, paragraph 7), it is later used for the unconstrained and disinterested (i.e., without specific purpose) entertainment of the mental faculties (*"freie und unbestimmt-zweckmässige Unterhaltung der Gemütskräfte"*) that mark our experience of beauty.[10]

Friedrich Schiller's appreciative identification of the aesthetic with the realm of play and appearance recognizes the positive human need of entertainment as expressed through the concept of play: "man plays only when he is a human being in the fullest sense of the term, and he is only fully a human being when he plays."[11] Schiller likewise insists on the ennobling value of play as both an expression of human freedom and a noncoercive, effective form of moral edification. As Kant's *Critique of Judgment* maintained a fragile balance in the notion of entertainment for both interested and free pursuits, and thus a consequent bivalence of the term between the lower realm of the agreeable and the higher cognitive realm of the beautiful, so Schiller's ideal of play suggests that entertainment itself, in its nobler forms, provides and symbolizes the perfect equilibrium of ideal form and material life.

This balanced view of entertainment is decisively disturbed by Hegel's influential aesthetics, with its fateful spiritualizing turn toward the ideal. With Hegel, entertainment seems unequivocally identified with what is unworthy of the name of art. In his initial remarks to affirm the worthiness of art in his *Vorlesungen über die Ästhetik*, Hegel feels he must sharply distinguish between "true art" and the "servile" artistic distractions that are merely "a fleeting game in the service of pleasure and entertainment" and of other "external" ends of "life-related pleasantness." Entertainment thus marks the inferior realm of servitude to pleasure and its external ends. In contrast, the fine arts only become true art when they are free from this subservience. This Hegelian attitude still sadly dominates contemporary aesthetics, whose idealist turn has privileged, in the realm of art, truth over beauty and pleasure, while also aesthetically privileging the realm of art high above natural splendors.

Nietzsche presents a more complex and salutary view of entertainment and its relationship to art and thought. He can deploy the term very pejoratively to denote a trivial concern with shallow pleasure and the passing of time to alleviate boredom. On the other hand, in *Ecce Homo* ("Why I Am So Clever," section 3), Nietzsche expresses the positive power of entertainment through the notion of "recreation" ("*Erholung*"), which he regards, along with choice of climate and nourishment, as essential to self-care, as what allows him to escape himself and his own self-demanding "seriousness." Nietzsche in fact claims, "Every kind of reading belongs among my recreations."[12] An intense practitioner of self-meditation like Montaigne, Nietzsche seems to affirm the productive paradox of entertainment's distraction that we earlier gleaned from etymology and from Montaigne—that the self is sustained and strengthened by being freed from attention to itself, that serious self-care also entails amusing distraction from oneself. And this paradox, I think, implies a further dialectical lesson: that the self is enlarged and improved by forgetting itself and plunging its interest in the wider world.

 After Nietzsche, the dominant trend in German philosophy to denigrate the entertainment function of art reasserts itself. Martin Heidegger insists that artworks are not truly presented or preserved when they "are offered for merely artistic enjoyment," since art's defining essence is not pleasure or entertainment but "the becoming and happening of truth."[13] The Hegelian trend in German aesthetics to privilege truth over pleasure and even over beauty is still more strikingly dominant in Adorno, who together with Max Horkheimer introduced the disparaging notion of "the culture industry" to denigrate the entertainments of popular art whose allegedly passive and mindless pleasures "fill empty time with more emptiness." For Adorno, it almost seems that the entertaining pleasures of art are starkly opposed to cognition: "People enjoy works of art the less, the more they know about them, and vice versa." In the contest of artistic values, Adorno is clear that pleasure must be sacrificed to truth. "In a false world, all hedone is false. This goes for artistic pleasure too. . . . In short, the very idea that enjoyment is of the essence of art needs to be thrown overboard. . . . What works of art really demand from us is knowledge or, better, a cognitive faculty of judging justly."[14]

KNOWLEDGE AND ENJOYMENT

But why should it be assumed that there is an essential opposition between truth and entertainment, knowledge and pleasure? Note how one influential Anglo-American poet-critic-theorist wisely maintains the fruitful interconnection of these terms and therefore can affirm art's entertainment without denying its cognitive import. T. S. Eliot, inspired by the ideas of Remy de Gourmont, famously defined poetry as "a superior amusement," while immediately cautioning that this does "not mean an amusement for superior people." The arts constitute a superior amusement, Eliot argues, because their pleasure appeals not just to the senses but to the understanding. "To understand a poem comes to the same thing as to enjoy it for the right reasons. One might say that it means getting from the poem such enjoyment as it is capable of giving; to enjoy a poem under a misunderstanding as to what it is, is to enjoy what is merely a projection of our own mind. . . . It is certain that we do not fully enjoy a poem unless we understand it; and, on the other hand, it is equally true that we do not fully understand a poem unless we enjoy it. And that means, enjoying it to the right degree and in the right way, relative to other poems."[15]

By deconstructing the opposition between aesthetic pleasure and cognition, Eliot also sought to challenge the dichotomy between high art—presumably devoted (in Hegelian fashion) to sublime truth—and, on the other hand, vulgar popular entertainments that presumably pander to mere pleasure. Seeing instead a continuum between high art and entertainment, Eliot insists that the good poet "would like to be something of a popular entertainer . . . would like to convey the pleasures of poetry." In mordant demystification of romanticist notions of the poet as prophetic genius whose divine function is to reveal sublime truths, Eliot insists he would be pleased to secure for the poet "a part to play in society as worthy as that of the music-hall comedian," and deliberately turned his poetic efforts to the theater so as to reach a wider audience. Yet he likewise insisted that poetry's entertainment could convey valuable knowledge, indeed that poetry "is the language most capable of communicating wisdom." An avid fan of the music hall, which represented the values, voice, and taste of "the lower classes," Eliot nevertheless realized that it is naive to speak of the audiences of high and popular art as if they are disjoint publics, just as it is wrong to think that works of high art cannot acquire a broad popularity or that works of vernacular popular culture cannot achieve high aesthetic value and the level of "art."[16]

In today's popular culture, rap music provides a voice of dominated classes which can nonetheless appeal beyond that population to middle- and upper-class admirers, including intellectuals. Rap also provides a powerfully sustained argument that pleasure and knowledge can be combined in a popular entertainment that can fiercely claim the status of "fine art" (in Ice-T's words), displaying both intrinsic and instrumental value as it thrills its audience with the exhilarating pleasures of its dancing beat while educating to raise black consciousness and "teach the bourgeois" (Public Enemy) about social injustice, thus achieving its undeniable "penetration to the core of the nation" (Ice-T).[17] This emphasis on rap's cognitive dimension is found in many rap artists who identify with the "knowledge rap" tradition of teaching "science" while providing musical and dancing pleasure. But the most durably prominent representative of this hip-hop genre is BDP's KRS-One who identifies himself in his lyrics as a "poet," "a teacher and artist, startin' new concepts at their hardest," but also as a "philosopher" whose ethical and social commentary is complemented by "metaphysical teachings." And he emphatically underlines rap's artistic ideal of uniting knowledge with enjoyment by naming one of his major albums "Edutainment."[18]

KRS-One grasps the urgent need for "edutainment" through his perception of the limits of both education's and entertainment's dominant forms. Our schools, he argues, are instruments of institutional power aimed at reproducing the oppressive social hierarchy, and thus they systematically ignore or diminish the importance of black culture and the enormity of the enduring injustice suffered by the black lower classes. "Due to religious and political power / We must be denied the facts every hour." "Education doesn't come from simply obeyin' / the curriculum, of the school criteria. / In fact what I learned I found inferior." He is likewise critical of the dominant forms of entertainment that seek only pleasurable sound without any serious intellectual substance and moral content or any urgent social critique to educate and "uplift" the audience. "If I say stop the violence, I won't chart. / Maybe I should write some songs like Mozart / 'Cause many people don't believe rap is an art." KRS-One defines himself as the "teacher" to affirm his difference from the ordinary commercial rap artists whose lyrics of "ignorance" uncritically reflect the unexamined values of a corrupt, dysfunctional society. "Well, the teacher comes to you, in effect / From a different style, a whole different sect. / I inject force and intellect / When I hit the mic, suckers hit the deck. / . . . Reason for this is very simple indeed / When it comes to music, everyone's in need. / You got wealthy artists, spending money loosely. / You ask about the culture, they talk about Gucci." The powerful pleasures of music are an essential ingredient of good living, but popular audiences, he insists, should get their entertaining beats with a more meaningful and edifying message. KRS-One's goal "in the hip-hop field of art" is to provide such enjoyably enlightening and motivating "edutainment," in which cognitive pleasures are not purveyed simply for their own sake but to improve the individual and society, for example, by using "rap music as a tool in changing the structure of racist America." "Dear it's simple edutainment. / Rap needed a teacher, so I became it. / Rough and ready, the beats are very steady / With lyrics sharp as a machete."

Of course, many cultural critics will still want to sharply contrast art and entertainment, identifying the latter with idle pleasure seeking and lower-class vulgarity. Many factors of cultural history have made this identification so seductive. As the notion of pleasure centrally includes pleasures of the flesh, so idealist philosophy and otherworldly Christianity conspired to distance their realms of value from such low, corporeal taints. The Protestant ethic of work and thrift, long entrenched in North America and Europe, has also given pleasure a bad name. Moreover, the intellectual asceticism that constitutes the typical *habitus* of theorists prompts them to resist full recognition of pleasure's rich values. With modernity's secularization of the natural world and the loss of traditional religious faith, art increasingly came to function as a locus for our habits of sacralization. Even if the sacred aura of art has been challenged (as Walter Benjamin argues) by the mechanical reproduction of artworks, the desire to sustain art as a transcendental, spiritual value remains. In secular society, museums have replaced churches as the place where one visits on the weekend for one's spiritual edification.

But if art is to be sacralized, it must be sharply distinguished from entertainment, since entertainment is associated with profane earthy pleasures that serve to refresh embodied human life, rather than devoting itself entirely to the transcendental realm of spiritual immortality celebrated by romantic "theologies" of art. Pleasure and service to life—two of the crucial values affirmed by pragmatist aesthetics and embodied in popular art—are paradoxically two of the cardinal sins for which entertainment is condemned. The next section therefore brings some arguments in their defense, though common sense would think that none are needed.

PLEASURE AND FUNCTIONALITY

I begin with pleasure, since my aesthetics has frequently been criticized for hedonism, even though I never claim that pleasure is the only or the highest value in art and life.[19] I do, however, think that post-Kantian aesthetics wrongly tends to dismiss the importance of pleasure by failing to realize the complexity of its logic and the diversity of its forms and uses. This diversity is even suggested in the vast vocabulary of pleasure that far exceeds the single word. Besides the traditional contrast between sensual voluptuousness (*voluptas*) and the sacred heights of religious joy (*gaudium*), there is delight, pleasantness, gratification, gladness, elation, titillation, fun, exhilaration, enjoyment, exultation, bliss, rapture, ecstasy, and more. While fun and pleasantness convey a sense of lightness that could suggest triviality, the notions of rapture, bliss, and ecstasy clearly evoke just how profound and potently meaningful pleasures can be. Such pleasures, as much as truth, help constitute our sense of the sacred and can establish or reinforce our deepest values.[20]

Modern empiricism understands pleasure (and experience more generally) in terms of passive sensations existing only in the private mental world of the experiencing subject. So conceived, pleasure could seem trivial. But pleasure is not such an isolated passive sensation; it is, rather, as Aristotle recognized, a quality of any activity that "completes" or enhances that activity by making the activity more zestful or rewarding and thus promoting it by intensifying our interest in it. Pleasure (even when its quality is felt through one's sensations) is thus inseparable from the activity in which it is experienced. To enjoy tennis is not to experience intensely agreeable feelings in one's sweating racket hand or running feet (feelings which would distract us from the game); it is, rather, to play the game with gusto and absorbed attention. Likewise, to enjoy art is not to have certain pleasant sensations that we might obtain from something else, like a good espresso or a steam bath; enjoying an artwork is, rather, to take pleasure in perceiving and understanding the particular work's qualities and meanings, where such pleasure tends to intensify our attention to the work in a way that aids our perception and understanding of it. This Aristotelian conception lies behind Eliot's view of the essential connection of poetic enjoyment and understanding.

By strengthening our activity, pleasure contributes to the perfection of life. Far from a radical voluptuary, Spinoza actually defines pleasure "as the transition of man from a less to a greater perfection"; "the greater the pleasure whereby we are affected, the greater the perfection to which we pass." And the sober Aristotle also insists, "Whether we choose life for the sake of pleasure or pleasure for the sake of life, they seem to be bound up together and not admit of separation, since without activity pleasure does not arise and every activity is completed by the attendant pleasure."[21]

Contemporary evolutionary theory confirms this linkage of life and pleasure. Some of life's most powerful pleasures are closely linked to the activities of nourishment and procreation that are (or, at least before the new genetic technology, were) necessary for the survival of the species. Pleasure's logic of desire guides us to what we need more quickly and more powerfully than deliberative reason can. More than making life sweet, pleasure makes continued life also more possible by offering the promise that it is worth living. Aesthetic entertainment certainly contributes to these life-fulfilling pleasures.

Though a powerful Kantian tradition insists on a very specific type of aesthetic pleasure, narrowly defined as the intellectual pleasure of pure form arising from the harmonious play of our cognitive faculties, the pragmatist tradition construes aesthetic pleasure more generously. First and most simply, there are the variegated pleasures of sense—rich qualities of color, shape, sound, movement, and so on. The pleasures of heightened perception, stirred by an artwork's appealing sensory qualities, are part of what makes it stand out from the ordinary flow of perception as a special aesthetic experience worthy of the name of art, an experience that so absorbs our attention that it also constitutes an entertaining distraction from the humdrum routine of life.

Indeed, aesthetic pleasures are often so intensely delightful that they suggest metaphysical or religious transcendence to a higher realm of reality. Indian philosophy claims that the aesthetic pleasure of *rasa* (the special emotion expressed in art, most paradigmatically in drama) is "transcendental" or "unworldly" in its power and quality of "bliss."[22] The sense of divine pleasure is also clear in the original meaning of the Japanese term for entertainment (*goraku*), which indicates the receiving of hospitality from a heavenly maiden.[23] Aesthetic pleasures include the experience of intense yet well-ordered feelings, but also the satisfactions of meaning and expression that satisfy our need for significance and communication. Such pleasures motivate not only the creative artist or entertainer but also the critic and public who engage in interpretation both to explain the pleasures they experience and to deepen them through enriching analysis.

The pleasures of meaning and expression point to another aspect of aesthetic pleasure that is often obscured—its social dimension. Too often it is assumed that the enjoyment of art or entertainment is simply subjective, hence essentially private and narrowly individualistic. But there is a radiating feature in pleasure that takes it beyond mere individual satisfaction. Pleasures are contagious; when we see a child enjoying a song, we will be inclined to take pleasure in her pleasure, even if we do not know the child and do not think that the song is especially beautiful. When we experience joy, we typically want to share it with others; and we *can* share our aesthetic pleasures in the same way we share an aesthetic experience. Though every fan attending a rock concert feels aesthetic pleasure through his or her own consciousness, this does not deny the shared character of our enjoyment, nor the fact that our enjoyment is heightened by our sense of its being shared. Aesthetic experience gains intensity from a sense of sharing something meaningful and valuable together, and this includes the feeling of shared pleasures. Art's power to unite society through its enchanting pleasures of communication is a theme that resounds from Schiller to Dewey, but the unifying power of mass-media entertainment is likewise recognized, though vilified, by the critics of popular art.

In arguing that we should not trivialize the aesthetic pleasures of art and entertainment because they contribute in so many significant ways to the maintenance, meaning, and enrichment of life, I must address the problem that service to life is precisely the reason why some philosophers denigrate entertainment as trivial, low, and devoid of cultural value. Combining Kant's idea of the aesthetic as disinterested and purposeless with Hegel's idealist notion of the freedom and spiritual transcendence of fine art, this line of argument sharply contrasts art and entertainment by asserting that only the latter has practical functionality in serving life, while true works of art eschew this petty role of means or function and indeed transcend the realm of mortal life. Hannah Arendt offers a powerful example of this approach.

Entertainment, she admits, has real utility for "the life process of society" because it relaxingly fills "vacant time" in "the biologically conditioned cycle of labor" with enjoyable commodities for experiential consumption. But Arendt still scorns "the noisy futility of mass entertainment" by contrast to art's creation of permanent things that she sees as belonging to the special enduring world of culture that stands entirely outside the realm and necessities of "biological life" and whose beauty and value are beyond all needs and function, inhabiting an immortal realm of freedom.[24] "Culture relates to objects and is a phenomenon of the world; entertainment relates to people and is a phenomenon of life."[25] Though "we all stand in need of entertainment and amusement in some form or other, because we are all subject to life's great cycle," we must not confuse it for an aesthetic or cultural pursuit. "Entertainment, like labor and sleep, is irrevocably part of the biological life process," which is "a metab-olism" of consumption. Entertainment thus provides mere "commodities" for experiential consumption, functional "consumer goods" to be used and "used up."[26] "They serve . . . to while away time . . . which . . . is biological in nature, left over after labor and sleep have received their due."[27] In contrast, works of art are not used but appreciated through a purely "disinterested" contempla-tion; their "durability is the very opposite of functionality" or use in the process of life (since, for Arendt, such use implies being "used up"). "They are the only things without any function in the life process of society; strictly speaking, they are fabricated not for men, but for the world which is meant to outlast the life-span of mortals."[28] In short, whereas entertainment is a "means" that serves to sustain and improve human life, artworks are pure ends, things of "intrinsic, independent worth," "things which exist independently of all utilitarian and functional references, and whose quality remains always the same."[29] For Arendt, art's "beauty is the very manifestation of imperishability," while "the entertainment industry" is a danger that threatens to pillage and corrupt the permanent, imperishable beautiful things of art, turning them into disposable commodities of human consumption.[30]

Arendt's position has a sense of noble grandeur and disinterested selfless purity that may strike us as initially attractive. Surely art is more than a mere means for the smooth functioning of life's biological processes of consump-tion. But why should we identify life and functionality with such a narrow physiological conception? Human life is always more than biological; it in-trinsically involves meaning, making, and conduct. And what would the world of culture be without human life and the experience of mortal people to ani-mate it? A collection of things that are lifeless rather than immortal. Functions and means need not be low and menial. Is the study of philosophy or art a slavish pursuit because it serves the end of wisdom or beauty? Underlying Arendt's theory is an aristocratic attitude that philosophy inherited from the Athenian class system, an attitude that associated all means and acts of mak-ing with the lower class of laboring servants and that contrasted this "banau-sic" work with the pure contemplation of "the most noble group of the free-born men." For Arendt, the danger of "fabrication in all forms ["includ-ing the production of art"] is that it is utilitarian by its very nature" and thus "always involves means" and so promotes "the banausic mentality."[31] Pragma-tism, a philosophy with a more democratic vision, argues instead that if you value the ends, you must also value the means necessary to achieve those ends. Moreover, it reconstructs our concept of means to show how they are actually integrated into the ends they serve, the way the means of a painting—its brushstrokes, paint, and so on—form part of the final work of painting.

Arendt's advocacy of a world of culture, art, and beauty that exists beyond the needs and purposes of human life may appeal to theorists who are weary of modern aesthetics' preoccupation with the human perspective on things. But pragmatism's affirmation of the life values of art, beauty, and entertainment need not be construed as confined exclusively to the human realm. Beauty of color, shape, movement, and song are part of the dance of life of the wider natural world that humans belong to and through which they are constituted. The energies and material that constitute aesthetic experience for the human subject belong to the wider environing world; aesthetic experience, properly speaking, is never located only in the head of the human subject but always exists in the wider context that frames the subject's interaction with the object of art or natural beauty. And, for pragmatism, the human subject itself is but a shifting, temporary construction from the materials and energies of the larger world of nature and history. Ironically, in advocating art (against entertainment) as a way of transcending the service of human life, Arendt is arguing from a perspective that she explicitly identifies as "humanism"—the glorification of the enduring man-made world of culture and its "cultura animi."[32] Still more paradoxically, though she claims to regard art and beauty as pure ends of delightful appearance with no functional reference to life, she actually ends up insisting that they perform perhaps the greatest service to life—its justification through immortalization. "The fleeting greatness of word and deed can endure in the world to the extent that beauty is bestowed upon it [through works of art]. . . . Without the beauty, that is, the radiant glory in which potential immortality is made manifest in the human world, all human life would be futile and no greatness could endure."[33] Conversely, beauty, in her account, seems to need the public-objecthood of human cultural creation as a medium in order to endure and achieve its immortality. If art serves life with immortalization, then entertainment is condemned because its meanings and pleasures are alleged to be more transient.

Pragmatism does not scorn the pleasures of art and entertainment because they are transitory in contrast to the imperishability of beauty claimed by Arendt. Regarding our entire universe as a realm of flux with no absolute permanence but only relative stabilities, pragmatism appreciates beauty and pleasure all the more because of its fragile, fleeting nature. By refusing to equate reality with permanence, it recognizes that short-lived loveliness or brief spasms of delight are no less real or moving or cherished because they are momentary. Indeed, some pleasures of beauty, art, and entertainment are not only valuable without being everlasting but are even more valuable because they are not. The beauties of cherry blossoms are cherished and savored all the more because we know they are so fleeting.

The Platonic prejudice for certainty and permanence is one reason for disvaluing the passing delights of entertainment. But the ancient prejudice against instrumentality as inimically conflicting with intrinsic value is just as powerful and just as manifest in Arendt's critique, which insists that real aesthetic and cultural values, because of their "intrinsic" worth, should "exist independently of all utilitarian and functional references." We need to examine more closely the notion of intrinsic value and its relationship to functional or instrumental value.

INTRINSIC VALUE

Analytic philosophy's most famous account of intrinsic value is that offered in the *Principia Ethica* of G. E. Moore. Here Moore provides a method (albeit an extremely intuitive one) for correctly judging the "intrinsic value" of things and their degrees of such value: "It is necessary to consider what things are such that, if they existed *by themselves*, in absolute isolation, we should yet judge their existence to be good; and, in order to decide upon the relative *degrees* of value of different things, we must similarly consider what comparative value seems to attach to the isolated value of each."[34]

Moore deploys this "method of absolute isolation" to argue, against radical hedonism, that the mere conscious sensation of pleasure is neither the only value nor even the highest value.[35] If we consider the conscious sensation of pleasure alone, isolated from consciousness of the activity in which that pleasure is expressed, and then compare the intuited value of the isolated pleasure to the value of the combined consciousness of pleasure and its associated activity (an organic whole that Moore calls "enjoyment"), we will readily recognize that the organic whole of enjoyment could easily be greater in value.[36] For instance, we can see that the value of enjoying a fine poem is more than a mere pleasurable consciousness existing in its own right without any relation to a

POPULAR ART AND ENTERTAINMENT VALUE

meaningful object or activity such as reading the poem. Relying on his method of absolute isolation, Moore claims, "By far the most valuable things, which we know or can imagine, are certain states of consciousness, which may be roughly described as the pleasures of human intercourse and the enjoyment of beautiful objects."[37] Though appreciating Moore's case against hedonism and sympathizing with his aesthetic and ethic ideals, I wish to challenge the method of absolute isolation as the proper way of defining or assessing intrinsic value.

This method, which Moore advocates to argue the objectivity of values, is paradoxically based on the psychology of subjective intuition and personal judgment. Moreover, its precise act of absolute isolation—of considering the value of something as "*existing absolutely by itself*"—seems psychologically, if not also logically, impossible to perform.[38] The very idea of one's judging the value of something as if it existed by itself alone clearly courts a performative contradiction, since that very act of judging or imagining or assessing implies a relationship of intentionality between the thinking subject and the object. A further problem is simply the arbitrariness of isolating the intrinsically valued thing from other things that help define its meaning and value. It seems perverse, for example, to value Picasso's *Desmoiselles d'Avignon* in absolute isolation from all previous and consequent painting, because part of the meaning of any artwork is determined by its perceived relations to other works in its genre or its tradition. And how can we isolate Moore's valued states involving consciousness of human intercourse from the multiplicity of real-world objects and relationships that define that intercourse and thus shape the attractive forms of its presence in our consciousness?

In contrast to Moore, pragmatism does not see values as existing autonomously in fixed isolation or as residing in unchanging objects, but instead regards them as pertaining to a complex, dynamic field whose relations shape the field's values. This field is broadly the behavioral field of human action, involving a plurality of communicative, active subjects facing multiple objects and choices. Moreover, the field of values is a temporally shifting field that is altered by the consequences of changing circumstances and behavior. It thus involves not only synchronic relations but also diachronic relations. As dynamically relational or (in Dewey's term) "transactional," all values are subject to change, even intrinsic values. A good meal is intrinsically valuable and enjoyed as such when the person eating it has some appetite. But the same meal no longer has that value if it must be immediately eaten again when one is already satiated. We can speak of the beauty of a tree as being intrinsically valuable, but we should not assume that this entails some fixed set of autonomous beauty properties isolatable in the tree itself. The tree's beauty is never the same in different seasons; nor is its beauty a pure function of the tree itself but instead also involves the environing conditions (such as light, space, etc.) that frame the tree's perception and allow its beauty to show forth. This idea of the interdependent, transactional character of an object's beauty—its emergence through the wider forces of environing nature—is expressed in an ancient, anonymous haiku cited by Nō theatre's most illustrious dramatist and theorist, Zeami Motokiyo (1363–1443):

> Break open the cherry tree
> And look at it:
> There are no flowers,
> For they themselves have bloomed
> In the spring sky.

The blossoms do not emerge from the sole autonomous inner power of the tree; they emerge through its interaction with the encompassing natural energies and surrounding frame (such as the spring sky) in which it can unfold its beauty, since (in Zeami's words) "the world of nature is the vessel that gives birth to all things."[39]

Moore's isolationist notion of intrinsic value is meant to resist the relational approach to value, which he thinks leads toward a kind of relativism, even if not always to a strict subjectivism with respect to value. This worry about relational accounts of intrinsic value is clearly expressed in his paper "The Conception of Intrinsic Value," where he defines intrinsic value in such a way that for anything to have intrinsic value, it "or anything exactly like it would *necessarily* or *must* always, under all circumstances, possess it in exactly the same degree."[40] If intrinsic value involves relationships, the value of a thing could change as its relationships change. But, for Moore, this would mean that the value did not really inhere in the thing itself but only in the thing as part of the larger whole determined by the relationship. How could a value be objectively intrinsic if it were subject to change simply through the mere changes of the things with which it is related? And how could intrinsic value be understood, if not as something that depended entirely on the properties of the thing itself apart from its changing relations to other things? What other sense could we give to the notion of intrinsic value that could distinguish it from instrumental value, which is a relational value of serving some other end or value?

A satisfactory theory of intrinsic value is too difficult a project for me to undertake here, but let me close by briefly sketching a possible approach toward answering these questions. Moore understandably takes intrinsic value to mean being valued in itself, but he then most radically construes "in itself" as "in absolute isolation." However, it also seems possible and more reasonable to regard being valued *in itself* as meaning valued *for itself* (or in its own right, for its own sake, or on its own account). We can then speak of intrinsic value when something is appreciated for itself and not simply in terms of its serving as a means to a further end that is valued. This would allow us to distinguish intrinsic value from instrumental value without implying that being instrumentally valuable is inconsistent with having intrinsic value and vice versa. Though food is nutritious, a good meal is intrinsically valuable because a person enjoys its taste in its own right, without having to think of the instrumental nourishment the meal gives. Even if we do also think of its nourishment or instrumentality, as long as we are enjoying the taste of the meal, we are appreciating the meal as intrinsically valuable.

What sense of objectivity could survive a relational account of intrinsic value? None that would ensure that things will have permanent unchanging values that are independent of all circumstances. But we could still say that the intrinsic value of this good meal is objective in at least two senses: that it involves objective factors (e.g., that the food is of good quality and well prepared rather than rotten and burned to a crisp) and that it is manifest in objectively observable behavioral responses (zest of eating, gestures of approval or satisfaction, neurological patterns, etc.) that indicate that the meal is being directly enjoyed and not simply being endured because of its instrumental value in procuring some further end taken to be intrinsically valuable. Objective value, as Moore himself realizes, does not exclude relational accounts. A person may be objectively better than another in terms of some job description or (using Moore's example) in evolutionary terms of survival given existing circumstances. But the problem for Moore is that since existing circumstances or desired functions can change, relational accounts of value (though based on objective conditions) cannot guarantee the sort of absoluteness and "fixity" of value that Moore wants our intrinsic values (as our deepest or most ultimate values) to have. This is why Moore's account of intrinsic value insists on going beyond mere "objectivity" to what he calls "internality."[41] The demand that intrinsic value must depend entirely on what is internal or intrinsic to a thing in such a way that it "*must* always, under all circumstances, possess it in exactly the same degree" is the only way of ensuring the absolute "kind and degree of fixity" that Moore demands of intrinsic value.[42]

In this radically internalist sense, the intrinsic value of a thing seems, strictly speaking, more correctly contrasted with a notion of extrinsic value (i.e., value that is entirely or primarily dependent on properties that are not internal to the object) than with the notion of instrumental value. The value of a winning lottery ticket, for example, would be essentially extrinsic to the internal properties of the ticket itself, such as color, shape, size, and so on. Parallel to such an intrinsic/extrinsic opposition, we could then explain that what is strictly opposed to instrumental value is not intrinsic value but "final" or unmediated value in the sense that such value would be directly appreciated as an end for itself and not just as a means for a further end.

Nonetheless, to the extent that instrumentalities obviously relate to ends, activities, and properties that lie beyond the purely internal properties of the particular object used as a means, instrumental value implies some extrinsic dimension (especially when intrinsic is defined in Moore's radically "internal" sense). We can thus understand how the ideas of extrinsic and instrumental value might be equated. However, as already suggested, Moore's internalist notion of intrinsic value is very problematic. It is very difficult to isolate the value of something in terms of that thing's purely intrinsic properties, since it is not at all clear how these intrinsic properties are to be identified and to what extent they can indeed exist or be identified independently from other properties that constitute that thing's relationships to other things and that often are essential to the generation or existence of that thing itself.[43]

Intrinsic value, as I prefer to construe this notion, does not, strictly speaking, belong permanently to isolated things in their internal autonomy but instead belongs to the particular situations or specific fields of transaction in which those things of alleged intrinsic value play a central role. The intrinsic value of a painting, for example, depends not only on the physically colored canvas itself but also on the fact that there are people who have the sense organs and understanding to appreciate its colors and the forms and meanings to which these colors contribute. We can still speak here of intrinsic value in the sense that the pictorial properties of the canvas itself constitute the crucial focus for the appreciated value in question. But there is no pretension that all the appreciated properties of the painting (including its expressive and meaning properties) can be conceived as purely internal to the canvas and independent of any relation to things beyond it.

Let me conclude by returning to the notion of entertainment value. Much of my case for entertainment has been dedicated to the instrumental uses of entertainment for other ends, such as the maintenance, relaxation, refreshment, and cognitive recreation of the individual and, by extension, the sustenance, harmonious cohesion, and revitalization of the society in which the individual self is situated. But besides such instrumentality, entertainment also has intrinsic value in its immediately enjoyed satisfactions. The expression "entertainment value" as distinguished from the value of entertainment can more specifically connote this sort of directly experienced enjoyment that is grasped as valuable for itself rather than as simply being appreciated for its instrumental value in achieving other ends. But such intrinsic value must not be confused with a permanently fixed value. The fact that values are transient does not mean they are not real. To equate the truly valuable with the unchanging is an understandably human impulse that is linked to our desire for security and permanence. But it is an error that senselessly degrades many of our valuable but fleeting pleasures and thus sadly tends to impoverish the range of values that we realize in our experience.

This respect for temporality and the transient is, I think, essential to the appreciation of popular art. Rap music affirms it with a vengeance, not simply by its appropriative sampling technique that refuses to treat admired musical works as untouchable eternal values and instead cuts them apart to make new "fresh" sounds, but also by its distinctive "time tags" that highlight the temporality of its musical experience and value—and of experience and value in general. Thus KRS-One's lyrics often describe his tracks as "Fresh for 88" or "Fresh for 90," implying that they may be neither fresh nor appreciated in later times. If these songs are still celebrated and enjoyed today, their value and "freshness" is inevitably different, for they are appreciated within a historically different transactional field whose difference includes the consciousness of these works as past classics of hip-hop, and such consciousness can enrich the enjoyment of our current lived experience in hearing them. Temporality thus not only can erode entertainment value, but it can also enhance it.

NOTES

1. See Richard Shusterman, *Pragmatist Aesthetics* (Oxford: Blackwell, 1992), chap. 7.

2. See ibid., and my *Performing Live* (Ithaca, NY: Cornell University Press, 2000).

3. Pierre Bourdieu, *Distinction* (Cambridge, MA: Harvard University Press, 1984).

4. See my article "Entertainment: A Question for Aesthetics," *British Journal of Aesthetics*, 43 (2003): 289–307, which provides a fuller account of this concept's philosophical history and anticipates some of the points I make here.

5. See Oxford English Dictionary, 2nd ed. (Oxford: Clarendon Press), 10:125.

6. See Lawrence W. Levine, *Highbrow/Lowbrow: the Emergence of Cultural Hierarchy in America* (Cambridge, MA: Harvard University Press, 1988).

7. Aristotle's *Poetics*, 1451b, trans. Ingram Bywater (Oxford: Clarendon Press, 1909), 27.

8. Michel de Montaigne, *Essais (édition conforme au texte de l'exemplaire de Bordeaux avec les additions de l'édition posthume)*, ed. Maurice Rat (Paris: Garnier, 1962), 1:447–62, 2:237–61. The parenthetical page references are to Donald Frame's excellent translation, which I generally adopt. See Donald Frame, *The Complete Works of Montaigne* (Stanford, CA: Stanford University Press, 1957).

9. See "Entertainment" in *The Oxford English Dictionary* (Oxford: Clarendon Press, 1933), 3:214.

10. Immanuel Kant, *Kritik der Urteliskraft* (Hamburg: Felix Meiner, 1974), 50, 84 ("Allgemeine Anmerkung zum ersten Abschnitte der Analytik"); cf. in English, *The Critique of Judgement*, trans. J. C. Meredith (Oxford: Oxford University Press, 1952), 53, 88; Meredith awkwardly renders the German phrase "free and indeterminately final entertainment of the mental powers."

11. Friedrich Schiller, *On the Aesthetic Education of Man*, bilingual edition (Oxford: Clarendon Press, 1982), 107.

12. Friedrich Nietzsche, *Ecce Homo* ("Warum ich so klug bin," sec. 3), in *Sämmtliche Werke* (Stuttgart: Alfred Körner, 1978), 320–21. Later, in sec. 8, he suggests that recreation involves "an instinct of self-preservation" (329); cf. the English translation, by Walter Kaufmann, (New York: Vintage, 1969), 242, 252.

13. Martin Heidegger, "The Origin of the Work of Art," in *Poetry, Language, Thought* (New York: Harper, 1975), 68, 71.

14. Theodor Adorno and Max Horkheimer, *Dialectic of Enlightenment* (New York: Continuum, 1986), 121; Theodor Adorno, *Aesthetic Theory* (London: Routledge, 1984), 18–21.

15. See T. S. Eliot, preface to *The Sacred Wood* (London: Methuen, 1968), viii–ix; and *Of Poetry and Poets* (London: Faber, 1957), 115. This means that we should not enjoy the bad poems that we understand, "unless their badness is of a sort that appeals to our sense of humor." The subsequent quote from Eliot is from his *The Use of Poetry and the Use of Criticism* (London: Faber, 1964), 154.

16. T. S. Eliot, *On Poetry and Poets*, 226; and Selected Essays (London: Faber, 1953), 457, 458. The complexity of the so-called popular audience is a point likewise made by two of the twentieth century's strongest theoretical defenders of popular art, Antonio Gramsci and Mikhail Bakhtin, who also recognize that the entertainment function does not deprive popular cultural expression of important aesthetic, cognitive, and political functions. Both theorists define the popular essentially in terms of its opposition to official culture, not in terms of its origin in a particular class identified as "the people," because, as Gramsci notes, "the people themselves are not a homogeneous cultural collectivity." See A. Gramsci, *Selections from Cultural Writings* (Cambridge, MA: Harvard University Press, 1991), 195. In stressing that the popular aesthetic of carnival festivity embraces all strata of society and works to enhance their communication by a momentary erasure of official hierarchies, Bakhtin highlights the role of play and entertainment. In a variation of the dialectical argument for the productive power of distraction, Bakhtin suggests that carnival entertainment has recuperative power in letting us momentarily forget the constraints of official roles and established truths and helping us to open our hearts and minds to utopian ideals and new possibilities. Because this recuperative, utopian function can serve all strata of the population, the appeal of popular entertainment is not narrowly linked to one particular social class.

17. See Ice-T's "Hit the Deck" and "Heartbeat" and Public Enemy's "Don't Believe the Hype." For more on rap's combination of passionate enjoyment and cognition, see *Pragmatist Aesthetics*, chap. 8, and my *Practicing Philosophy* (London: Routledge, 1997), chap. 5.

18. See KRS-One's "My Philosophy," "Gimme Dat, (Woy)," and "The Real Holy Place," which comes from the *Edutainment* album. All the quotations in the following two paragraphs are from tracks on this album from 1990.

19. See, for example, the criticisms made by Rainer Rochlitz, "Esthétiques Hédonistes," *Critique* 540 (1992): 353–73; Alexander Nehamas, "Richard Shusterman on Pleasure and Aesthetic Experience," *Journal of Aesthetics and Art Criticism* 56 (1998): 49–51; and Kathleen Higgins, "Living and Feeling at Home: Shusterman's *Performing Live*," in *Journal of Aesthetic Education*, 36 (2002): 84–92.

20. In underlining the power and significance of these exalted pleasures, it is wrong to dismiss the value of the lighter ones. Merriment can offer a welcome relief from the strains of ecstasy, but also provides a useful contrast to highlight its sublimity. Besides these uses of diversion, lighter pleasures have their own intrinsic charms. The purpose in learning the diversity of pleasures is not to select only the highest and reject the rest, but to profit best from enjoying them all, at least all that we can happily manage.

21. Benedict de Spinoza, *The Ethics*, in *Works of Spinoza* (New York: Dover, 1955), 174. Aristotle, *Nicomachean Ethics*, 1175a, in *The Basic Works of Aristotle* (New York: Random House, 1968), 1100.

22. P. J. Chaudhury, "The Theory of Rasa," *Journal of Aesthetics and Art Criticism*, 24 (1965), 145, 146. The great Indian aesthetician Abinovagupta, writing in the tenth century, describes the pleasure of *rasa* as "like the relish of the ultimate reality" (see ibid., 148). For a brief comparison of *rasa* theory to the pragmatist view of aesthetic experience and pleasure, see my "Definition, Dramatization, and Rasa," *Journal of Aesthetics and Art Criticism* 61 (2003): 295–98.

23. This early Japanese meaning of *goraku* can be found in the Japanese literary classics *Konjaku-monogatari* (twelfth century) and *Taiheiki* (fourteen century). The *kanji* (or character) that forms the word suggests a person's head tilted back with the mouth wide open in joyful laughter (and perhaps also some other pleasure).

24. Hannah Arendt, "The Crisis of Culture," in *Between Past and Future* (New York: Viking, 1961), 197–226. Quotations in this sentence are from pages 205–6.

25. Arendt, 208.

26. Arendt, 205, 206, 208.

27. Arendt, 205.

28. Arendt, 208, 209, 210.

29. Arendt, 215–16.

30. Arendt, 207, 218.

31. Arendt, 215, 216, 219.

32. Arendt, 225.

33. Arendt, 218.

34. G. E. Moore, *Principia Ethica* (Cambridge: Cambridge University Press, 1959), 187 (italics in the original); hereafter PE.

35. PE, 188.

36. PE, 96, 188.

37. PE, 188.

38. PE, 188.

39. See J. T. Rimer and Y. Masakazu, eds., *On the Art of Nō Drama: The Major Treatises of Zeami* (Princeton, NJ: Princeton University Press, 1984), 119.

40. G. E. Moore, "The Conception of Intrinsic Values," in *Philosophical Studies* (London: Routledge, 1970), 253–75, citation from p. 265, hereafter PS. In this paper, Moore carefully distinguishes between the objectivity of a value and its intrinsic nature. For example, a trait that has evolutionary value is objectively valuable but not intrinsically valuable, since its value depends also on the circumstances that in fact make it a better fit for survival and thus does not entirely depend on the trait's own nature by itself (PS 255–57).

41. PS, 255.

42. PS, 257.

43. The claim that any thing has (and must have to be a thing) a set of autonomous internal properties that constitute that thing's identity is a difficult metaphysical question that divides analytic philosophy from the organic tradition (stretching from Hegel to contemporary poststructuralism), according to which things are holistically constituted in terms of their relationships to other things. For a more detailed survey of the arguments and stakes of this debate, see Shusterman, *Pragmatist Aesthetics*, chap. 3.

II

INTERPRETATION AND POPULAR ART FORMS

8

Popular Culture and Spontaneous Order, or How I Learned To Stop Worrying and Love the Tube

Paul A. Cantor

SHAKESPEARE AND *THE SIMPSONS*

In studying popular culture, especially when working on my book *Gilligan Unbound*, I quickly ran into hermeneutical difficulties. I wanted to discuss television shows as works of art, to demonstrate how they present a meaningful view of the world in a skillful and sometimes even masterful manner. I was interested in how a sequence of television shows expressed changes in the way Americans perceived their place in the world, and, more specifically, the way their attitudes toward globalization evolved. This project involved making statements such as, "*The Simpsons* portrays the national government negatively and celebrates a turn to the local and the global," or, "*The X-Files* suggests that modern technology is at war with the power of the state." In short, like many of my colleagues, I surreptitiously imputed intentionality to something inanimate and truly unconscious—a television series. One could claim that in such circumstances, saying "*The Simpsons*" is simply shorthand for saying "the team that created *The Simpsons*," but I suspect that something more is at work here, an attempt to elide and evade the difficult questions about intentionality and artistic purpose that analyzing a television show raises.

Our basic model of aesthetic intentionality in literature is the lyric poem. When Yeats sat down to write "Sailing to Byzantium," we like to think that he was free to shape the poem any way he chose. Thus we want to say that the resulting poem was wholly the product of Yeats's intentions and his alone, and that means that every word in the poem is aesthetically meaningful.[1] One can therefore in good conscience worry over the most minor details in a poem like "Sailing to Byzantium" and make something of the fact that Yeats chose to use one particular word rather than another. But is this kind of close reading appropriate to television shows, when we know that they are not produced the way lyric poems are? No television show is created by a single author. Scripts are typically the product of a team of writers, and even the list of people officially credited with writing a given script does not include all those who had a hand in it. Writing for television resembles committee work rather than what we normally think of as artistic activity. Scripts generally involve compromises and may end up embodying different conceptions of the work in question, and sometimes even contradictory ones.

Moreover, a script is only the rough blueprint for creating a television show. In the process of actually shooting the show, the director, and sometimes even cast members, will modify the script, perhaps because it has led to problems in production or simply because, on the spur of the moment, they think that they can improve it. A show has not taken its final form even after it has been shot. Network executives, censors, and potential sponsors may well demand further changes in the show before it can be aired. The result of the complicated production process of a television show is that the work that finally reaches the screen will never correspond exactly to the idea of the person who first conceived it and will usually in fact be quite remote from the initial conception.

It thus becomes problematic to speak of intentionality in the case of television shows when it is difficult just to identify whose intentions one is talking about. Moreover, the nature of television production is such that an element of contingency is inevitably introduced into the final product. As an interpreter, one might, for example, try to make something of the darkening of the light in a particular scene and claim that it was intended to achieve a darkening of mood. But if one asked the producer about this particular "effect," he might say something like this: "It was two days till airtime, and we needed to finish the lakeside scene; I knew I was running out of light, but we were also running out of money, and I hoped nobody would notice the difference." So much for any attempt to find the changed lighting of the scene aesthetically meaningful. In the course of researching *Gilligan Unbound*, I found many cases where developments in a television program could not be explained in terms of purely aesthetic considerations. In the second season of *The X-Files*, for example, Agent Dana Scully was abducted, possibly by aliens, and for several episodes the audience was wrapped up in the question of her fate. One might marvel at the ingenuity of the show's creators in mapping out this dramatic turn of events, until one learns that, far from planning it in advance, they were scrambling to cope with the fact that the actress who portrayed Scully, Gillian Anderson, had become pregnant and was going to be unavailable for shooting in the middle of the season. For all that *The X-Files* managed to make of Scully's abduction, at root it was a plot device to cover over a production snag.[2] The more one reads about the history of shows like *The X-Files*, the more one realizes that this kind of improvising, rather than careful planning in advance, is typical of television production.

With considerations such as these in mind, I grew uneasy in the course of working on *Gilligan Unbound*. Was I wrong to look for artistic unity in television shows, when so many aspects of their creation point to a disunity of conception and an even greater disunity of the ultimate product? I had come to the study of popular culture with the training of a literary critic, and had devoted much of my career to analyzing Shakespeare. Thus it was natural that when I viewed television, I was looking for masterpieces, for shows that used traditional artistic techniques to convey important truths about the world we live in. But can masterpieces be produced on a weekly schedule and a tight budget, and also please sponsors? My *Gilligan Unbound* project was haunted by the fear that I was illegitimately using categories derived from high culture in my study of popular culture.

And yet, despite everything I learned in the course of researching television shows, I could not ignore what had originally drawn me to some of them— what looked like a high level of artistic achievement. In theoretical terms, the application of the concept of intentionality to television shows seems dubious, but I could not help seeing signs of artistic intentions at work in some of them. Despite the general messiness of the medium, some of the shows seem extremely well crafted and appear to make coherent statements when carefully analyzed. Even the best of the shows do not achieve the artistic coherence of a perfect Yeats lyric, but that does not mean that one should label them incoherent. I began to ask, is it fair to judge television programs by the standard of artistic coherence achieved in lyric poetry at its best?

On reflection, it does seem inappropriate to use standards of artistic coherence derived from one medium to understand an entirely different medium. A sixteen-line lyric poem is, at least in material terms, much easier to produce than a one-hour television program, and one can imagine the poem issuing from a single consciousness in a way that seems impossible for the television show, which must necessarily be a cooperative effort. Notice that this distinction is not simply one between high culture and popular culture.[3] A lyric poem may not be the appropriate model for understanding a Shakespeare play either. Shakespeare was of course a great poet, and there is much that is poetic in his plays. Nevertheless, their conditions of production more closely resemble those of a television show than those of a lyric poem. As a dramatist, and specifically a commercial dramatist, Shakespeare was working in a cooperative medium, and no doubt the finished form his plays took on the stage involved the kind of compromises we can observe in television production today. We do not have the detailed information about the production history of Shakespeare's plays that is available for television, but historical research has uncovered elements of contingency even in Shakespeare.

For example, we know something about the casting in Shakespeare's theater company. Its principal comedian was originally a man named Will Kempe, who specialized in comic dances and little dialogues with himself. When Kempe left Shakespeare's troupe—like a television actor today leaving a successful series—he was replaced by a man named Robert Armin, who excelled in different forms of comic business. Armin evidently sang well, and he also specialized in playing the part of a fool. This change in personnel in Shakespeare's company helps explain the fact that in roughly the first half of his career, the chief comic figure in his plays was a clown, such as Launcelot Gobbo in *The Merchant of Venice*, whereas in the second half, Shakespeare switched to a fool, such as Touchstone in *As You Like It*.[4] This may seem relatively insignificant until one realizes that one of Shakespeare's most distinctive strokes of genius—his inclusion of a fool in his greatest tragedy, *King Lear*—was not a move he pulled out of thin air, so to speak. It is indeed a good question: if Robert Armin had not replaced Will Kempe in Shakespeare's company, would the dramatist have come up with the brilliant idea of counterpointing Lear's tragedy with the fool's comedy? We have reason to believe, then, that much like television writers today, Shakespeare wrote with specific actors in mind and sometimes tailored his plays to their peculiar talents.

ORGANIC FORM AND ROMANTIC AESTHETICS
Thus my efforts to reassure myself about the legitimacy of what I was doing in *Gilligan Unbound* led me to more general reflections about the nature of

culture. Perhaps contingency is a more important factor in the artistic process than the example of lyric poetry would lead us to believe. Perhaps in this regard, popular culture may provide a better model for culture in general than the relatively elite activity of poetry. The domination of lyric poetry as our model of artistic creation is itself a historically contingent development. Poetry is one of the oldest of the arts, and it certainly had a considerable head start over television in offering a model of artistic activity. Already in Aristotle, one can observe the tendency to think of all art as a form of *poiesis*, and his *Poetics* introduced the organic model of poetry and art more generally— the crucial notion that a true work of art must form an organic whole. Given Aristotle's conception of organism, that means that in a true work of art, every part has a function to play in the whole (*Poetics*, 1451a). That in turn means that every part of a true work of art is there by design, not by chance. Aristotle was the first to try to theorize contingency out of the realm of art.[5] His organic model of art proved to be extremely durable and powerful, especially as a heuristic device. Precisely because critics were guided by the conception of the work of art as perfectly designed, they were impelled to study the often hidden ways in which artworks hang together. Elements that might at first look anomalous in a work proved on closer inspection to have a role to play in its overall aesthetic logic. Aristotle's organic model of art was so useful that it even survived one of the great revolutions in criticism—the shift beginning in the late eighteenth century from classic to Romantic aesthetics. However much the Romantics revolutionized our conception of artistic form, they still maintained that it is organic in nature. In fact, they tended to make their argument against classic conceptions of form by insisting that they are mechanical, and only the new Romantic conceptions are genuinely organic. The Romantics opened up the concept of the organic unity of art, allowing for more complex forms of unification and for more heterogeneous elements to be unified, but they still remained true to the Aristotelian ideal of the artwork as perfectly designed. The difference is that the Romantics introduced the idea of artistic genius. The artwork takes organic form, not because the artist follows patterns inherent in the nature of the genre (as in the Aristotelian tradition), but because the artistic genius shatters old models that have become mechanical and divines new forms that restore life to his art.[6]

The Romantic reconception of organic form was developed in Germany but reached England chiefly in the writings of Samuel Taylor Coleridge. Coleridge did much to establish the organic model of poetry in particular and art in general in the English-speaking world, and he was especially influential on the development of one of its chief incarnations in twentieth-century aesthetics: the New Criticism.[7] Our tendency to think of organic form in poetry as our model of art in general is largely the result of the way the New Criticism dominated American academics in the 1950s and 1960s. The New Critics did not simply take lyric poetry as their model of art; more specifically, they operated with a certain kind of poetry in mind—basically the modernist lyric of Eliot and Yeats. They came to read not just all poetry, but eventually drama and fiction as well, on the model of works like "The Love Song of J. Alfred Prufrock" or "Sailing to Byzantium."[8] It is remarkable how many genuine insights the New Critics were able to produce, even though they were generalizing from a small sample of what actually constitutes literature. But the very specific nature of their model of artistic form leads to misperceptions when one tries to apply it to the realm of popular culture.

This is especially true because the New Criticism and the Romantic/modernist aesthetic out of which it grew were biased against popular culture from the start. In fact, both Romantic and modernist aesthetics defined themselves in opposition to popular culture. The very idea of a split between high culture and popular culture is basically an invention of the late eighteenth and the early nineteenth century. Given economic, social, and political developments in the late eighteenth century, the Romantic generation was the first group of artists to confront mass commercial culture in the modern sense. The Romantics found themselves competing in a newly developed cultural marketplace, in which commercial success was replacing aristocratic and ecclesiastical patronage as the chief support for the arts. The ideal of organic form became a weapon in their struggle with their competitors in the cultural marketplace. The Romantics identified organic form with what they now defined as high or true culture, and they cordoned off a lower realm of popular or mass culture, which fails to measure up to the exalted standard of organic form. As Alvin Kernan formulates their position, "Isolated from society, exiled from and hostile to the world of industrial capitalism, they have spoken in poetry the truth and beauty known only to the imagination, defended the authentic human self with its ancient ways of thinking and feeling against science and crude utilitarianism, and created perfect works of art, organic in structure, crystalline in form."[9] Whereas the Romantics as geniuses could re-

POPULAR CULTURE AND SPONTANEOUS ORDER 167

main true to the purity of their inspiration and achieve perfection of organic design in their creations, they deemed the products of commercial culture imperfect because artistically impure.[10] Motives other than the purely aesthetic supposedly corrupt works of art produced for commercial markets. This Romantic attitude linked up with the idea of the autonomy of art, developed by Kant in his *Critique of Judgment.* The Romantics claimed that true art could be produced only by the artistic genius operating in total independence and splendid isolation. The artist has to be relieved from the demands of the commercial world in order to be free to pursue his artistic vision and produce works that will be completely faithful to his own design and hence genuinely organic in form.[11]

If, on the other hand, the artist is forced to work with commercial success as his motive, his vision will inevitably be compromised. He will have to introduce elements into his art to please others, rather than himself, and thereby corrupt the organic purity of his creations. One can see the thrust of Romantic aesthetics in the way that nineteenth-century critics tended to look down upon the novel as a popular form, hardly a form of literature at all.[12] Since it was created with a commercial market in mind, the novel was not viewed as authentic art, but rather as an impure form, filled with aesthetically extraneous elements whose only function was to please the public and sell copies. According to Romantic aesthetics, in a poem, every word has an artistic function to perform in the work as a whole, but in a novel, many words are there simply because the novelist was being paid by the word.

In short, an anticommercial bias was built into the Romantic aesthetic from the start, and hence it is hardly surprising that when we apply a late form of that aesthetic, the New Criticism, to popular culture, it looks suspect to us as an artistic realm. We need to recognize how the Romantic heritage in our aesthetics has prejudiced us against popular culture. We assume that only if an artist is given complete autonomy will he be able to achieve anything great. Unity of design demands a single designer, who out of his own inner depths molds his material into pure organic form. Many of the institutions in our culture today are designed to shield artists from external pressures and particularly commercial ones. This is especially true of universities, foundations, and government granting agencies, which pride themselves on providing artists with financial support and thus freeing them from any need to please the public.[13] Supposedly this freedom will make their art better.

This glance at the historical development of our aesthetic assumptions helps clarify what is at stake in the debate over popular culture. When we find that the conditions of production in television are not the same as in the writing of poetry, we assume that this is a bad thing and will make television less of an art form than poetry. It is the Romantic ideal of the solitary genius that makes us wary of multiple authorship in television writing. We are also put off by all the elements of contingency involved in television production. We think that great works of art must be carefully planned in advance, and are suspicious of any work improvised on the spur of the moment. And we are right to have these suspicions. Much of our greatest art was produced by individual geniuses, working according to the Romantic aesthetic and with an organic view of form in mind. Many great artists have complained about interference with their aesthetic autonomy, and have been particularly bitter when commercial demands have intruded into what they hoped would be the self-contained world of their art. This attitude prevails even in the realm of television. In researching *Gilligan Unbound*, I noted how frequently television producers railed against network executives who had interfered in the production process.[14] Like all artists, these producers crave a free hand to create their shows as they see fit. They do not want network executives or censors or sponsors telling them how to do their job, and they view outside interference as a source of corruption in their work. And in many cases they are justified in this view. Network executives often failed to understand what these television creators were trying to do and would have ruined their shows if the producers had not stood their ground and maintained their integrity as artists, in the Romantic understanding of the term. If the most creative talent in television distrusts conditions in the medium, surely critics trained in traditional high culture can feel justified in their doubts about it. And television spews out enough garbage every year to make anyone with taste wonder if there is not something inherently inartistic about the medium.

And yet I keep coming back to the fact that somehow, amongst all this trash, television manages to produce works of genuine artistic quality. How is this possible? We have been talking about the distinctive production process in television, but implying that insofar as it is distinctive, it has a negative effect on what is produced. But perhaps there is something in the process that is positive, that actually contributes to the artistic quality of the resulting product. To put the question in the simplest terms, is commercial art necessarily inferior to noncommercial art?

IN PRAISE OF MULTIPLE AUTHORSHIP AND IMPROVISATION

Consider the issue of multiple authorship in television. It is certainly true that too many cooks can spoil the broth in art as well as life. The result of continually rewriting scripts is often to make them bland, to take out any originality and assimilate them to familiar patterns. But there is no reason why several minds coming together to write a script could not in some cases improve the final product. Different writers may bring different talents and strengths to the task and help to inspire each other and spur each other on. And no writer—not even Shakespeare—is so great that he never makes mistakes and cannot benefit from some criticism and correction. Most television writers, far from wishing to be left alone, speak positively about script conferences and look forward to continual feedback on their work. The writers of *The X-Files*, for example, in their accounts of the genesis of their script ideas, talk about how helpful Chris Carter, the creator-producer of the show, was to them in refining their original conceptions and making them work in the context of the series.[15] Upholders of the autonomy of art insist that in creation, the individual artist knows it all and does it all. But this is not always true even in the most rarefied realms of high culture. In fact, multiple authorship is not as uncommon in serious literature as the Romantic aesthetic would lead us to believe.[16] I am not just thinking of famous teams of authors, such as the English Renaissance dramatists, Beaumont and Fletcher. In fact, we now know that multiple authorship was quite common in English Renaissance drama—another parallel between Shakespeare's medium and television.[17] From what we know of the rewriting of plays such as Marlowe's *Doctor Faustus*, it seems that the Elizabethan Age even had its own script doctors.[18] Shakespeare himself may have served as one—we see his hand at work at a few points in a play called *The Book of Sir Thomas More*. Indeed, in the only dramatic passage we may have in Shakespeare's own handwriting, he is to our eternal frustration evidently working on somebody else's play.[19]

Even in the very bastion of the Romantic aesthetic—the writing of Romantic lyrics—artistic collaboration is not unknown. Wordsworth and Coleridge are among our models of the Romantic solitary genius, and yet they worked together on the volume of poetry that made them both famous, *Lyrical Ballads*. And, although today each of the poems in this volume is credited to one author or the other, their handiwork was not distinguished in the original edition, and we now know that some of the poems were in effect joint productions—that some of the lines in the poems credited to Wordsworth were in fact written by Coleridge and vice versa.[20] Wordsworth and Coleridge were constantly commenting on each other's work and were willing to take advice from each other, much to the benefit of the published work. Perhaps the most famous modernist poem is *The Waste Land*, and it is of course ascribed to T. S. Eliot. But the publication of the original manuscript has revealed that Ezra Pound's editing played such a role in the finished form the poem took that he might as well be credited as coauthor.[21] The degree to which Eliot was willing to accept Pound's editorial suggestions seems incredible to us, raised as we are on the Romantic aesthetic. And yet we must also admit that much of what we think of as the distinctively modernist character of *The Waste Land* is the result of Pound's efforts to edit the text down from Eliot's original inspiration.

Someone might object that these are cases of solitary geniuses working together and thus are quite different from the kind of collaboration characteristic of television, which often more closely resembles the case of a writer working with a commercial editor rather than a fellow artist. But even in this case, studies have shown that editors at commercial publishing houses have sometimes played an important role in the shaping of certain literary masterpieces. One of the most famous editorial collaborations in American literature involved the novelist Thomas Wolfe and the editor Maxwell Perkins of Charles Scribner's Sons. As Jack Stillinger writes, "Perkins's most publicized accomplishment . . . was the virtual creation of *Look Homeward, Angel* (1929) and *Of Time and the River* (1935) out of huge masses of manuscript that Wolfe had brought him in despair."[22] Thus the issue of multiple authorship does not allow us to draw a sharp line between high culture and popular culture. And although multiple authorship may introduce contradictions into a work of art or result in a kind of "lowest common denominator" effect, it may instead, through the benefits of synergy or feedback, improve the ultimate product. The demands of the marketplace, far from always ruining literary works, have in many cases improved them. Commercial pressures can exercise a disciplining effect on artists, if nothing else forcing them to finish a work by a certain date or to keep it at a reasonable length. The record of art produced with foundation or government grants does not offer convincing evidence that being released from having to please the public is a sure path to greatness for an artist.[23] Thus, the fact that a popular medium such as television does not afford complete autonomy to individual artists is not an effective argument against it.

Rethinking the issue of contingency in television production leads to a similar conclusion. When we see producers scrambling to finish shows by a deadline, rewriting scenes up until the last possible moment and jerry-rigging special effects, it is hard for us to believe that what they are creating can be genuine art. This is especially true because of the way critics tend to approach artworks. They are generally looking to uncover a plan in the work, a pattern by which it is structured, and they assume that the artist had this plan fully elaborated in his mind before constructing it. What the critic discovers retrospectively, the artist must have divined prospectively.[24] It is natural for such critics to question the artistic potential of television as a medium when it does not seem to allow for this kind of advance planning.

But, once again, our knowledge of high culture does not support this critique of popular culture. To be sure, we know many cases of artists who did in fact plan out their masterpieces well in advance, sometimes down to the smallest details. But for every example of the advantages of advance planning in the arts, we can find counterexamples of the corresponding advantages of improvisation. Many great literary masterpieces have been churned out with deadlines fast approaching and the authors desperately struggling to finish them in the quickest way possible. Some artists seem to need the pressure of deadlines to produce their best work.[25] And some arts have incorporated improvisation as one of their fundamental principles. Think of the importance of improvisation in the careers of such musical geniuses as J. S. Bach, Mozart, and Beethoven. In short, many creators in the realms of high culture have had to come to terms with an element of contingency in their art and have even learned to turn it to their advantage. Consider the role of the found object in surrealism, for example.[26] The Slavics scholar Gary Saul Morson has argued that certain authors have even made contingency the fundamental principle of their literary art—chiefly, in his view, Dostoevsky and Tolstoy. He shows how Dostoevsky, for example, allowed breaking stories in newspapers to alter the plot lines of a novel in the course of publication:

> In *The Idiot*, real crime reports that first appeared between installments are read by the characters, who seem to be following the press along with the readers and the author. These real crimes shape characters' imagination, discussion, and future actions. Because those crimes took place after some sections of the work had appeared [in print], the reader recognizes that they *could not* have been part of an original plan, and that forces outside the author's control shape his work as it goes along.[27]

This case is analogous to the way television shows often incorporate references to contemporary events at the last minute.[28] Morson shows how Dostoevsky deliberately created open-ended narratives, in which he himself did not know in advance in which direction the story was headed.[29] He in effect left the course of the action up to his characters, waiting until the last minute to see what decisions the characters would make and thus shape the outcome of the story. Morson argues that contingency becomes an aesthetic value in the novels of Dostoevsky; the open-ended narrative is a way of celebrating the reality of human freedom.

Thus, dealing with elements of contingency turns out to be something popular culture has in common with many forms of high culture. It may be possible to eliminate all elements of chance from a brief lyric poem, but it is much more difficult to do so in a long novel. Some novelists have failed to catch minor changes in their works when typesetters accidentally introduced them in the printing process.[30] The larger the work, the more likely it will admit imperfections by the rigorous standards of tight, poetic form. But, for critics such as Morson, what looks like imperfection from the perspective of the Romantic aesthetic of organic form may be a higher kind of perfection according to a different aesthetic. The famous bagginess of the novel, which makes it seem loosely organized and even shapeless by comparison with lyric poetry, can also be viewed as a virtue and indeed seems to be related to the novel's greater realism and above all its ability to capture a wider range of ordinary human experience. Insofar as contingency is an important element of human life, any form of art that strives to eliminate it risks becoming untrue to the way we actually experience our existence.[31]

Recognizing that contingency is an inevitable component of both life and art, many artists, even in high culture, choose not to sketch out their plans in advance and prefer to develop them as they go along, to try a variety of possibilities and see what works and what does not. The alternative to a "perfect plan" model of artistic creation is a "feedback" model, in which the imperfections of a work of art are gradually corrected in a process of trial and error (or sometimes even left in place to achieve a variety of effects, according to Morson). The feedback model is far more common in high culture than the Romantic aesthetic would lead us to believe. Many artists crave contact with their audience precisely because of the valuable feedback it can supply.[32] Sometimes an artist's audience is able to judge when he is doing his best work more easily than he himself can. For this reason, the way contemporary artists are shielded by institutional grants from the need to please an audience may actually have a deleterious effect on their art. Being free of the public's demands may be every artist's dream, but it can easily turn into a nightmare of aesthetic isolation, cut off from all sources of guidance and legitimate criticism, and perhaps even from the ultimate source of artistic inspiration itself.[33] There are many cases of artists who did their best work when they still felt a need to cater to their audience, and lost their way artistically when they began to feel that pleasing the public was beneath their dignity as autonomous geniuses.

If feedback from an audience is actually valuable to artists, popular culture has certain advantages over high culture (especially in its more elite forms). In particular, many of the aspects of the production process in television that look dubious from the viewpoint of the Romantic aesthetic may turn out to work to the benefit of those who labor in the medium. What from one angle looks like harmful interference with the integrity of the artist in television, from another angle looks like helpful feedback. Not all the advice from network executives is wrongheaded; although their primary consideration may be the infamous bottom line, their very concern with audience reaction may sometimes make their suggestions improve a program. One of the things that struck me in my research on *Gilligan Unbound* was the way successful television producers actively seek out feedback from all sources and look to it for guidance.

In the case of *The X-Files*, the producers discovered a new feedback mechanism—the Internet. They carefully monitored the many websites that sprung up to discuss and celebrate the show and learned a great deal in the process. For example, when in a first-season episode entitled "E.B.E." *The X-Files* introduced a new set of characters called the Lone Gunmen—three paranoid conspiracy theorists and computer experts who help the hero of the show, Fox Mulder, in his struggle against the government—the writers who thought them up (Glen Morgan and James Wong) felt that they were a failure and were ready to drop them from future episodes. But the Lone Gunmen caught on immediately with one of the core segments of the *X-Files* audience. As technological nerds, they appealed to precisely the fans who were among the first to take advantage of the Internet. Because of the popularity of the Lone Gunmen as judged by the *X-Files* websites, the producers decided to bring the characters back.[34] If the rest is not exactly television history, the quirkiness of the Lone Gunmen certainly contributed something to *The X-Files*, especially an element of humor that helped lighten the prevailing dark mood of the show. Somehow the show's audience, or a segment of it, was better able than the producers to sense the potential long-term contribution these characters might make to the series. The Romantic aesthetic tells us that giving in to audience demands can only corrupt an artist's vision. But the customer may occasionally be right, and artists who listen to their audience may learn to improve their art.[35]

As this example from the history of *The X-Files* reminds us, unlike many forms of art, a television series cannot be created all at once but must of necessity be produced over long stretches of time—weeks at first, but over years if the series is successful. This is one reason the television series does not fit the "perfect plan" model of artistic creation, but it is very well suited to the feedback model. Creating episode after episode and unable to go back and alter earlier efforts in light of subsequent developments, television producers often find themselves in the embarrassing position of having introduced lapses in continuity into their shows, if not outright contradictions.[36] A devoted fan may have fun pointing out such inconsistencies, but they mark television shows as failures according to the strict demands of coherence imposed by the organic model of poetic form. But what a television series loses in coherence over the years it gains in its ability to experiment with new possibilities and find ways to improve the show and expand its range. As the case of the Lone Gunmen demonstrates, in its long run, a successful television series will often introduce new characters and see which ones click with its audience. Characters who prove to be unpopular will be dropped, and characters who are popular will see their roles expanded.[37] Although the addition of a popular character may not always improve a show artistically, it often does and can sometimes revitalize the whole series. And in the serial character of much television production, it yet again proves impossible to maintain a strict division between high culture and popular.

For television did not invent the mode of serial production. It goes all the way back to the eighteenth century, when novels were first published serially. This method of producing novels reached its peak in the Victorian Era, when Charles Dickens led the way in making the serial novel the most popular and financially rewarding form of entertainment in England.[38] The novels we now study reverently in universities as masterpieces of fiction and hence high culture were at the time of their creation serially produced and consumed, much like the weekly installments of shows on television today. And we can observe the same feedback process at work in the Victorian novel. Novelists often killed off or otherwise disposed of characters who were proving unpopular with their audience, and devoted more pages to those who were evidently increasing weekly or monthly sales.[39] Jennifer Hayward has argued that the serial in its many incarnations—the serialized novel, the comic strip, the movie serial with its cliffhanger endings, the radio soap opera, the television soap opera, and other forms of serialized television—is the distinctive form of modern culture.[40] The fact that serial production, by allowing for all sorts of audience feedback, facilitates communication between artists and their public may go a long way toward explaining the prevalence of the form.[41] Serially produced works will usually be looser in form and fail to achieve the level of artistic coherence possible in lyric poetry, but, on the positive side, they can be more experimental and pursue a wider range of possibilities in terms of both form and content. And this is just as true when one compares a Victorian novel with a lyric poem as when one compares a television series.[42] Observing the similarities in the way serial production functioned in the nineteenth-century novel and in twentieth-century television is a good way of seeing how much high culture and popular culture have in common.

FEEDBACK MECHANISMS VS. THE PERFECT PLAN

To place my argument about popular culture in a larger context, I want to examine briefly the broader implications of the contrast I have been drawing between the "perfect plan" model of artistic creation and the "feedback" model. The "perfect plan" model of artistic creation has its deepest roots in Western theology and the teleological understanding of the universe to which it is related. To think of the artist planning out his works perfectly and in advance is to think of him on the model of God creating the universe, especially as understood in Christianity. According to this view, for any kind of meaningful structure to come into being and function, it must be the work of a single designer, who can bring all its elements into harmony. This way of understanding the world long dominated thought in a wide variety of areas. It seems natural to human beings to trace order anywhere they find it to some kind of orderer, someone who brings the field into order.[43] In politics, this way of thinking produced the theoretical support for monarchy—the claim that a country is ruled best when a single authority is in place to give it order. In economics, this way of thinking leads to the belief that the government must intervene to introduce order into the marketplace—to set prices, for example, or, more generally, to impose restrictions on commerce in order to make the common good prevail. In biology, this way of thinking leads to what is called creationism, the idea that the perfection of form we observe in biological phenomena can be explained only as the work of a single divine creator. To borrow a term from economics, all these approaches to understanding order celebrate the virtues of "central planning." Given the prevalence of this kind of thinking, it is understandable that it came to dominate aesthetics; the traditional idea of organic form in poetry is another way of celebrating central planning as the only route to order. Indeed, as long as people thought that only a single, divine creator could be responsible for the order we see in the biological realm, it was logical to view order in the aesthetic realm as having a similar origin.[44] The ideal of central planning is actually more plausible in aesthetics than in any other realm. In poetry, we can in fact observe poets at work and watch them achieve perfection of form by carefully designing their poems.

It is therefore not surprising that the central planning model of order survived in aesthetics long after it began to be challenged in other areas. Probably the most famous challenge to this way of thinking came in Darwin's theory of evolution. Darwin showed how the perfection we observe in the structure of animals and plants can be explained without recourse to the notion of a divine creator of that structure. His idea of natural selection is basically what we have been calling a feedback model of order. Evolution proceeds by what we now call random mutations, which lead to a proliferation of biological forms—experiments in life forms, as it were. In Darwin's view, the environment provides the feedback in this system, selecting out new forms that work and rejecting those that do not. If this sounds like my description of how a television series develops, that is just my point.[45] What looks anomalous from the viewpoint of traditional poetics fits the Darwinian model of how form can be perfected in a system that does not have a central orderer or planner. Darwin in fact provides a way of questioning traditional poetics by questioning its fundamental conception of organic form. Both Aristotelian and Romantic poetics stake their claims on the principle of organic form. But since Darwin, we have come to understand that organic form need not be the result of conscious design or preplanning. Franco Moretti and Gary Saul Morson have led the way in showing how Darwin's ideas can help us rethink our notion of literary form.[46] Drawing upon the work of Stephen Jay Gould, both have stressed how Darwin, as opposed to Aristotle, allows for an element of contingency in biological form.[47] The truth of Darwin's theory in fact hinges on our ability to find evidence of imperfection in biological form—elements of an organism which do not fulfill the Aristotelian criterion of being integral parts of the whole and which therefore do not appear to be the result of divine creation. The presence of vestigial organs in animals, for example, can be explained, not by any theory of perfect design (since they in fact have no function), but only by reference to an animal's evolutionary history, and history is the realm of the contingent. As Gould writes,

> If feathers are perfect, they may as well have been designed from scratch by an omnipotent God as from previous anatomy by a natural process. Darwin recognized that the primary evidence for evolution must be sought in quirks, oddities, and imperfections that lay bare the pathways of history. Whales, with their vestigial pelvic bones, must have descended from terrestrial ancestors with functional legs. . . . If whales retained no trace of their terrestrial heritage, . . . then history would not inhere in the productions of nature.[48]

If the biological realm allows for contingency of form, then, according to Moretti and Morson, literary form can admit contingent elements as well.

Darwin's revolution in how to conceive order was preceded by a revolution in economic thinking that we associate with Adam Smith and classical economics. Darwin himself admitted to being influenced by classical economics in the person of Thomas Malthus, and indeed in retrospect we can see that Malthus's theory of population was crucial to Darwin's understanding of natural selection.[49] Smith and his followers attacked central planning in its root economic form, the idea that only government intervention can achieve order in markets that would otherwise, if left to themselves, break down into chaos. Smith showed just the opposite—that markets are self-regulating and self-ordering, and it is government intervention that throws them out of balance and produces chaos. In Smith's analysis, the pricing mechanism of free markets produces the feedback that orders economic phenomena. Rising prices are a signal to producers to turn out more of a good, and falling prices a signal to turn out less. The price mechanism thus works to bring supply into line with demand and thereby to make the market move toward equilibrium.

When the government intervenes and tries artificially to raise or lower prices, it sends the wrong signals to producers, and that leads to surpluses or shortages in the market, which is to say, economic chaos.

Thus in both Smith's economics and Darwin's biology, systems generate order from within themselves and on their own. In the traditional theological model of order, a force outside or above the system is necessary to intervene and introduce order into what would otherwise be chaos. In the Smith/Darwin model, a system becomes self-regulating through a feedback mechanism. Such a system does not achieve perfection all at once by an act of divine creation; rather, it is always striving toward perfection by a process of evolution; it is, in effect, self-perfecting rather than perfect. The Austrian economist Friedrich Hayek has popularized the use of the term "spontaneous order" to describe this sort of system, and he did much to develop a general theory of spontaneous order, showing how the concept is applicable in a wide range of fields beyond economics and biology, from linguistics to law.[50] What I have been trying to do in this chapter is to apply the concept of spontaneous order to popular culture. The realm of popular culture looks messy and disordered to us, and we have a hard time understanding how any kind of artistic form could emerge out of this seeming chaos. The idea of spontaneous order always seems counterintuitive to us; as human beings, we evidently are conditioned to attribute order to an individual orderer. That is why the ideas of both Smith and Darwin (not to mention Hayek) encountered so much initial resistance and are rejected to this day by many people. But if one recognizes the various kinds of feedback mechanisms at work in popular culture, one begins to see that it is possible for it to lack a centrally ordering agent and yet be self-regulating and self-perfecting.

To return to my initial questions, if we find that authorship is, as it were, "corporate" rather than individual in television production, that does not rule out the serious study of television programs. As we have already seen, even in high culture the concept of the single perfect author is perhaps best understood as a heuristic device. We may never encounter a work of literature actually produced entirely and perfectly by a single author, but it is useful for us to read literature and especially lyric poetry as if this were the case. We will find more in a literary work if we are looking for perfection in it, and that is why the New Criticism, for all the dubious aspects of its theoretical foundations, proved to be fruitful in its application to analyzing literature. Thus, when we turn to

popular culture, even if we see that single authorship is not the norm of production, we can still "read" individual shows as if they had artistic integrity, and
this will help us to find whatever artistic merit they may in fact have.

In short, the typical critique of popular culture is a version of the genetic
fallacy. By concentrating on how works of popular culture are produced, it
prejudices us against taking the products seriously. But, as we have seen, in
both high culture and popular culture, the genesis of a work does not necessarily tell us anything about its artistic quality. A work produced by a seemingly haphazard process may not turn out to be haphazard in form (by the
same token, a perfectly planned work may turn out to be lifeless and dull). Instead of focusing on the original intentions of the creators in popular culture
and worrying whether they have been carried out faithfully, we should dwell
upon the intentionality of the finished product—whether in the end it has become, by whatever process, a work of art. And we must beware of taking the
perfectly unified lyric poem as our only model of aesthetic achievement. As
studies of the novel are increasingly revealing, a work of literature may embrace various forms of what would be regarded as imperfection in lyric poetry
and still have aesthetic value. Indeed, as Morson and Moretti have argued,
novels may make those imperfections serve new artistic purposes. The same
may be true of what are often considered to be the aesthetic shortcomings of
popular culture. We should be careful about judging the new media of popular culture by the artistic standards of the older media of high culture. We
should instead be looking for the unprecedented aesthetic possibilities suddenly opened up whenever a new artistic medium comes along. In sum, we
can take the artistic forms of popular culture seriously without assuming that
they will conform to the norms of high culture in the past; indeed, the genuine excitement of studying popular culture may well be to discover the new
conceptions of artistic form it is developing.

The spontaneous order model also helps us rethink our negative reaction
when we encounter the element of contingency in television production. We
have begun to realize that to eliminate all contingency from art might well be
to take the life out of it—especially now that Darwin has given us a concept of
biological form that includes contingency, rather than banishing it as the Aristotelian tradition tried to do. Another way of saying that television production
inevitably involves an element of contingency is to say that it inevitably takes
place over time, sometimes long periods of time.[51] In the model of a divine

moment of perfect creation, time is seen as the great corrupting force. The
world is perfect at the moment of creation and can only degenerate thereafter.
A similar view is embodied in the idea of the moment of perfect poetic creation. The poet's vision is at its purest at the instant of inspiration, and his efforts to work out his original idea over time and embody it in material form
only lead him away from its initial perfection. In the classic formulation of
Percy Shelley, "When composition begins, inspiration is already on the decline,
and the most glorious poetry that has ever been communicated to the world is
probably a feeble shadow of the original conception of the poet."[52] By contrast,
in the spontaneous order model, time is the friend rather than the enemy of
creation. In both Adam Smith and Darwin, systems perfect themselves over
time, and, on a smaller scale, the same process can be observed in the evolution
of a television series. If Rome was not built in a day, neither was *The X-Files*.

None of this is to say that the conditions of television production *guarantee* high artistic quality and the automatic evolution of every show to perfection by its sixth or seventh season. Obviously from what we observe on
television, something closer to the opposite seems to be the case. All I am
claiming is that the typical conditions of television production do not simply
preclude artistic quality, as some critics of the medium have argued. As Hayward writes,

> The ability to alter narratives in response to the success or failure of subplots or
> characters is seen as negative because we have constructed ideologies of the
> "true" artist and writer as governed only by individual genius and never by the
> demands of the marketplace. . . . There is no inherent flaw in a kind of "just in
> time" production of stories; neither does this method preclude the inspiration
> of creative genius. Instead, both market forces and artistic gifts can work to-
> gether to produce texts crafted by an individual or creative team but flexible
> enough to respond to good and relevant ideas from outside, whether in the
> form of audience response, news events, or other sources.[53]

I have tried to suggest some of the ways in which the various feedback mechanisms in television production can help to improve the quality of shows, but
that still requires the talent of a creative producer to take advantage of the circumstances. Because that talent is rare (although perhaps no rarer in popular
culture than in high culture), the overall level of aesthetic quality of television

programs may remain low, even while oases of genuine art spring up from time to time in the vast television wasteland.

My main goal has been to identify and try to overcome the prejudices we have inherited from the tradition of Romantic aesthetics. This tradition has been anticommercial since its inception; the Romantics were the first to set up the autonomous creative genius in opposition to the vulgarity of the market-place. In trying to rethink our view of popular culture, I have drawn upon the idea of spontaneous order, particularly because in its economic form, it shows that commerce can be an ordering and indeed a creative force. The ultimate objection to popular culture among its many critics on the left and on the right is that it is commercial culture, and in the Romantic tradition, commerce and culture are seen at odds. But once we begin to think of popular culture—and perhaps culture in general—as a form of spontaneous order, we can begin to understand how commerce and culture can work together for their mutual benefit.[54] To put the matter in the most unromantic terms possible: just because a television show is a commercial success does not mean that it is an artistic failure.

NOTES

1. This principle was the cornerstone of the New Criticism. See, for example, Cleanth Brooks, *The Well Wrought Urn* (New York: Harcourt Brace, 1947), where he defends "the proposition that *every word* in a poem plays its part" (221, italics in the original).

2. For more on this bit of television history, see my book *Gilligan Unbound: Pop Culture in the Age of Globalization* (Lanham, MD: Rowman & Littlefield, 2001), xxxv–vi.

3. For general discussions of the relation between popular culture and high culture, see Herbert J. Gans, *Popular Culture & High Culture: An Analysis and Evaluation of Taste* (New York: Basic Books, 1999); and Richard Keller Simon, *Trash Culture and the Great Tradition* (Berkeley, CA: University of California Press, 1999). On this specific point, see Gans, 37, and also Jack Stillinger, *Multiple Authorship and the Myth of Solitary Genius* (Oxford: Oxford University Press, 1991), 163.

4. See David Bevington, ed., "General Introduction," *The Complete Works of Shakespeare* (New York: Addison-Wesley, 1997), lxvii.

5. See Gary Saul Morson, "The Prosaics of Process," *Literary Imagination* 2 (2000): 379.

6. For a brilliant and concise account of these developments in aesthetics, see Martha Woodmansee, *The Author, Art, and the Market: Rereading the History of Aesthetics* (New York: Columbia University Press, 1994).

7. For examples of the influence of Coleridge on the New Criticism, see Brooks, 7–8, 26–27, 258. For the idea of the "structure of the poem as an organism" in New Criticism, see 213. See Woodmansee, 98, for the more general connection between Romanticism and the New Criticism.

8. For further discussion of this point, see my essay "The Primacy of the Literary Imagination, or, Which Came First: The Critic or the Author?" *Literary Imagination* 1 (1999): 133–37.

9. Alvin Kernan, *Samuel Johnson & the Impact of Print* (Princeton, NJ: Princeton University Press, 1987), 293. See also Gans, 66; and Lee Erickson, *The Economy of Literary Form: English Literature and the Industrialization of Publishing, 1800–1850* (Baltimore, MD: Johns Hopkins University Press, 1996), 104–105. For a thorough critique of the Romantic ideology of the autonomous creative genius, see Jerome J. McGann, *The Romantic Ideology: A Critical Investigation* (Chicago: University of Chicago Press, 1983); and *A Critique of Modern Textual Criticism* (Chicago: University of Chicago Press, 1983), 8, 40, 42.

10. For one of the earliest attempts in English to condemn the emergence of mass culture, see Wordsworth's preface to the 1800 second edition of *Lyrical Ballads*.

11. On the connection between the idea of genius and the idea of organic form, see Woodmansee, 53–54.

12. For the critical hostility to the novel, see Woodmansee, 89–92. For further examples of nineteenth-century critiques of novel reading, see Jennifer Hayward, *Consuming Pleasures: Active Audiences and Serial Fictions from Dickens to Soap Opera* (Lexington, KY: University Press of Kentucky, 1997), 6, 26–27; and Erickson, 139–41. For a full treatment of the subject, see John Tinnon Taylor, *Early Opposition to the English Novel: The Popular Reaction from 1760 to 1830* (New York: King's Crown, 1943). What is striking in reading all these accounts is to see that in the nineteenth century, reading novels was criticized for exactly the same reasons watching television is criticized today.

13. On this point, see Erickson, 15, 105, 171–72.

14. For some examples, see Cantor, *Gilligan Unbound*, xxxvii, esp. 214n6.

15. See Cantor, xxxvii and 215n8. For specific examples of *X-Files* writers praising Chris Carter's intervention in their work, see Brian Lowry, *Trust No One: The X-Files* (New York: Harper, 1996), 227–29; and Andy Meisler, *The X-Files: I Want to Believe* (New York: Harper, 1998), 122.

16. Jack Stillinger has assembled a list of prominent examples of multiple authorship in the history of British and American literature (Stillinger, 204–13).

17. See Stillinger, 164–69.

18. See Michael Mangan, *Christopher Marlowe: Doctor Faustus* (London: Penguin, 1989), 21.

19. See G. Blakemore Evans, *The Riverside Shakespeare* (Boston: Houghton Mifflin, 1974), 1683–1700; and Scott McMillin, *The Elizabethan Theatre & The Book of Sir Thomas More* (Ithaca, NY: Cornell University Press, 1987), 135–59.

20. For example, Coleridge wrote the opening line of Wordsworth's "We are Seven," and Wordsworth wrote lines 19–20 of the original version of Coleridge's "The Rime of the Ancyent Marinere" (lines 15–16 of the later "The Rime of the Ancient Mariner").

21. For a full account of Pound's contribution to Eliot's poem, see the chapter "Pound's *Waste Land*" in Stillinger, 121–38.

22. Stillinger, 146. For further discussion of the Wolfe/Perkins collaboration, see McGann, *Textual Criticism*, 53, 78–79. For further discussion of the general issue of authors working with editors and publishers, see McGann, *Textual Criticism*, 34–35, 42–44, 52–53, 75.

23. Paul Delany offers a particularly trenchant critique of government attempts to subsidize art under socialism in his *Literature, Money and the Market* (London: Palgrave, 2002), esp. 122, 172–74.

24. See Stillinger, 173.

25. Samuel Johnson provides an excellent example of an author who seemed to need deadlines to get him to write; see Kernan, 94–96. For the example of Thackeray, see Alan C. Dooley, *Author and Printer in Victorian England* (Charlottesville, VA: University Press of Virginia, 1992), 40. For a discussion of Dostoevsky and deadlines, see Gary Saul Morson, *Narrative and Freedom: The Shadows of Time* (New Haven, CT: Yale University Press, 1994), esp. 202–3.

26. See Sarane Alexandrian, *Surrealist Art* (New York: Thames and Hudson, 1985), 140–50.

27. Morson, "Prosaics," 386.

28. For examples of these sorts of contemporary references in television soap operas, see Hayward, 187–88. Hayward discusses analogous contemporary references in the serialized novels of the nineteenth century (30, 44), including cases of Dickens working from newspaper incidents (47).

29. See Morson, "Prosaics," 381, and "Sideshadowing and Tempics," *New Literary History* 29 (1998): 608–9.

30. For some specific examples of authors failing to spot textual changes introduced during the printing process by mistake, see Dooley, 40, 45, and 48 (George Eliot), 40 (William Makepeace Thackeray), and 41 (Charles Dickens).

31. See Morson, "Sideshadowing," 599–600.

32. For an example early in the history of the English novel, see Lennard J. Davis's discussion of the procedures of Samuel Richardson, *Factual Fictions: The Origins of the English Novel* (Philadelphia, PA: University of Pennsylvania Press, 1996), 189–90. For a later example of this kind of literary feedback, involving Tennyson, see Dooley, 21, 52.

33. For a provocative discussion of the problematic aspects of efforts by the Modernist movement to shield artists from commercial pressures, see Lawrence Rainey, *Institutions of Modernism: Literary Elites & Public Culture* (New Haven, CT: Yale University Press, 1998), esp. 40, 148–49, 156, 168. For further discussion of attempts "to establish a modernist literary economy in isolation from the literary marketplace" (146), see Delaney, "Paying for Modernism" and "T. S. Eliot's Personal Finances, 1915–1929" in *Literature, Money and the Market*, 146–71.

34. Brian Lowry, *The Truth Is Out There: The Official Guide to the X-Files* (New York: Harper, 1995), 140; and Cantor, *Gilligan Unbound*, 167–68.

35. In the crisp formulation of Franco Moretti, "The Slaughterhouse of Literature," *Modern Language Quarterly* 61 (2000): 219n12: "if it is perverse to believe that the market always rewards the better solution, it is just as perverse to believe that it always rewards the worse one!"

36. For some concrete examples, see Cantor, *Gilligan Unbound*, xxxvi; and Hayward, 154.

37. See Hayward, 170, 174–85 for a detailed study of the development of one character in a television soap opera in response to audience feedback.

38. For discussion of some of the aspects and implications of serial publication, see Erickson, 158–68; and Morson, "Prosaics," 385–86.

39. For examples of Dickens expanding the role of his characters or killing them off in response to sales figures, see Hayward, 58–59, 61.

40. See Hayward, 2–3.

41. For the various forms of audience feedback in television soap operas, see Hayward, 165.

42. See Hayward, *Consuming Pleasures*, for examples of both discontinuity in Victorian serial novels (82) and the greater potential for character development (37, 50).

43. See Friedrich Hayek, *Law, Legislation and Liberty* (London: Routledge, 1982), 1:9–10, 26–27; and *The Fatal Conceit: The Errors of Socialism* (Chicago: University of Chicago Press, 1988), 24.

44. On the theological model in Romantic aesthetics, see Woodmansee, 18–19.

45. Let me stress that I am talking about an analogy here, not an identity. For the differences between biological and cultural evolution, see Hayek (1988), 23–28.

46. For Franco Moretti, see "On Literary Evolution," *Signs Taken for Wonders: Essays in the Sociology of Literary Forms* (London: Verso, 1988), 262–78; *Modern Epic: The World System from Goethe to García Márquez* (London: Verso, 1996), 20, 22, 94, 150, 177–78, 184, 188–91; and "Slaughterhouse of Literature," 207–27. For Gary Saul Morson, see *Narrative and Freedom*; "Sideshadowing and Tempics"; and "Contingency and Freedom, Prosaics and Process," *New Literary History* 29 (1998): 599–624, 673–86; and "Prosaics," 377–88.

47. For the element of contingency in Darwinian biology, see Stephen Jay Gould, *Wonderful Life: The Burgess Shale and the Nature of History* (New York: W. W. Norton, 1989), esp. 51, 283–91, 299–301, 317–18.

48. Gould, 300–301. For the application of these ideas to literature, see Morson, "Sideshadowing," 618–21.

49. See the introduction to *Origin of Species*, where Darwin writes, "This is the doctrine of Malthus, applied to the whole animal and vegetable kingdom." Quoted

from the edition of Gillian Beer—Charles Darwin, *The Origin of Species* (Oxford: Oxford University Press, 1996), 6.

50. For Hayek's understanding of spontaneous order, see chaps. 1 and 2, "Reason and Evolution" and "Cosmos and Taxis," of the first volume, *Rules and Order*, of his trilogy *Law, Legislation and Liberty*, 1:8–54. See also the essays "The Theory of Complex Phenomena" and "The Results of Human Action but Not of Human Design" in his *Studies in Philosophy, Politics and Economics* (New York: Simon & Schuster, 1967), 22–42, 96–105. For a brief but comprehensive survey of the development of the idea of spontaneous order, see Steven Horwitz, "From Smith to Menger to Hayek: Liberalism in the Spontaneous-Order Tradition," *The Independent Review: A Journal of Political Economy* 6 (2001): 81–97.

51. For the importance of the time element in serial forms, see Hayward, 136.

52. From *A Defence of Poetry*, quoted from Donald H. Reiman and Sharon B. Powers, eds., *Shelley's Poetry and Prose* (New York: W. W. Norton, 1977), 504. For a critical assessment of this understanding of literary composition, see Dooley, 171; and McGann, *Textual Criticism*, 102–3.

53. Hayward, 62.

54. For a comprehensive treatment of this possibility, see Tyler Cowen, *In Praise of Commercial Culture* (Cambridge, MA: Harvard University Press, 1998).

9

From Horror to Hero: Film Interpretations of Stoker's *Dracula*

Jorge J. E. Gracia

Films based on Bram Stoker's *Dracula* (1897) pose some of the most challenging questions surrounding interpretation. I would like to take up three: First, can we justifiably characterize the films I discuss below as interpretations of Stoker's novel? Second, if they are interpretations, what kind are they? And third, what implications do the answers to these two questions have for the understanding of popular interpretations of literary works in general?

These questions arise because most *Dracula* films contain major differences with Stoker's novel. Some of these result from the difference in medium between Stoker's work and the films, whereas others do not. Here, I concentrate on those that do not, although I shall have something to say in passing about the ones that do.

I begin by examining pertinent details in Stoker's novel. Then I turn to the six films that I have chosen for my purposes: F. W. Murnau's *Nosferatu: A Symphony of Horror* (1922; with Max Schrek, and produced by Albin Grau); Tod Browning's *Dracula* (1931; with Béla Lugosi, and produced by Carl Laemmle Jr. and Tod Browning); Paul Morrisey's *Dracula* (1974; with Udo Kier, and produced by Andy Warhol); Werner Herzog's *Nosferatu: The Vampyre* (1979; with Klaus Kinski, and produced by Werner Herzog); John Badham's *Dracula* (1979; with Frank Langella, and produced by Walter Mirisch); and Francis Ford Coppola's *Bram Stoker's Dracula* (1992; with Gary Oldman, and produced by Francis Ford Coppola and others). I have selected these films for three reasons: they are recognized classics in the genre; they display the typical kinds of differences found in film renditions of Stoker's novel; and they play important roles in the evolution that films about Dracula have undergone over time, particularly with respect to the central character of the novel. Next, I discuss briefly several common, but inadequate, ways in which the relation between these films and Stoker's *Dracula* is conceived, and this leads me in turn to a different way of understanding this relation.

STOKER'S *DRACULA*

Stoker's novel begins with a diary entry made in Bistritz by the aspiring solicitor, Jonathan Harker, who is on his way to Count Dracula's castle in Transylvania. The purpose of the trip is to have the count sign the purchase of a piece of property in London. Harker is doing this on behalf of the law firm for which he works, whose chief solicitor is Peter Hawkins.

Strange happenings occur as Harker gets closer to the count's dwelling. There are howling wolves and strange actions and comments by the driver sent to pick him up. Events turn even more bizarre after Harker arrives at his destination. While shaving, he cuts himself, and the count reacts violently, barely managing to control himself. Harker becomes a prisoner in the castle and has an encounter with three lascivious women. Eventually, Harker succeeds in escaping, taking advantage of Dracula's absence while the count is on his way to England by sea.

Back in London, Harker's fiancée, Mina Murray, is worried because she receives no news from him, but when she is notified that he is in a hospital in Budapest, she goes to fetch him. In the meantime, Mina's friend, Lucy Westenra, has fallen prey to Dracula. One of Lucy's admirers, Dr. John Seward, runs an insane asylum next to the ruined house which Dracula has purchased. Puzzled by Lucy's disease, he asks a "philosopher," "metaphysician," and "scientist" from the Continent, Dr. Abraham Van Helsing, for a consultation. Van Helsing figures out the nature of Lucy's ailment and begins to take measures against the disease, intended to provide more blood for her and to prevent further action by the vampire he suspects is preying on her. He fails, and Lucy dies, becoming herself a vampire who preys on children.

After Harker recovers, he and Mina return to England and are apprised of the situation there. Mina reads the diary Harker composed while he was staying at Dracula's castle and gives it to Van Helsing, who organizes the resistance against the count. The fighting group includes Harker; Van Helsing; Seward; Lucy's former fiancé, the Honorable Arthur Holmwood (later Lord Godalming); Lucy's Texan admirer, Quincey Morris; and Mina. While they deliberate on the strategy to follow, Dracula tempts and convinces an inmate in Seward's asylum, R. N. Renfield, to invite him into the building, where Mina and the others are staying. Dracula thus gets access to Mina and not only begins to drink her blood, but makes her drink his. Van Helsing describes the latter as "the Vampire's baptism of blood." As a result, a bond between the two is established that allows each of them to have access to some of the other's thoughts and perceptions. This serves Dracula to learn of the group's efforts to find and destroy him, but it also provides information on Dracula's whereabouts for the group when Van Helsing succeeds in hypnotizing Mina. Dracula manages to escape, but his foes follow. The chase succeeds when Harker and Morris pierce Dracula's heart and cut off his head. These actions end the curse.

Several things stand out in the story. Most important is the portrayal of Count Dracula. He is presented as a formidable being, with supernatural powers, who is the personification of evil. He has the strength of twenty men and can transform himself into various animals (e.g., a bat, a wolf). He can also change himself into fog, mist, or elemental dust, thus making it possible for him to pass through small cracks. He can control lower animals, and he can direct elements, such as a storm, fog, and thunder. He can become big or small, and he can disappear and appear at will. He can look old and young, he does not cast a shadow or a reflection in mirrors, and the vision of a flame is not obstructed by his body. There is not a speck of color about him except for the intense vermilion of his lips and the occasional redness of the eyes, and he is always dressed in black. The eyebrows are massive; the hair is bushy; a cruel and hard-looking mouth has peculiarly sharp, white canine teeth protruding over the lips; the ears are pointed; the hands appear coarse and have squat fingers and hairs on their palms; the nails are long and cut to a sharp point; and his breath is rank. Apart from this extraordinary appearance, we are told that Dracula has a strong hold on all those whose blood he has tasted.

Dracula also has weaknesses. He has to sleep during the day in his coffin and in dirt from his native soil; he suffers when he is exposed to the light of the sun, the cross, garlic, holy water, the wild rose, and the Eucharist, among other things; and he needs to feed on human blood. He cannot enter an abode into which he is not invited. His power ceases with the coming of the day, and he can only change himself at noon or at the exact moment of sunrise or sunset. He can willingly pass through running water only at the slack or the flood of the tide, and both he and everything about him inspire terror, horror, fear, abhorrence, revulsion, and even nausea.

Dracula is described as full of hate and as diabolical, indescribably evil, wicked, callous, and malicious. He has no heart, conscience, or pity, and he preys on young children and helpless creatures. He desires and is attracted to women, but he has no love. Dracula never loves at present, although there is one allusion to past love in the book. He forces himself with passion on the women he chooses, but they are terrified of him, even at times when they feel a certain unholy attraction for him. After encounters with him, they feel polluted and unclean.

Stoker's story contains holes and obscurities, and some subsequent interpretations try to fill the first and clarify the second. For example, we are never clearly told how Dracula became a vampire, why he wishes to move to London in particular, why he is especially attracted to Mina, why he has a hold on certain animals and not others, and why he is adversely affected by light. And questions also arise about other characters, such as Renfield.

Perhaps most important of all, the aim of what appears to be the count's quest is never made explicit. In one place, Stoker identifies it as power, suggesting perhaps that Dracula aims to establish a fellowship or kingdom of evil and a new order of beings based on death, in which he would be master and others slaves. But it is common to think of the novel as an allegory in which Christianity fights evil, or as an exploration of the relation between sex, blood, and evil.

The hero of Stoker's novel is Harker.[1] He is the champion of good over evil, an exemplary lover, and capable of self-sacrifice. Indeed, he is willing to become a vampire so as not to abandon Mina if she should become one. The love he has for her reveals the rationale of the action in the story and contrasts with Dracula's selfish, loveless figure. In the last line of the book, Van Helsing is holding a boy, the son of Mina and Harker, and referring to him says, "He will understand how some men so loved her (i.e., Mina) that they did dare much for her sake."

SIX FILMS BASED ON STOKER'S *DRACULA*

Stoker's novel undergoes drastic changes in its popular film renditions. The following six films illustrate them.

Murnau's *Nosferatu*

This is the first film based on Dracula still extant. The word *nosferatu* is used by Stoker. It is a modern word, derived from an Old Slavonic term meaning "plague carrier." It came to be used to refer to "vampires," and Stoker extends its meaning to the "undead."

The differences between Stoker's tale and the story presented in the film are significant. Dracula is named Graf Orlock and is transformed into a truly horrific figure. He is largely bald and stooped; he has extremely long clawlike fingernails and fingers; and his front teeth are elongated, coming out of the front of his mouth like those of a rat. He moves deliberately, slowly, and with difficulty. You would not want to meet him around a corner on a dark night. Other characters in the novel are also changed. Harker becomes Waldemar Hutter, and Mina, named Ellen, is his wife from the beginning. Renfield, renamed Knock, is turned into Hutter's boss in the movie (Mr. Hawkins, for Stoker). And Van Helsing, renamed Professor Bulwar, devotes his time to experiments on meat-eating plants and other vegetable vampire creatures.

There are also differences in the action. The film presents an explanation of the Bremen outbreak of the plague (1838). It opens with a quote from a historian who states that the plague was brought about by *nosferatu*. Next we see Hutter happily gardening and Ellen receiving a bouquet of flowers from him. Then Knock is presented as reading a letter from Orlock in which he is instructed to buy property for him. He appears malicious and cunning and suggests to Hutter that he travel to Transylvania to arrange the deal, even if "it should cause him a bit of pain and some loss of blood." He aims to sell the count a house across the channel from Hutter's home.

When Hutter informs Ellen of the trip, she appears to have a bad presentiment. Hutter travels to Transylvania but has difficulty reaching the place because the driver of the carriage in which he is traveling does not want to go beyond a certain point. Hutter walks to the appointed place, is picked up, and is taken to Orlock's castle. While eating, he cuts his finger, prompting Orlock to reveal his desire for blood and eventually to attack Hutter. The next day, while discussing the contract, the count sees a picture of Ellen and is attracted to "her lovely neck."

Hutter discovers the count in his coffin and later observes how he loads boxes of dirt in a cart and gets into one before the cart moves away. Hutter manages to escape, but Orlock has already left for Bremen, where the plague breaks out after his arrival. We see the count carrying his own box full of dirt from his native soil to his new home.

Ellen reads *The Book of Vampires* after Hutter returns to Bremen, and she finds the prescription for destroying *nosferatu*: only a woman who is pure of heart can break the spell, by freely offering her blood to the vampire and keeping him by her side until after the cock has crowed. After much agony, Ellen decides to sacrifice herself to save Hutter and end the curse. In the final scene, we see her in bed, with Hutter asleep sitting on a chair in the room. She wakes up and opens the window, from which she can see the expectant Orlock looking at her from across the street. She is horrified, wakes Hutter, and faints. Hutter goes to fetch Professor Bulwar, but in the meantime, Ellen regains consciousness and sees the horrific shadow of Orlock entering the room. Ellen falls on her bed but willingly lets him feed on her. The cock crows, and Orlock realizes he must leave, but it is too late. The light of the sun is already out, and he turns into flames. Ellen appears dead, but when Hutter arrives, she has a last conscious moment in which they embrace. This moment marks the end of the plague in Bremen.

Two important departures from Stoker's novel stand out in Murnau's film. One is the introduction of extraordinary female love and sacrifice in the way the count is destroyed. Ellen gives up her life and faces an indescribable horror in order to save her husband and the town. Clearly, she is the heroine of the story. The other is the presentation of Dracula himself, who as Orlock becomes even more horrific than the creature presented by Stoker.

Browning's *Dracula*

This film version of *Dracula* has become a favorite of Dracula fans. Part of the appeal is the performance of Béla Lugosi, which many find fascinating. Although the film claims to be based on Stoker's tale, it departs from the story line in a variety of ways.

The film begins with a conversation among passengers in a coach traveling in Transylvania. They tell Renfield, who is on his way to Dracula's castle, about the *nosferatu*, the undead who feed on the living. When they get to the inn and Renfield notifies the innkeeper that he needs to continue his trip to the Borgo Pass, the innkeeper informs him that Dracula is a vampire. Renfield pays no attention and goes on to the pass.

Next we see the castle in the mountains and its dungeon. A hand creeps out of a coffin, mice move away, wolves howl, and we see Dracula. He is dressed in black, wrapped in a cape. His most prominent feature are his eyes—big, intense, piercing, shining with a special light, and fixed on the audience. This is one of the main elements of Lugosi's performance, repeated almost every time he comes on screen, and passed on to those who join him as undead.

In the meantime, Renfield has reached the Borgo Pass, where he meets a coach that takes him to the castle. Here we see again Dracula's eyes, for he is the driver of the coach. The castle Renfield enters is in ruins, with rats and armadillos among the debris. Dracula enters by coming down imperial stairs very slowly, dressed elegantly in white tie, with a medal hanging from his neck, and the piercing eyes fixed on Renfield. After a polite welcome, they move up, Dracula going through cobwebs without disturbing them. Wolves howl, giving Dracula the opportunity to say the famous line: "Listen to them, children of the night! What music they make!"

While at supper, Dracula informs Renfield that they are leaving the next day. Renfield cuts his finger, and Dracula is attracted by the blood but is stopped by the cross on the rosary that the wife of the innkeeper had given Renfield. That night, three women try to attack Renfield, but Dracula stops them and takes him himself. From then on, Renfield becomes Dracula's slave.

After a sea voyage to England, Dracula appears in London, dressed elegantly as usual, attending the symphony. Here he meets Dr. Seward and his daughter Mina, who is engaged to Jonathan Harker. Lucy is a friend who accompanies them and is immediately attracted to Dracula. She tells Mina that she finds him fascinating and romantic when they are back at Mina's home. That night, Dracula enters Lucy's room and makes her a vampire.

Next is Mina, but here there is no attraction. Mina is frightened of Dracula, and when he attacks her, it is always while she is asleep. Van Helsing suspects the count and confronts him. Harker and Seward have difficulties accepting Van Helsing's surmises but eventually help him. The count now has Mina in his power and takes her to his dungeon. Van Helsing and Harker find them there. Dracula is resting in his coffin, where Van Helsing destroys him (something we hear, but do not see). Mina is still not a full vampire and recovers after Dracula's demise.

The story as told in the film differs in many ways from the written tale. Most important are three elements that it includes. First is the pleasant physical appearance of Dracula and his behavior as an elegant aristocrat. He often appears wrapped in a cape, sometimes looking like a statue, but more often showing an impeccable attire of white tie. His manner is always suave in the extreme. Even the attacks upon his victims are not violent. The victims are always in a kind of swoon by the time he gets to their necks. Second is the romantic and erotic attraction that Dracula exercises over Lucy. Although Dracula forces himself on other victims, such as Mina and a flower girl, Lucy is attracted to Dracula and appears to invite his advances. Mina only does so after he has forced himself once on her, but Lucy does it before he has taken her. Third, although Dracula does not inspire pity, we get a hint that he does not consider himself happy. When he first meets the other main characters of the story, he tells them that "to die, to be really dead . . . that must be glorious. There are far worse things awaiting man than death."

Morrisey's *Dracula*

Although some elements of Stoker's story are preserved in Morrisey's film, its innovations are substantial. The film is not only original and humorous, but also sexy. Lots of flesh gets exposed. Moreover, Warhol answers some of the questions left unanswered by Stoker, such as the reason why Dracula has to leave his homeland.

The film begins with Dracula dying his gray eyebrows and hair black and putting color on his lips. This is followed by a scene in which his amanuensis, Anton—probably the counterpart of Renfield in Stoker's novel but this time with a heavy German accent and a kind of Nazi military air to him—convinces the count that he needs to leave for Italy. The reason is that Dracula is dying, and the only thing that can save him is the blood of a virgin. Unfortunately, virgins are scarce in his country, and he is well known for his need. Anton suggests Italy because this country's religious fervor makes families keep their daughters virginal.

Dracula is not thrilled to go and is quite willing to end it all. He appears as a weak, diffident young man, pale and thin and suffering from anorexia, who is bullied and manipulated by the amanuensis. But he eventually relents and departs for Italy with both his coffin and a wheelchair that helps him to move around, loaded on top of the car driven by Anton.

When they reach their destination, they learn that there is an impoverished Italian noble family with four unmarried daughters in the area: an old spinster, a fourteen-year-old girl, and two marriageable sisters. Anton asks whether the family is religious, and the innkeeper responds, "I'm sure they are religious; they have a very nice house." This ironic humor pervades the movie.

Anton visits the family and arranges for the count to move into the palazzo. Dracula is in a bad way, retching from lack of proper food and subject to attacks that leave him weak. The marquesses are eager to marry their daughters with solvent suitors and, after some pro forma initial resistance, welcome the possibility of having the count marry one of them.

The amanuensis' plan is to tap the two marriageable daughters, but he unfortunately does not know that they are far from being virgins. Indeed, they are thoroughly promiscuous and regularly enjoy the attentions of the only hired hand the marquesses can afford. He is presented as a gardener and factotum on the property, with a vigorous libido and a Marxist political agenda.

Dracula needs blood, so after questioning one of the sisters about her virginity, he sucks her blood. At first, he is in a state of glory, but suddenly he turns green and vomits every drop of blood he had drunk; he cannot tolerate blood from nonvirgins. After this scene is repeated with the other marriageable sister, Anton suggests the younger sister. She is a virgin, but the servant is secretly attracted to her and interferes. He saves her by forcing himself on her, even though after some initial, tepid resistance on her part, she appears to enjoy the affair. The marquess finds them in the act and blames the servant: "You are just an employee; how could you dare?"

In the meantime, the old spinster had approached Dracula, whose strength had been restored thanks to her virginal blood. Unfortunately for the count, it is too late, because the gardener figures out that he is a vampire and goes after him with an ax. He pursues him through the palazzo, first hacking away an arm, then another, and then the legs. Blood squirts everywhere, and the old spinster comes to the rescue, but not before the servant drives a stake through Dracula's helpless torso. In desperation, the spinster throws herself on top of Dracula and is also pierced by the stake. They die simultaneously. The film ends with the servant taking the younger sister out of the room in which this scene takes place.

The most significant differences between this story and Stoker's concern Dracula. He looks young but weak and has none of the powers of Stoker's character. He cannot transform himself into a bat, or anything else for that matter. At the same time, although the sun bothers him a little, he is not affected by it in the way Stoker's count is. He does not like garlic, but its consumption does not seem to have major consequences, and in one scene, he takes a crucifix and puts it in a drawer. Dracula has become more human in this portrayal. Indeed, he is hardly evil, and we feel sorry for him when he dies.

The connection he makes at the end with the spinster is both pathetic and moving, and the audience's sympathy (at least mine) is with him.

The role of Harker in Morrisey's movie is intended to be taken by the gardener, although Harker's purity and selfless love is transformed into something very different in the movie. The servant spends most of his time in bed with two of the sisters, but his interest in them is exclusively prurient, and he often insults them and even roughs them up a bit. Moreover, the political formulas he spouts about a decaying aristocracy, the exploited proletariat, and the future revolution, while concomitantly doing his work on the sisters, are stale Marxism. The only hint of true love in the movie is found in the old spinster's feelings for the count. The role of Mina is taken up by the youngest sister, who is saved by the servant, although in ways that would have raised eyebrows in Stoker's time. The two promiscuous sisters may be intended to take the place of the three lascivious women that accost Harker in the count's castle in Stoker's story, and perhaps also of Lucy, once she has become a vampire. The characters of Van Helsing, Seward, and Morris are missing, and Morrisey has added the droll roles of the Marquesses.

Herzog's *Nosferatu*

This is the most visually beautiful version of *Dracula* to date, and the acting is superb. It is a remake of Murnau's film, shot simultaneously in German and English in various picturesque locations in Europe. Like Murnau's film, it departs in important ways from Stoker's text, although the legal reasons that may have prompted many of the departures in the earlier film did not apply any longer. The story is very similar to Murnau's and bears no restatement. But Herzog added significant elements and elaborated some of Murnau's insights.

At least three major changes need to be noted: First is the appearance and behavior of the count. He looks more like a sick man than a threatening monster. He is bald, very thin, and dressed in a long black coat, but he is diffident and appears weak, as if he were very tired. His speech is slow, not like Lugosi's in Browning's *Dracula*, but because of lack of energy. We hear his labored breathing throughout the film. He looks hopelessly sad, a defeated man.

This picture is emphasized by a second departure from Murnau and Stoker: Dracula complains explicitly about his fate, inspiring pity and sympathy. He tells Harker how terrible it is to be unable to grow old. "There are things more horrible than death. Can you imagine enduring centuries experiencing each day the same?" And to Lucy, in her bedroom, he moans, "Death is not everything. It is more cruel not to be able to die." He longs for love: "I wish I could partake of the love between you and Jonathan. . . . The absence of love is the most abject pain." He looks miserable, painfully aware of the hopelessness of his suffering and his endless loneliness.

Also important is the ironic and humorous twist added to the end. Dracula is destroyed by Mina and Van Helsing, but Harker becomes the new Dracula, one full of energy, for he is new to this "life." Having been bitten by the count, the disease has done its work, and Harker grows to look like Dracula, with rodentlike teeth, a pale visage, and a malicious reddish shine in his eyes. Ironically, Van Helsing is sent to jail for the murder of the count.

Badham's *Dracula*

Just as with the other films discussed, this one changes substantial elements in the story, although the changes are different from those in the other films. Most significant is that, in this film, Dracula is portrayed as a handsome, debonair, and dashing aristocrat who attracts the attention of women. He does not force himself on them, but rather effortlessly seduces them. One of the high points of the film occurs when Dracula enters Lucy's bedroom and shares his blood with her. (In this movie, the original character of Mina is called Lucy.) Here, horror has given way to sensuality and tenderness, and although horror is not absent altogether from the film, particularly at the beginning, it ceases to be an important factor in the conception of Dracula. It would be difficult to imagine any woman being attracted to the horrific figure of Orlock in Murnau's film, or of Dracula in Herzog's *Nosferatu*. Indeed, in Morrisey's version, it is only the pitiful old spinster who falls for the count, and in Browning's film, only Lucy is attracted to Dracula. Langella's Dracula, however, is presented as an easy object of romantic feelings.

This is not the only departure from Stoker. The film opens with the sea raging against the ship that carries Dracula to England. Inside, the count is doing his grim job. The ship is beached, and Dracula abandons it in the form of a wolf. It is still in semianimal form that Mina finds him in a cave and succumbs to him. In Badham's film, Mina is presented as Van Helsing's daughter and plays the role of Lucy in the novel. She is spending time with Lucy, who is in turn presented as Dr. Seward's daughter and is engaged to Harker. Some characters are missing altogether.

Next, Harker is seen as taking charge of the count's property at the ship-wreck. Renfield is introduced as an agent of the count, and Dr. Seward sends the count an invitation to dinner. Then we find ourselves in the living room of Dr. Seward's home. Lucy, Mina, Harker, and Seward are waiting for the count, who makes a grand entrance. He captivates the general attention with his good looks and sophisticated manner. Mina is pale and looks at him with longing eyes, and Lucy is clearly captivated by his presence. Harker becomes particularly jealous when Lucy and the count dance romantically to one of Strauss's popular tunes.

After Mina inexplicably dies and is buried, her father is summoned. Be-cause Dr. Seward has to meet him at the station, Lucy goes to dinner at the count's dwelling by herself. The abbey is lighted with innumerable candles, and the conversation over dinner becomes intimate. Dracula warns her, but her attraction for him is unstoppable. The meeting seals their love.

Meanwhile, Van Helsing suspects the truth about Mina, but that night, Dracula visits Lucy, and they unite in a passionate love scene in which he takes her in his arms and carries her to bed, as a groom is expected to do with his bride. In a state of ecstasy, they drink each other's blood.

An encounter of Van Helsing with the count confirms the former's suspi-cions, and Van Helsing enlists the aid of Seward and Harker in a pursuit to de-stroy Dracula. The count takes Lucy with him, and the pursuers find them resting in Dracula's coffin. They succeed in taking Lucy away, but Dracula es-capes. They finally catch up with him in a ship bound for Romania. In a ter-rific fight, the count impales Van Helsing, and he is about to kill Harker when the half-dead Van Helsing throws a hook at his back, piercing it and, with Harker's help, lifting him out from the darkness of the ship's hold, all the way to the top of the mast, into the full light of the sun. Dracula burns while Lucy and Harker watch. After moments of agony in which Lucy suffers for him, Dracula appears to be dead, and Lucy, sadly, extends a hand to Harker. Then she sees the count's cape, flying away in the wind, in the shape of a bat. She smiles knowingly, happy to guess that he has somehow managed to survive.

Coppola's *Bram Stoker's Dracula*

Coppola intended his film to be an accurate version of Stoker's novel, and some critics claim that in fact it does rely more closely on the book than any previous film. Still, from its very beginning, it is clear that it deviates from the text in significant ways. For example, Dracula's initial colorful appearance as an old man dressed in a long red cape and with an elaborate coiffure is quite different from that suggested in the book, where he is always dressed in black and has a solemn demeanor.

The most important changes introduced by Coppola result from his attempt to answer the issues that Stoker left unresolved. Three of these stand out: the rationale for why Dracula became a vampire, the reason he pursues Mina in London, and the mode and purpose of his death. These are significant because they modify the character of Dracula, turning him into a romantic hero in a way that no other Dracula movie had done before. Dracula is portrayed as a tragic figure in the Greek heroic tradition: an extraordinary person who falls prey to a fault which is a byproduct of his strengths and pays a heavy price for it. Yet, at the end, there is redemption in suffering. Dracula becomes something of an Oedipus, inspiring respect, admiration, and pity. The romantic dimension lies in the role that love and death play in the story—Dracula dies for love.

The first two changes mentioned are introduced at the beginning and end of the film respectively, the two places where audiences are most effectively influenced by the action, but they color also the famous scene in which Dracula shares his blood with Mina. Indeed, these are also the three most dramatic moments in the film. Even audiences jaded by the seemingly endless number of bad Dracula movies cannot but be moved by their power.

In the prelude, Coppola tells the story of Vlad the Impaler, a fifteenth-century Romanian prince who is the basis for the supposedly historical Dracula. He battles the Turkish hordes that were invading his country in 1462, after the fall of Constantinople. Elisabeta, who is Vlad's love, knows the odds are against him, and, expecting defeat, she believes a false message sent by the Turks. Thinking that her lover is dead, she commits suicide rather than face life without him. When the victorious Dracula returns, he learns of Elisabeta's suicide and is told by a priest that her soul cannot go to heaven because of it. In a fit of fury in the chapel where her body lies, he renounces Christ and swears to rise from death and summon all the powers of darkness in revenge. Taking out his sword, he strikes at the cross, which bleeds profusely. He then gathers some of the blood in a golden cup and defiantly drinks it. This apparently transforms him into Dracula.[2]

Dracula's identification of Mina with Elisabeta provides the rationale for why he pursues Mina in London. When he sees a picture of Mina that Harker has carried with him to the castle, Dracula believes her to be the reincarnation of Elisabeta and hopes to recapture his long lost love. Once he arrives in London, he pursues her relentlessly as a lover, and she in turn falls in love with him. In one of the three most dramatic scenes of the film, they share each other's blood. They both desire it, but Dracula's love for Mina makes him plead with her not to drink his blood; in spite of what appears to be unbearable passion, he is willing to sacrifice it for her well-being. However, she refuses his sacrifice, and they consummate their union.

Perhaps the most dramatic moment of the film occurs at the end, when Dracula is pursued by Morris, Holmwood, and Seward, who, with the encouragement of Van Helsing, have sworn to destroy the count. They reach him before the sun goes down, and Harker drives a sword through his chest. Dracula staggers, but before the pursuers finish the job, Mina interferes. She and Dracula are then allowed to enter the chapel where originally Dracula had faced the corpse of Elisabeta. The count, transformed into one of his animal-like appearances, is kissed by Mina, and at that moment, her love releases both her and Dracula from the power of darkness: love proves stronger than death and evil. In a final moment of drama, Mina pushes the sword completely through Dracula's chest, and he again looks young while he dies. She immediately cuts his head off. He is now redeemed, and she is free.

Stoker conceived Dracula as the incarnation of evil, a malicious, perverse, and cruel monster. Coppola, by contrast, portrays him as a great tragic knight who sins because of his inordinate love for his beloved. He pays for this excess by becoming everything that he was not, until love again redeems him. The horror that Dracula inspires in Stoker's novel is changed in Coppola's version into admiration for Dracula's extraordinary character and pity for his fall and the fate he endures.[3] There are a few scenes in the film in which Dracula is portrayed as horrific, but this happens only when he feels attacked and in peril, and never in relation to Mina. Dracula's true nature is revealed in his love for her, and this ultimately saves him.

THE PROBLEM

Four of the films considered here explicitly claim to be based on Stoker's book, at least one of them was intended as a faithful rendition of it, and all six deal with Count Dracula. Yet all six films introduce substantial changes in the story. Some changes are the result of the different medium; a film cannot do the same things that a written work can do. For example, films need to be relatively short, whereas a written work can have thousands of pages. Even the longest movies rarely go much beyond three hours. Indeed, none of the films discussed is much longer than a couple of hours, and some are considerably shorter. In a film, much of the written material needs to be abbreviated, consolidated, or left out altogether. Moreover, in films, visual images are directly presented to the audience and take precedence over words, whereas in a written work, images are always mediated through words, the primary medium of meaning. It is one thing to imagine Dracula climbing down a wall and another to see him do so. Both films and text leave out different things, and different things are made more specific or clear in them.[4] For example, Stoker seldom dwells on the garments used by his characters, but films cannot avoid presenting us with persons whose clothes are evident. And the detailed inner states of consciousness of the characters described in the book are often rendered in abbreviation through facial expressions in the films. Finally, sound and music are important factors in films but are missing in a written work.

These and other differences resulting from a change of medium are significant and pose interesting questions. Here I shall not deal primarily with these, but rather with changes that are not particularly medium related. Let me begin by recounting a few examples taken from the films described earlier, some of which concern the story line and some the characters.

First, the location of the action changes. In Stoker, the two primary locations are Transylvania and London. The first is kept in all of the films, but the second is changed in two of them: London becomes Bremen in the *Nosferatu* films and a town in Italy in Morrisey's film.

Second, the point at which the story begins is also changed. In Stoker's novel, it is in Bistritz, after Harker had started his trip to Dracula's castle, but none of the films follows the story in this. Murnau's *Nosferatu* opens in Bremen with Hutter's preparations for the trip to Transylvania. Browning and Herzog begin with a scene in the coach where Renfield travels to Transylvania (in Herzog, this is preceded by a bat flying into undefined space). Morrisey's film opens in Transylvania, when the count is considering how to address his precarious situation. In Badham's version, the action starts at sea, on the ship that is transporting Dracula to London. And in Coppola's film, the story of Vlad the Impaler is presented first, as a prologue.

Third, many different dimensions are added in the films that are missing in Stoker. For example, Morrisey's film contains strong elements of sex, eroticism, nudity, ironic political commentary, gore, and humor. We see much flesh from the two sisters who are the first targets of Dracula and the male servant who cooperates with them. We are also presented with explicit sexual situations and activities as well as what comes across as Marxist political dribble from the servant. The scene in which Dracula is hacked to death is as gory as anything currently popular in movies, and humor and irony are evident throughout.

Sexuality and eroticism are also present in Badham's and Coppola's films, although neither contains the explicit sexuality and nudity of Morrisey's version. These two films, and Browning's version, also bring out a romantic dimension related to Dracula that is missing in the others. In Stoker's novel and in Murnau's *Nosferatu*, there is love and romance, but these do not involve Dracula. But Browning has Lucy attracted to Dracula. Langella's portrayal makes Dracula the object of erotic attraction by Lucy and Mina, and there is more than sex in the feelings that they and Dracula share with each other. In Coppola's film, love is at the center of the story: it causes Dracula to become a vampire, it leads him to sacrifice himself for Mina, and it eventually redeems him. In Herzog's film, we do not see any love exchanges except between Lucy and Jonathan, but the count longs for love, and in the scene in which he feeds on Lucy, his hand pushes up Lucy's gown and caresses her thighs with evident desire.

Fourth, the conditions of vampirism change considerably in some of the movies. According to Stoker, light seriously weakens vampires, but for Morrisey, it constitutes only a minor inconvenience. In Stoker, the effective method of destroying vampires is driving a stake through their heart and cutting off their head, whereas for Browning it is only the first. But in the *Nosferatu* films and Badham's version, light seems to be the decisive factor, although in Herzog's movie, Van Helsing cuts off Dracula's head. For Stoker, vampires need to sleep in their coffins and on dirt from their place of origin, but Morrisey's count sleeps on a bed, away from both his coffin and dirt from Transylvania. And in the novel, Dracula casts no shadow, but in the most terror-inspiring scene in *Nosferatu*, Orlock's shadow is projected on a wall.

Fifth, the role of horror changes in the films. Indeed, in some of the movies, horror is eliminated altogether or limited substantially, whereas in at least one it is emphasized. In Morrisey's *Dracula*, there is no horror to speak of, and in Langella's portrayal, Dracula inspires some fear but little horror.[5] Indeed, the horror in the movie is usually related to other characters, such as the undead Mina. And Browning's aristocratic Dracula seldom inspires horror. Likewise, Coppola's Dracula is rarely horrific, and never with Mina. Yet, for Stoker, horror is central to the story. Even in places where the count exerts attraction over females, they always speak of him with terror. By contrast, Murnau's *Nosferatu* goes well beyond the novel in horror, and Herzog's remake of *Nosferatu* also emphasizes horror, although Dracula himself is not so horrific.

Apart from these changes in the story, the movies also introduce substantial changes in the characters and their roles. First, some characters are added, and some are dropped. In Morrisey's *Dracula*, most characters present in Stoker's novel (Mina, Lucy, Harker, Van Helsing, Holmwood, and Morris) are dropped, whereas several others are added—two lecherous sisters, an old spinster, a young virgin, a solicitous mother, an irresponsibly gambling father, and the central figure of the male servant. Holmwood, Morris, and Seward also disappear in the *Nosferatu* films. In Murnau's *Nosferatu*, the names of the characters and some roles are modified: Mina becomes Ellen and is presented as Hutter's (i.e., Harker's) wife from the beginning; Renfield is renamed Knock and is turned into Hutter's boss (i.e., Mr. Hawkins); and Van Helsing, renamed Bulwar, is a professor who devotes his time to the experiments mentioned earlier. Herzog follows Murnau in some of this but introduces other changes: Lucy plays the role of Mina and is Harker's wife, Renfield is Harker's boss, and Van Helsing includes the role of Seward. In Badham, Lucy plays the role of Mina and vice versa; Seward is Lucy's father rather than one of her suitors, Van Helsing is Mina's father, and Morris and Holmwood are missing altogether. And in Browning, Renfield occupies center stage, taking the place of Harker in the trip to the count's castle, while Seward is Mina's father, and Holmwood and Morris drop out.

More than anything else, however, it is the changes in the central figure of the story that mark significant departures in the films. First, there are changes in Dracula's outward appearance. In Murnau's *Nosferatu*, Orlock is a kind of monstrous, rodentlike, repugnant creature whose sight is sufficient to inspire terror. Morrisey's count looks puny and pitiful. In Herzog's *Nosferatu*, the count looks sick, and his manner is diffident. By contrast, Browning presents him as an elegant aristocrat of the old school, and in Badham he is handsome and fashionable. And Coppola's Dracula appears alternatively as a colorful old man, a heroic knight, and a brooding lovesick gentleman. All of these contrast with Stoker's portrayal of the count as a thin, commanding figure, dressed in black, with piercing eyes.

Second, Dracula's moral value also changes. The count, a paragon of evil for Stoker, becomes a victim of circumstances in Morrisey's *Dracula*, a man aware of his horrible fate in Herzog's and Browning's movies, an attentive lover who wants to make Lucy his queen in Badham's film, and a self-sacrificing hero for Coppola.[6] Indeed, there is a marked evolution in this character. It begins in one direction with Murnau's *Nosferatu*, where Dracula becomes a creature whose mere sight inspires more horror than that suggested by Stoker. But it moves in a different direction in later films, away from this horrific conception. Browning's count seldom inspires horror, and the same is true for Herzog, whereas Morrisey's Dracula does not inspire horror at all, but rather pity and sympathy. Langella's count is attractive, an object of love rather than horror. And Coppola's protagonist turns into a hero worthy of admiration.

The path from Murnau's personification of horror to Coppola's romantic and heroic knight goes through stages. Some of these take place in films we are not considering here. But even in the six films discussed, we can see the evolution. First, the horrific characterization of Murnau's is effectively undermined first in Browning's portrayal of Dracula as an elegant aristocrat capable of inspiring romance, and then in Herzog's and Morrisey's films, when horror begins to fade and eventually gives in to pity: Dracula becomes an object of sympathy. Once this is accomplished, more appealing properties are added in the next step. This is illustrated by Badham's film, with its representation of Dracula as dashing, handsome, lovable, and loving. Finally, Coppola moves one step further and portrays Dracula as heroic and self-sacrificing.

The evolution is away from horror, but the means used to accomplish it differ somewhat in different films. I see at least three ways in which this deemphasis on horror takes place. One is through the introduction of a romantic element. This is first timidly introduced through the attraction of Lucy to Dracula in Browning's film, and is given full impetus in Badham's and Coppola's films. A second line in which horror is undermined is by the introduction of humor. This is most obvious in Morrisey's film, and also timidly in the ironic turn with which the tale ends in Herzog's *Nosferatu*. A third way used to deemphasize horror is through sympathy, caused by the awareness of Dracula's humanity and suffering. We get a hint of this in Browning's movie, when Dracula refers to fates worse than death. But it is by Herzog and Coppola that this is given full rein. In the first, Dracula talks explicitly about his suffering; apart from the reference to worse fates than death, he laments an endless, loveless life. In Coppola, we often see the tragic hero's plight echoed in the movie.

Curiously, in this evolutionary process, some of the laudable features of some of the key characters in Stoker's novel are transferred to Dracula. Harker's self-sacrificing heroism in the novel is transferred to Ellen in Murnau's film and Lucy in Herzog's *Nosferatu*, but ultimately rests with the count in Coppola's version. The objects of true love and devotion in Stoker are primarily Mina and Lucy, and to some extent Harker, Seward, Holmwood, and Morris, but in the films, this changes. In four of the films, Dracula becomes a primary object of romantic interest, love, or devotion: in Browning's, for Lucy; in Morrisey's, for the spinster; in Badham's, for Mina and particularly Lucy; and in Coppola's, for Mina. The role of devoted lover is played primarily by Harker in Stoker, but to a lesser extent by Seward, Holmwood, and Morris. But in Badham's and Coppola's films, the main devoted lover is Dracula. Tenderness is something that Stoker's Dracula never has; this quality is reserved for Mina and Harker in particular. However, in the films by Badham and Coppola, the count is the epitome of tenderness with Mina. And Herzog's Dracula is not tender but longs for the kind of love shared by Lucy and Harker.

These changes are both profound and significant, and they pose the question raised at the beginning of this chapter concerning the relation between Stoker's novel and the films we have been considering: how should we think of their relation?

INADEQUATE ANSWERS

Four main ways to answer this question suggest themselves. The first—call it the *topical view*—considers Stoker's novel and each of the films as independent works that explore a common topic, and it is this topic that justifies gathering them into a group. We could say, for example, that all of them deal with the character of Dracula, with vampires, or with both. A second—call it the *essentialist view*—considers them as being tied essentially. This requires all these works to satisfy certain conditions that are necessary and sufficient to qualify as members of the group. A third understands this relation as a kind of family resemblance: the conditions that apply to each work do not necessarily have to apply also to all the other works, although there may be common elements between any one of these works and at least some other work in the group. And a fourth considers the films to be interpretations of Stoker's novel. This would not preclude their status as works, but it would require them to be tied in some way to Stoker's book.

The first of these understandings of the relation between Stoker's *Dracula* and the films is inadequate for a variety of reasons. To say that Stoker's novel and the films are independent works which happen to deal with a common topic ignores the nonreciprocal history that ties the films to the novel. These films are based on Stoker, even if they change significant aspects of the story. They directly depend on Stoker's *Dracula*, something we could not say about films such as *Shadow of the Vampire*. This way of conceiving the relation between the six films and the novel does not account for the unique relation of Stoker's work to the films. Four of the films explicitly acknowledge being based on Stoker's novel, and even Murnau's *Nosferatu*, which does not acknowledge its debt to Stoker, is based on the novel, as documented by the successful legal action taken by Stoker's widow against its producers.

The topical view would make sense if we were speaking about works on vampires in general, for in this case we have a certain concept that is the basis of elaborations. It might even make sense to talk this way about Dracula films and stories in general when these are centered on the character of the count rather than on Stoker's novel. To do so would make room for works such as *Shadow of the Vampire*, which deal with Dracula but are not based on Stoker's book, or even for Anne Rice's novels and films, which concern vampires in general, but not Stoker's novel.

The essentialist view faces the problem that there seems to be no core of features common to all these works. Indeed, the changes that are introduced in the films are substantial and are at the center of the story. But even if there is a core of elements that all these works share, it is rather insignificant. Consider Morrisey's *Dracula*. What does this work have in common with Stoker's novel and the other films apart from the fact that the main character of the novel and the films is a count from Transylvania who feeds on human blood and gets killed? Indeed, the kind of blood on which the count feeds, the very conditions of vampirism, and the mode of his death are not shared by all of them. The burden to point to a set of significant elements that run through all of these works is just too great for the essentialist view to be successfully defended.

The family resemblance view also encounters difficulties in that it seems to open the doors to an endless number of works that would have to be considered part of the family. To refer to an example already cited, why should we exclude *Shadow of the Vampire* from the group we are considering, when in many ways there is much that this movie has in common with some Dracula films and even Stoker's novel? Indeed, in many ways, this film has more in common with some of the works we have considered than some of these works have among themselves. Are we entitled to accept Orlock, the main character in Murnau's *Nosferatu*, as a version of Dracula and reject the main character in *Shadow of the Vampire*, who appears to be the count himself? The family resemblance view may be useful to account for the relation of various works to a particular story or a character (say Faust, Don Juan, or even Dracula), but not for the relation between the kind of film we have been discussing here and Stoker's novel.

The inadequacies of the three solutions presented reveal something about the conditions that an adequate account should satisfy. The view that conceives this relation in terms of a common relation to a story or character does not properly explain the lack of reciprocity between Stoker's novel and Dracula films. Moreover, this position is too weak insofar as it makes it difficult, if not impossible, to draw a line between Dracula films and other films. The family resemblance view is similarly weak, failing to explain why these films can in fact be seen as somehow together, but separate from other films with similar topics. And the essentialist view fails because it is too strong. The problem with it is that it is not likely that one can find a strict set of conditions that are satisfied by films such as the ones we have discussed. We need a view, then, that avoids as strong a claim as essentialism makes, while making exclusion possible and maintaining a distinction between the films and their literary source.

A PROPOSAL

One way to do this is to conceive the relation in which Stoker's novel stands to the films as a work to its interpretations. Prima facie, this might sound lame, but I submit that it is not. However, in order to support this claim and explain what this position entails and how it functions in the case we are considering, I need to say a few things about interpretations in general.

Interpretations can be taken in at least two senses. In one, an interpretation is a kind of understanding of a work. In this sense, understandings that someone may have of Aristotle's *Metaphysics* or of Stoker's *Dracula* are interpretations of these works. But interpretations can also be works themselves, related in some specific ways to the works of which they are interpretations. In this sense, Aquinas's *Commentary on Aristotle's "Metaphysics"* is an interpretation of Aristotle's *Metaphysics*. Clearly, in this case the interpretation is itself a work that can in turn be the subject of other interpretations in both senses mentioned.

Regardless of whether one is concerned with interpretations as understandings or as works, they can also be classified in terms of their function. In one, the function of an interpretation is to understand a work or its meaning. If I write a commentary on Aristotle's *Metaphysics* with this primary aim in mind, for example, then the function of the interpretation would be to facilitate the understanding of the work by others. Let us call these *work-oriented interpretations* because their primary function concerns the work under interpretation.

But an interpretation may also have as its primary function to relate the work or its meaning to something else, such as historical facts, other works, societies, certain theories, special effects that interpreters want to produce, particular contexts, prevailing views or attitudes, and so on. The list here is endless, for a work or its meaning can be related to practically anything, even if it does not make sense to relate it to some things. If someone were to write a book on Stoker's novel with the intent of showing how the novel revealed certain aspects of Freudian theory, this would be an interpretation of this sort. The *relata* in this kind of interpretation are the work that is under interpretation on one hand and something else that is brought in by the interpreter on the other. The aim of this interpretation would not be an understanding of *Dracula*, but rather of the relation between *Dracula* and Freudian theory. Let us call this kind *relational interpretations*, to contrast them with work-oriented interpretations.

Of course, the interpreter may intend to produce an understanding of a work, and not of its relation to something else, but nonetheless may hold that the only way to do so is through some means outside the work. A Freudian interpreter of *Dracula* may want to understand the work but may also hold that the only way to understand Stoker's novel is in terms of Freudian theory. Freudian theory is the means necessary to get at the work, just as Greek is a necessary means to get at Aristotle's *Metaphysics*. In this case, the interpretation intended is work oriented, but the interpreter has a view of the world or of the method of producing interpretations that makes it necessary to relate the work to Freudian theory. Clearly, this is a work-oriented interpretation, but one that comes with certain baggage, and the baggage can be put into question. Does Freudian theory really make sense? Is Freudian theory necessary to understand *Dracula*? In these cases, we have several issues at stake: the interpreter's commitment to a certain theory, the interpreter's commitment to a certain theory as a proper means of interpreting a work, and the accuracy of the interpretation. It is important to keep these in mind when judging an interpretation.

I do not mean to argue that work-oriented and relational interpretations are always, or even frequently, kept apart. Most interpreters engage in the interpretative process without a clear distinction about these in mind, and they often mix different kinds of interpretations and objectives. Nor do I claim that work-oriented interpretations do not contain relational elements. Indeed, they often do. Most interpretations of Aristotle's *Metaphysics*, for example, refer to historical facts that are not part of the text and thus are brought into the interpretive process by the interpreter. The point to keep in mind, however, is that the establishment of the relation of these facts to the work need not be the primary function of the interpretation. And, indeed, if what we have is a work-oriented interpretation, then this function is rather to understand the work itself, and the relations the work has with these facts are used merely as ways to enhance that primary function.

Likewise, I do not claim that relational interpretations ignore the work or its understanding. Most of them do not. But this understanding is mediated through the primary aim of causing some other effect or achieving some other end, such as relating the work to a historical event. So, even though work-oriented and relational interpretations are seldom found in isolation from each other, and there are relational elements in work-oriented interpretations and work-oriented elements in relational interpretations, it is still useful to keep this distinction in order to facilitate the understanding of interpretations and their relation to the works they interpret.

The two distinctions I have drawn here can be used to explain the relation of Stoker's novel to the six films we have been discussing. The first distinction, between interpretations considered as the understanding of a work and those considered as works whose aim is to produce an understanding of the work, is useful because the six films in question are themselves works that can stand on their own. In this, they are not different from Stoker's novel. So, clearly they cannot be interpretations when these are taken as understandings. Rather, they must be taken as interpretations of the second sort, that is, as works intended to produce an understanding.

The second distinction, between work-oriented and relational interpretations, is even more pertinent. The first are interpretations focused on a work; the second aim at establishing or exploring the relation between a work and something else. This distinction explains the divergence between Stoker's novel and the six films we have considered, without having to fall into any one of the inadequate positions examined earlier.

These films are intended to stand on their own, as works in a new medium, although related in some way to Stoker's novel. Moreover, the films are not intended primarily to provide us with an understanding of Stoker's work; they are intended to do something else primarily.

What was Murnau trying to do in *Nosferatu*? His aim seems to have gone well beyond the understanding of Stoker's book. This seems quite evident when one considers the changes he introduced in the story, particularly in its central character. Count Orlock is without a doubt intended to inspire horror and repulsion in the audience. His deformities, the important role that rats play in the film, the slow pace at which he moves, and the shadowy and desperate mood that permeates the film introduce us to a dark and frightening world. Murnau seems to have wanted to create a world of extraordinary horror, and he succeeded. Moreover, he tried to present a story that shifted the burden of destroying the vampire from a competitor for the object of his desire to that very object. Ellen, rather than Hutter, destroys Nosferatu. And the vampire's destruction was achieved through love and self-sacrifice rather than violence. Clearly, Murnau's agenda was very different from Stoker's, and it was in this context that he used Stoker's book. Stoker's work is viewed through its relation to this agenda, which produces a relational interpretation.

Herzog's remake of Murnau's film clearly has as an agenda. Even more than Murnau, Herzog seems intent to make Lucy (Ellen, for Murnau) a true heroine—perhaps the modern woman, independent and able to make decisions for herself. He is obviously also concerned with visual and musical beauty. And he undermines the monstrosity of Dracula, presenting him trapped in his fate. Is this an allegory for our condition?

Browning's portrayal of Dracula as an appealing aristocrat points to another aim. Evil is now dressed in elegant clothes and can even be romantic. The message has been changed; the aim of the interpretation has a different direction from that of Stoker's work.

In Morrisey's film, we are again treated to a different agenda. Here the count is presented as weak and harmless, a truly pathetic figure. Horror is completely gone, and instead we are engaged in pity, humor, irony, and political commentary. Morrisey presents us with a piece of social criticism, both political and sexual. Virgins are scarce, even in a proverbially religious country like Italy, so virginity seems to be a hypocritical front for the upper classes in society, rather than a reality. Only ugly and very young women are virgins. The old aristocratic system is corrupt, but Marxism seems to amount to no more than stale, conveniently memorized formulas.

Critics frequently point out that Badham's *Dracula* seems to be intended as an exploration of the relation between horror and sensuality, but this may not be entirely right, because the role of horror is drastically diminished in the film. This is evident in the changes introduced in Dracula's appearance. Indeed, one could argue that the movie is intended to show how love and sensuality have the power to banish horror, for horror generally occurs in contexts that do not involve Lucy. Regardless of the correct explanation, however, it is clear that something else, in addition to Stoker's novel, is at play here and that it is the relation of this to the novel that determines which elements of the story are emphasized or changed.

Coppola set out to fill in what was missing in Stoker's tale, and in doing so he transformed Dracula into a romantic knight of heroic proportions, a tragic figure saved in the end. Whether his primary aim was to present a rationale for Stoker's novel or to reconceive the character of Dracula, he modified the story and its main character substantially as a result of it. Again, an idea is used to deal with Stoker's book, and the film that results is an outcome of that relation.

In all six cases, the films have an agenda that goes well beyond the understanding and representation of Stoker's novel. In part, the agenda is possible because of a change in context. Today, much more explicit sexual content is possible than in Stoker's time, for example. But this is not all, or even what is most important. The changes go beyond a desire to make the story more titillating, or even to understand the implications of Stoker's novel for the present day. Each film aims at the realization of an idea presented in the context and trappings of Stoker's book. A particular conception of Dracula not based on Stoker's novel is brought into the picture, and the story, as narrated by Stoker, is then presented in that light.

If I am right, we now have the answers to two of the questions posed at the beginning of this chapter, and we can also surmise the answer to the third. The three questions were, Can we justifiably hold that the six films discussed are interpretations of Stoker's novel? If they are interpretations, what kind are they? And what implications do the answers to these two questions have for the understanding of popular interpretations of literary works?

The answer to the first question is affirmative: yes, the films are interpretations of Stoker's book. To the second: they are relational, rather than work-oriented, interpretations. And, with respect to the third question, we need only say that the popular interpretations of literary works, such as Stoker's novel, often fall into the relational variety. They tend to be works that are themselves intended to relate the work of literature to factors extraneous to it. This allows the interpretations to introduce changes that otherwise would justify a different characterization of their nature, while maintaining a connection to the original work.

Why is this important? For at least two reasons. First, this explains the popularity of such interpretations. Relational interpretations can follow socially contextual leads that draw the attention of the public at large in ways that other kinds of interpretations do not. They can easily adapt themselves to the interests and needs of new audiences and social contexts. Work-oriented interpretations are often too scholarly, archaic, and stuffy to be of interest to the general public. Their emphasis is on the understanding of the original work in its historical context, and they tend to lose audiences whose interests are the here and now.

Second, it allows us to formulate better criteria for judging the value of popular interpretations of literary works. This is significant because it is one thing to consider films, such as the ones we have examined here, as independent works whose relation to Stoker's novel is irrelevant, and another to think of them as interpretations of that work. If the first, their value is completely divorced from a relation to Stoker's novel, but if they are considered interpretations of it, then it is not. It is one thing to think of and judge them on their own, and another to do so as interpretations of Stoker's book. But if they are regarded as interpretations, then it is also important to keep in mind the kind of interpretations they are, for work-oriented interpretations cannot be judged by the same criteria as relational ones. Unfortunately, it is common to find critics who adversely judge popular interpretations of literary works because they fail to meet the standards one would expect work-oriented interpretations to meet. Moreover, we also find responses to these that opt for the artificial separation of popular relational interpretations from the literary works on which they are based in order to provide favorable evaluations.

FILM INTERPRETATIONS OF STOKER'S *DRACULA*

The larger issue that has concerned me here is the relation of certain films to the literary works on which they are based. I have approached this issue by raising it in the context of the relation between six Dracula films and Stoker's famous novel. I considered three inadequate ways in which this relationship could be characterized. In one, the films and Stoker's novel are considered independent works dealing with common subject matter. In a second, they are considered to have an essential core of elements that they share. In a third, they are regarded as forming a kind of family, the members of which share some resemblance.

In place of these inadequate characterizations, I proposed to conceive the films as relational interpretations of Stoker's novel that are themselves works in their own right. And I suggested some reasons why this model could also be effective for the characterization of other popular interpretations of literary works. Whether the model is effective or not, however, will depend also on other factors. In the case of Mel Gibson's *The Passion of the Christ*, for example, the factors at work have to do with historical accuracy and the kind of text of which the film is an interpretation.[7] Other cases pose other challenges, but that is a story for another time.

NOTES

I am grateful to Paul A. Cantor, Noël Carroll, Cynthia A. Freeland, and William Irwin for their suggestions.

1. Some may disagree with this, insofar as Mina could also be considered a heroine. See Cynthia A. Freeland, *The Naked and the Undead: Evil and the Appeal of Horror* (Boulder, CO: Westview, 2000), 134. The point does not affect, one way or another, my argument here.

2. Apart from the heroic elements, Coppola's rendition also has religious overtones. See Freeland, 137–38, 142.

3. If Noël Carroll is right about the nature of horror, Coppola's film violates the rules of this genre insofar as in it the emotion of the characters and that of the audience are supposed to be synchronized, but they are not. Noël Carroll, *The Philosophy of Horror: Paradoxes of the Heart* (New York: Routledge, 1990), 18.

4. Although films often contain texts, generally they cannot be considered texts unless the notion of text is inflated. I dispute this view in Gracia, *A Theory of Textuality: The Logic and Epistemology* (Albany, NY: State University of New York Press, 1995), chap. 1.

5. I take it that fear and horror are not the same thing. One can fear things that do not necessarily inspire horror, such as death, contagion, and pain. See Carroll, 22.

6. But there is more to them. For example, Badham's Dracula speaks of making a new ruling race from his offspring with Lucy, and he is arrogant in demeanor and aristocratic in his thinking.

7. See my "How Can We Know What God Means? Gibson's Take on the Scriptures," in *Mel Gibson's* Passion *and Philosophy: The Cross, the Questions, the Controversy*, ed. Jorge J. E. Gracia (Chicago: Open Court, 2004), 137–50.

10

Socrates at Story Hour: Philosophy as a Subversive Motif in Children's Literature

Gareth B. Matthews

Morris, the moose, meets a cow. "You're a funny-looking moose," Morris says. "I'm a cow," the cow protests; "I'm no moose."

Morris persists. "You have four legs and a tail and things on your head," he points out quite correctly. "You're a moose," he concludes.

"But I say MOO," the cow objects.

Morris is unimpressed. "I can say MOO, too," he boasts.

The cow is not stumped. "I give milk to people," she says; "moose don't do that."

Morris remains unimpressed. "So," he says, "you're a moose who gives milk to people."

The cow then plays her trump card. "My mother is a cow," she points out.

Morris is unfazed. "She must be a moose," he rejoins coolly, "because you're a moose."

"What can I say?" pleads the cow.

"Say that you're a moose," replies Morris.

Morris and the cow look for a third party to adjudicate their dispute. They spot a deer.

"What am I?" the cow asks the deer.

"You have four legs and a tail and things on your head; you must be a deer," says the deer.

"She's a moose, like me!" shouts Morris.

"You're no moose," retorts the deer; "you're a deer, too."

The three go off together to find another judge. They come upon a horse, who greets them with "Hello, you horses," and then adds, "What are those funny things on your heads?"

Before the four of them seek yet another judge of their identities, they stop to drink from a cool stream. Looking at the reflection of himself in the stream, Morris decides that he is much better looking than the others, so much better looking, in fact, that the others can't be moose after all. The deer sees *his* reflection in the stream and decides that *he* is so much better looking than the others that they can't be deer. In the end, the moose, the cow, the deer, and the horse all recognize each other for what they are: a moose, a cow, a deer, and a horse.

NATURAL KINDS AND CONVENTIONAL KINDS

I remember reading *Morris the Moose*[1] to our first child, and later to her younger sister and brother. The first copy I bought, which we still have almost a half century later, is printed on cheap paper with black-and-white drawings.

Recently, I bought the latest edition of *Morris the Moose*.[2] It is an "I Can Read Book" fitted out with drawings in full color and a bad pun for a new ending. (On the last page, Morris is now made to admit, "I made a MOOSE-take!" Ugh!) But otherwise the plot is the same.

With the skill of a poet, the author, Bernard Wiseman, teases us into reflection on our animal classification system and the species it is meant to capture. His choice of a moose as the main character in his story is inspired. For one thing, a moose is strikingly marked with those "things on its head." Moreover, most of the book's readers, even the adults among us, are likely to be a little shaky about what exactly a moose is, and how a moose is related to a cow and a deer, but especially, perhaps, how a moose is related to an elk, a caribou, and a reindeer. A parent or teacher may be quizzed by a curious child on what the differences between these animal kinds are. Asked that question, most of us would be left mumbling that a moose has bigger, "clunkier," antlers, or something of the sort. But, even if that is right, why should having bigger, clunkier antlers make an animal anything more than a bigger, clunky-antlered reindeer? Most of us couldn't say.

I am not suggesting that *Morris the Moose* be considered a good introduction to the classification of animals—what is called "taxonomy." I am suggesting instead that it is a good first sample of a philosophical children's story. Why?

When Morris comments to the cow at the very beginning of the story, "You're a funny-looking moose," he makes two natural moves in one. First, he does something akin to anthropomorphizing; he assumes, without further thought, that the cow is the same kind of being he is. But, second, he assumes that obvious differences between him and the animal in front of him point up deficiencies in that animal. The cow, he thinks, is a "funny-looking" moose.

Another thing to note about this story is that what these animals are primarily interested in with respect to each other is not what philosophers would call their "accidental features," that is, whether this one has brown fur, whereas that one has white fur with black spots, or whether this one has blue eyes and that one brown eyes. What they are primarily interested in is their essential nature, their kind.

It was Aristotle who gave us the animal classification system we still use today. To be sure, Linnaeus (1707–1778) and other taxonomers have modified the system somewhat. But what we use today to classify animals and plants is still, basically, Aristotle's system.

It was also Aristotle who taught us to think of an animal's essence or nature as a stable cluster of features that normally gets passed on in reproduction. My essential nature, on this view, is something I have in common with all other human beings. Differences between me and other human beings, such as height, intelligence, and skin color, are accidental features and do not make me a different kind of being from someone with a different height, a different level of intelligence, or a different skin color.

Aristotle realized that it is no easy matter to distinguish those features that yield a different species from those features that mark variation within a species. We are much more conscious of the difficulties today, partly because we, unlike Aristotle, suppose that a new species may evolve from chance variations in individual organisms, that is, chance genetic mutations. Still, even if population biologists today would rather talk about gene pools than species, most of us, most of the time, even if we are biologists, continue to think about human beings and other animals by reference to Aristotle's classification scheme.

Like us, Aristotle also thought of artifacts, and their classification, in analogy to biological species. A tricycle, we are inclined to suppose, is not just a bicycle with an extra wheel; it is, instead, a different kind, a different "species," of self-propelled vehicle. And a motorcycle is not just a bicycle with an engine, but, again, another kind of two-wheeled vehicle.

One philosophical question that *Morris the Moose* raises is whether the moose, the cow, the deer, and the horse are indeed *real* kinds, as opposed to merely *conventional* kinds, or, as a philosopher might say, merely "nominal" kinds. Aristotle was impressed by how stable the biological species are. Think of songbirds. Every year, cardinals and blue jays and house finches (among a large number of other species) come to our birdfeeder just beyond the kitchen window. Every year, male cardinals mate with female cardinals, male blue jays with female blue jays, and male house finches with female house finches. Soon we see baby cardinals, blue jays, and house finches, immature birds that will grow up to look exactly like their parents. It is hard not to think of the reproduction of kinds of songbirds the way Aristotle did, as parents (he thought it was the father) passing on the cardinal form, or species, to the offspring, or the blue jay form or the house finch form, to the respective offspring.

Does a bird or animal of one species ever mate with a bird or animal of another species? Yes, we know that that sometimes happens. And Aristotle knew that too. Aristotle was particularly interested in the fact that a horse may mate with a donkey and thereby produce something different from each parent, namely a mule. But mules, as Aristotle also knew, tend to be sterile, as if to demonstrate that the natural offspring of a horse is another horse, and the natural offspring of a donkey is another donkey. These reflections tend to suggest that biological kinds are real and not merely conventional. Certainly Aristotle thought they suggested that conclusion.

One thing that makes the choice of a moose so instructive in *Morris the Moose* is that biologists actually consider a moose a kind of deer. So when the deer in the story says to Morris, "You're no moose; you're a deer too," what he should have said instead is, "You are a moose *and* you are a deer too." But one couldn't know that for sure without doing a little biology.

What about artifacts? Are there any real kinds among them, or are all kinds merely conventional?

It is quite plausible to say that kinds among artifacts are merely conventional. But we shouldn't be too smug about saying that. Consider the question about whether a motorcycle is a bicycle with an engine, or whether a bicycle is a motorcycle without the motor. What we should note here, I think, is that motorcycles did indeed evolve from pedaled bicycles. Indeed, it is still possible to get bicycles with a small motor that can be engaged to make it easier for the cyclist to get up hills.

Having noted that motorcycles evolved from bicycles, and not the other way around, we should also note that motorcycle design has moved far, far away from its bicycle heritage. A standard motorcycle today is quite unsuitable to be pedaled, even if the engine could be removed from it to leave pedaling as a last resort. Since motorcycles, like bicycles, are a human invention, there is something conventional about their nature. But, since motorcycle design has evolved in such a sophisticated way, it also seems appropriate to say that human society has, in the motorcycle, developed a distinctive kind of vehicle that is, indeed, a real kind of vehicle. Similar lines of thought might be pursued with respect to chairs and stools, say, or walking sticks and umbrellas.

When my own children were young, I invented a game in which we all had to make up definitions of artifacts and decide which ones were naturally appropriate and which were simply ad hoc. Thus, for example, we might decide that it is natural and correct to say that a stool is a chair without a back, but not correct to say that a chair is a stool with a back. Oftentimes our ideas about how artifacts evolved would play an important role in determining which definitions were natural and which not.

SUBVERSIVE SOCRATES

I have chosen *Morris the Moose* as my first example of a philosophically subversive children's story. I have already said something about the philosophical questions the story invites us to raise—questions about biological taxonomy, about taxonomy in general, about the idea of a species, and about the difference between essential features of a thing and its accidental features. Let's suppose you agree that this children's story is philosophical in the sense that it invites us to think about these issues. I still haven't said anything about why I consider the story subversive.

There are several different ways of being subversive in philosophy. One way is to become a skeptic. Skepticism has a very long tradition in philosophy. Skepticism was one of the great "schools" of Hellenistic philosophy. The writings of ancient skeptics culminated in Sextus Empiricus's great work, *Outlines of Pyrrhonism*. Skepticism was, and remains, an unsettling position in philosophy. It is subversive in that it unsettles our natural assumptions about our relation to ourselves and the world around us.

The stories I want to call to your attention, however, do not invite skepticism. Thus they are not subversive in that way. How then?

Well, another way to be philosophically subversive is to promote philosophical relativism. Again, relativism has a long and distinguished history in philosophy. It goes back at least to the ancient sophists. In the dialogue *Theaetetus*, Plato has Socrates characterize the views of the ancient Greek relativist, Protagoras, with the slogan, "Man is the measure of all things." Socrates interprets the slogan this way: "As each thing appears to me, so it is for me, and as it appears to you, so it is for you" (152a). Thus we cannot correctly say that the wind is hot or cold, only that "it is cold for the one who feels cold, and for the other, not cold" (152b).

Relativism is rampant in our society today. To many, if not most, of the college students I teach, relativism is the "cool" position to take. But relativism is also unsettling. Some of my students find it attractive just because it calls into question societal assumptions.

Certainly a children's story could be philosophically subversive by encouraging philosophical relativism. But the stories I have in mind are not subversive in that way. Instead, my model for philosophical subversion is Socrates. Socrates, as you will recall, went around asking the top people of Athens what piety is, what courage is, what justice is, and what virtue is. The top people of Athens were not able to say, at least not in a way that satisfied Socrates. Socrates concluded that he was wiser than they, simply by not thinking he knew what others thought they knew.

Of course, the top people of Athens came to resent Socratic questioning and eventually executed Socrates. Nobody likes to be shown up. Certainly the top people of Athens didn't. But, instead of trying to hold onto their pretences and resenting the way Socrates had exposed those pretences, they should have dropped them and joined with Socrates in the pursuit of philosophy.

The stories I want to call to your attention, and I think they belong to a prominent vein of children's stories, are philosophical by problematizing some important concept, typically a concept we don't see how we could do without. A child who reads one of these stories, or hears it read by an adult, naturally asks questions about the problematic concept or one of its applications. For example, the child who hears the story *Morris the Moose* may become puzzled about how we classify animals and why. That child may not have a well-defined concept of a species, or the concepts of essence and accident. But the child may wonder why we call something a moose and something else a deer, and what difference it makes.

Carolyn Korsmeyer tells us, in her contribution to this volume, that she is using *philosophy* as a "success" term. In her usage, *philosophy* refers to "works demanding imaginative engagement that results in the recognition, and perhaps the acceptance, of a philosophical position."[3] By contrast, I am here using *philosophy* as a "task" word, rather than as a "success" or "achievement" word.[4] My aim is to provide compelling examples of children's stories that problematize concepts and so challenge readers, whether children or adults, to clarify those concepts in their own minds so as to eliminate what is puzzling and problematic about them.

Asking questions about taxonomy, or about essentialism, is subversive because it challenges the assumed authority of adults, whether they are parents or teachers. Adults often assume, and lead the children around them to assume, that they, as adults, should be able to answer satisfactorily any question a young child is capable of asking. At most, they think, all they will need to do is look up the relevant information in an encyclopedia—or, these days, on the Internet. But a genuinely philosophical question about taxonomy, or about essence and accident, cannot be answered easily by consulting the Internet. And so the presumption of epistemic authority that many adults automatically accept is challenged. Fortunately, embarrassed parents and teachers are unlikely to put to death, the way Socrates was put to death, the children who ask them philosophical questions they cannot answer. But they are indeed likely to cover up their inability to respond to the philosophical question with an easy answer. So they may say, "We can talk about that when you're older," or they may use some other diversionary tactic to avoid having to do philosophy with their children.

Of course, the best thing to do when a child is moved to ask an interestingly philosophical question is to think *with* the child about what a good answer might be. Adults who do not put themselves on an epistemological pedestal with respect to their children may have the great blessing of enjoying a genuinely philosophical conversation with their kids. Genuinely philosophical conversations with kids foster respect for the children, as well as for the questions they raise and the puzzlement they express.

BUT IS IT ART?

Here is another philosophically subversive story. It's *Leese Webster* by Ursula K. LeGuin.[5]

Leese was a spider, born in the throne room of a deserted palace. Like every other member of the family (the "Webster" family), Leese knew, without having to learn, how to spin an elegant and efficient web of traditional design (the "spider-web" design!). She spun one, then another. Then, forsaking her heritage, she set out to produce webs of original design.

In her new creative freedom, Leese began to weave designs like the petals of flowers portrayed in the carpet of the throne room, even designs like the huntsmen, hounds, and horns in a painting on the wall. No doubt her images were at least twice removed from reality. But were they pictures at all?

"An image is not a picture," Wittgenstein tells us, "but a picture can correspond to it."[6] Perhaps, then, the designs in Leese's webs were images, but not pictures.

Sometimes one can see flowers or hunters in the clouds, or in driftwood. Could a cloud depict a hunter? Could a piece of driftwood do so? What about a piece of driftwood that has been sanded, shellacked, mounted on a base, and labeled "Hunter"? If the sanding, shellacking, mounting, and labeling make a difference, what difference do they make? And suppose a cloud could be frozen in its most suggestive shape and exhibited?

A visiting Webster, scornful of one of Leese's fancy webs, asked, "Will it catch flies?" "Not very well," admitted Leese; "the old pattern works better for that." A little embarrassed at having to give such an answer, Leese set out to make her webs more efficient. After a time, she was able to make fancy webs that would catch flies quite as well as those in the traditional pattern. (Of course, even good art can be functional.)

One day, cleaning women arrived. They came prepared to dust the webs away. But they stopped, struck by the beauty of Leese's tapestries. "Spiders can't make pictures, dear," said one, knowingly. Should the other cleaning woman have responded, "Yes, but they can make images"?

One cleaning woman ran off to tell "the Authorities," who had the webs carefully encased in glass and put on exhibit. Did the encasing change the metaphysical status of the webs? Suppose they were also labeled for exhibition. Would that have mattered?

With the webs safely preserved for posterity, the cleaning women returned to the task of cleaning up the throne room. In their dusting, they dusted Leese right out of the window.

Leese was at first devastated and then exhilarated by her move to the out-of-doors. She found her new "room" already "splendidly decorated" with leaves and flowers. But, hungry for a fly, she spun a web anyway. At dawn the next day, she was distressed to see that her web was dotted with drops of water. Then, when the sunshine shone on her handiwork, she saw that this web, with its jewels of refracted light, was "the most beautiful web I ever wove."

Suppose it turned out that those male birds of a given species that produce the songs we find aesthetically most pleasing also stand the best chance of mating successfully. And suppose that the female spiders of a given variety that spin webs we find most charming live, on average, a longer life—even though they don't catch more flies. Might we conclude that such data would establish that female birds of that species have an aesthetic sense, and that aesthetically gifted spiders lead more satisfying lives? Or do we know something about birds and spiders that would guarantee that such a reading of the data is fanciful and inappropriate?

And what about the remains of an ancient human civilization? Can we know that those beautiful bits of pottery belong, encased, in an *art* museum, before we know whether in that ancient society there was an intent to produce art? Or even the intent to depict leaves and flowers, or hunters? "Well," someone might say, "at least it can be art for us." And so also, perhaps, can the webs of Leese Webster.

Leese Webster offers a delightful opportunity to do some philosophy of art with children—but only to an adult willing to drop the pretence that adults should be able to answer any question a young child can ask.

PRETENCE AND DEVIANCE

Here is another philosophically subversive story.

Treehorn noticed one day that he couldn't reach the shelf in the closet where he usually hid his candy and bubble gum. Strange. He also realized that his clothes were too big for him. He seemed to be shrinking!

Neither Treehorn's mother nor his father would take any notice of the situation. "Do sit up, Treehorn," they scolded him at the dinner table.

"I *am* sitting up," Treehorn protested; "this is as far up as I come."

Treehorn's mother explained that it was all right to pretend to be shrinking, as long as Treehorn didn't do it at the dinner table.

"But I *am* shrinking," Treehorn insisted.

"Nobody shrinks," said Treehorn's father, who spoke with great authority.

Eventually Treehorn's parents did take in the fact that Treehorn was really shrinking. But, of course, they didn't know what to do. Neither did the school bus driver, or Treehorn's teacher.

When Treehorn told the school principal that he was shrinking, the principal said that he was very sorry. "You were right to come here," he added; "that's what I'm here for, to guide, not to punish, but to guide." Still, he had no guidance for Treehorn.

Home again, Treehorn retreated to his room, where he found a game to play. It was called "The Big Game—For Kids to Grow On." Treehorn played the game. As he played, he grew—except that when he reached the size he used to be, he stopped playing the game. (End of story.)

The most obvious fact about children is that they are small. A child may be too short to reach the door knocker, or to get a drink from the drinking fountain. Children who live in apartment buildings with elevators may measure their growth by seeing how many buttons they can reach without having to be lifted up by mummy or daddy.

Although tables and chairs at school may be the right size for children in kindergarten or second grade, for most of the furniture of the world, children are misfits. They are the naturally handicapped. When we call children "the little people," we may express affection, but we also express condescension.

Size is important in our culture, but especially height. A few people are, of course, too tall. Except among basketball players, excessive height is also a handicap. But to be a little taller than one's peer group, especially among boys, is a very good thing.

A second fact about children—not quite as obvious as the first, but equally important—is that they are essentially in transition. In particular, they are growing. True, they grow at different rates. One seventh grader may be as tall as the teacher, or even taller, whereas another could still pass as a fifth grader. But all of them, even the tall ones, are in transition.

In fact, all of us are really in transition. We're in high school preparing for college. Or we're in college preparing for "the real world," or for graduate or professional school. Or we're single preparing for marriage, or married preparing for children. And all along, there is the advancement to senior status, the "golden years," and then death.

Of course the "normal" transition through life's stages is often cut short, dramatically these days, with school killings, AIDS, and violence on our city streets. Still, the pattern of a standard progression through life, with adulthood up to retirement as the normative plateau toward which childhood is taken to aim, is built into our ways of thinking about what it is to be a human person.

When Treehorn deviates from the expected progression toward becoming a standard, fully real, adult human person, his parents are unable to see what is happening. When Treehorn deviates from the norm by actually shrinking, we sense immediately that this is either comedy or tragedy. Florence Parry Heide's whimsical writing style, in her classic tale *The Shrinking of Treehorn*,[7] tips us off that this is comedy. And Edward Gorey's mock antique drawings remove any lingering doubt. Yet the joke is on us, especially on those of us parents, teachers, and counselors who undertake to guide and nurture children's growth. For we, many of us, have such unyielding preconceptions as to how children should be developing that we fail to notice what is happening in and to the real children around us.

One thing that has made this story a favorite among children, I strongly suspect, is the way it mocks adult pretence and their concern with what the neighbors will think. When a girl becomes a tomboy, this may or may not be a family problem. But when a boy wants to wear dresses, this is almost sure to be a family problem. When Treehorn's mother finally sees that her son is shrinking, she asks her husband, "What will people say?"

"Why, they'll say that he is getting smaller," replies the father, in what is surely his best line in the story. But just when the father has won a few points with enlightened readers, he blows it all by adding, "I wonder if he's doing it on purpose, just to be different." How we adults like to be in control, even if it is only by analyzing the motivation of our kids.

The shrinking of Treehorn is a metaphor for deviance in child development. As parents and teachers, we all want our children to develop "normally," perhaps also to excel, but not so as to become "oddballs," and certainly not to retrogress. Most of us adults assume that our children should develop in roughly the ways that we did, or anyway, in the way we *like to think* we did. But that may well not happen, either because they as individuals are too different from us, or because the society in which they are growing up is too different from the one we grew up in.

What makes *The Shrinking of Treehorn* subversive is not only the way it exposes adult pretence to ridicule. Also subversive is the way it problematizes the idea of child development and the conception of normalcy that goes with it. Ideas of normal development in children—physical, emotional, social, and intellectual—can certainly be a great help in understanding our children. But those ideas can also lead us to stereotype our children and treat them, not as individuals, but as age types. Children can help us to accept the fact that they may be different from their peers, or from the way we think of ourselves as having been at their age. A subversive story like *Treehorn* can be the stimulus for discussing the possible oppressiveness of our developmental models and of the expectations we have for our children.

POST HOC, ERGO PROPTER HOC

When I am asked to recommend a children's story that is clearly philosophical, I often pick one of the stories from Arnold Lobel's remarkable collection, *Frog and Toad Together*.[8] The second story in the collection is called "The Garden." It goes this way:

Frog was in his garden.

Toad came walking by.

"What a fine garden you have, Frog," he said.

"Yes," said Frog. "It is very nice, but it was hard work."

"I wish I had a garden," said Toad.

"Here are some flower seeds. Plant them in the ground," said Frog, "and soon you will have a garden."

"How soon?" asked Toad.

"Quite soon," said Frog.

Toad ran home. He planted the flower seeds. "Now seeds," said Toad, "start growing."

Toad walked up and down a few times. The seeds did not start to grow. Toad put his head close to the ground and said loudly, "Now seeds, start growing!"

Toad looked at the ground again. The seeds did not start to grow. Toad put his head very close to the ground and shouted, "NOW SEEDS, START GROWING!"

Frog came running up the path. "What is all this noise?" he asked.

"My seeds will not grow," said Toad.

"You are shouting too much," said Frog. "These poor seeds are afraid to grow."

"My seeds are afraid to grow?" asked Toad.

"Of course," said Frog. "Leave them alone for a few days. Let the sun shine on them, let the rain fall on them. Soon your seeds will start to grow."

That night Toad looked out of his window. "Drat!" said Toad. "My seeds have not started to grow. They must be afraid of the dark."

Toad went out to his garden with some candles. "I will read the seeds a story," said Toad. "Then they will not be afraid."

Toad read a long story to his seeds. All the next day, Toad sang songs to his seeds. And all the next day, Toad read poems to his seeds. And all the next day, Toad played music for his seeds.

Toad looked at the ground. The seeds still did not start to grow. "What shall I do?" cried Toad. "These must be the most frightened seeds in the whole world!"

Then Toad felt very tired, and he fell asleep.

"Toad, Toad, wake up," said Frog. "Look at your garden!"

Toad looked at his garden. Little green plants were coming up out of the ground.

"At last," shouted Toad, "my seeds have stopped being afraid to grow!"

"And now you will have a nice garden too," said Frog.

"Yes," said Toad, "but you were right, Frog. It was very hard work."

Some years ago, I sat on an advisory committee for a series in children's literature produced for television by an educational TV station in Boston. The advisory committee was made up of academics, like me, who were supposed to lend respectability to the literature series. More crassly, having professors from well-known universities, including Harvard and Princeton, was supposed to make it more likely that the TV station would be able to raise money for its series from the National Endowment for the Humanities. (My understanding is that we successfully performed that function.)

At one meeting of our committee, we screened a number of TV animations of children's stories, including, as I recall, "The Wind in the Willows," two or three folktales from central European countries, and Arnold Lobel's "The Garden," the story I have just recounted. Some of the committee members, being specialists in children's literature, were able to point out the literary merits of this or that story. Some members, being developmental or educational psychologists, were able to point out ways in which this story or that would or would not be appropriate for a preschool child, or for a second or third grader. But my fellow committee members all took a rather condescending attitude toward the frog-and-toad episode, "The Garden." Its vocabulary is certainly very simple. It is, like the second edition of *Morris the Moose*, an "I Can Read Book," which means that the vocabulary is deliberately restricted. The characters, Frog and Toad, are also rather simply drawn. The episode certainly has none of the *literary* complexity of, say, "The Wind in the Willows." My colleagues on that advisory committee pointed out these limitations in solemn tones and gave the story only a qualified "pass."

After listening for a while to that condescending assessment of "The Garden," I finally could stand it no longer. "The collection of stories from which

'The Garden' comes, *Frog and Toad Together*, is," I asserted, "a philosophical classic." I listed the other stories in the collection, mentioned the philosophical questions they raise, and, for each question, pointed to a classic discussion of that question in Plato or Aristotle or Hume or Descartes. "As for 'The Garden,'" I said, building up to my climax, "that story exposes, in simple language worthy of a great poet, the classic fallacy, post hoc, ergo propter hoc, 'after this, therefore because of this.'" The story, I explained, is about causality and about how we can distinguish a true cause, in this case, the true cause of the seeds growing, from preceding events that in fact have no causal efficacy. Causality, I went on, remains a much discussed and highly problematic concept in philosophy. Hume's skeptical stance toward establishing anything as causal necessity continues to present a challenge. But what are called "Mill's Methods," in honor of John Stuart Mill, might provide practical help in considering what Toad ought to do the next time he plants seeds.

As for the causal efficacy of reading poetry or playing music to make seeds grow, there are, I pointed out, commercial suppliers who sell music makers to help gardens grow, and my colleagues in botany even report that academic botanists are quite gingerly considering whether they ought to include research on the psychology of plants at their annual professional meetings.

My outburst had the effect of ending the condescension toward "The Garden." Perhaps my colleagues were most impressed by the Latin phrase, "post hoc, ergo propter hoc," which I threw at them in my effort to generate respect for Arnold Lobel's story. They laughed good-naturedly and teased me a bit after the meeting, but even the most eminent authority on children's literature on our committee, and he is really quite eminent, admitted that he had failed to appreciate the profundity of this simple story.

Causality certainly is problematic, both in general and in a particular case such as Toad's garden. My wife frets about what she needs to do to keep her orchids blooming. The metaphor for her insecurity is her worry about whether she has a "green thumb," either in general, or for orchids in particular. It's fun to discuss these issues with children, perhaps in connection with houseplants, or with some school botany project.

THE COPPER MAN AND CONSCIOUSNESS

Suppose a parent or teacher were to take up the challenge I have laid down here. Suppose that adults were to welcome a child's questions about one of the stories I have retold, were even, perhaps, to encourage a discussion of the philosophically problematic concepts of taxonomy, essentialism, art, child development, or causality. Would anything really significant result? I am going to add to the last story I recount for you something from a discussion of this story with some third and fourth graders I read this story to.

This passage from chapter 4 of Frank Baum's *Ozma of Oz* is one of my favorites:

Standing within the narrow chamber of rock, was the form of a man—or, at least, it seemed like a man, in the dim light. He was only about as tall as Dorothy herself, and his body was round as a ball and made out of burnished copper. Also his head and limbs were copper, and these were jointed or hinged to his body in a peculiar way, with metal caps over the joints, like the armor worn by knights in days of old. He stood perfectly still, and where the light struck upon his form it glittered as if made of pure gold.

"Don't be frightened," called [her companion, the hen,] Billina, . . . "It isn't alive."

"I see it isn't," replied [Dorothy], drawing a long breath.

"It is only made out of copper, like the old kettle in the barn-yard at home," continued the hen, turning her head first to one side and then to the other, so that both her little round eyes could examine the object.

"'Once," said Dorothy, "I knew a man made out of tin, who was a wood-man named Nick Chopper. But he was as alive as we are, 'cause he was born a real man, and got his tin body a little at a time—for the reason that he had so many accidents with his axe, and cut himself up in a very careless manner."

"Oh," said [Billina], with a sniff, as if she did not believe the story.

"But this copper man," continued Dorothy, looking at it with big eyes, "is not alive at all, and I wonder what it was made for, and why it was locked up in this queer place."

"That is a mystery," remarked [Billina]. . . .

Dorothy stepped inside the little room to get a back view of the copper man, and in this way discovered a printed card that hung between his shoulders, it being suspended from a small copper peg at the back of his neck. She unfastened this card and returned to the path, where the light was better, and sat herself down upon a slab of rock to read the printing.

"What does it say?" asked [Billina], curiously.

Dorothy read the card aloud, spelling out the big words with some difficulty; and this is what she read:

SMITH & TINKER'S
Patent Double-Action, Extra-Responsive, Thought-Creating, Perfect-Talking

MECHANICAL MAN
Fitted with our Special Clock-Work Attachment
Thinks, Speaks, Acts, and Does Everything but Live

"How queer!" said [Billina]. "Do you think that is all true, my dear?"
"I don't know," answered Dorothy, who had more to read. "Listen to this, Billina:"

DIRECTIONS FOR USING:
FOR THINKING:—Wind the Clock-work Man under his left arm, (marked No. 1.)
FOR SPEAKING:—Wind the Clock-work Man under his right arm, (marked No. 2.)
FOR WALKING AND ACTION:—Wind Clock-work in the middle of his back, (marked No. 3.)

"Well, I declare!" gasped [Bellina], in amazement; "if the copper man can do half of these things he is a very wonderful machine. But I suppose it is all humbug, like so many other patented articles."
"We might wind him up," suggested Dorothy, "and see what he'll do." . . .
Dorothy had already taken the clock key from the peg.
"Which shall I wind up first?" she asked, looking again at the directions on the card.
"Number One, I should think," returned Billina. "That makes him think, doesn't it?"
"Yes," said Dorothy, and wound up Number One, under the left arm.
"He doesn't seem any different," remarked [Billina], critically.
"Why of course not; he is only thinking, now," said Dorothy.
"I wonder what he is thinking about."
"I'll wind up his talk, and then perhaps he can tell us," said the girl.
So she wound up Number Two, and immediately the clockwork man said, without moving any part of his body except his lips:
"Good morn-ing, lit-tle girl. Good morn-ing, Mrs. Hen."[9]

I have discussed this passage with children of different ages and in many different countries. One of the most memorable discussions I have had took place in an elementary school in Newton, Massachusetts, near Boston. The children were third and fourth graders who had volunteered to join my discussion group.

I asked these kids whether a robot could think.

"There's no proof," said both Ross and Sam, "that a robot cannot think."

Rachel suggested that a real brain could be put into a robot and then the robot could think.

Nick was unimpressed. "If it had a real brain," he objected, "it wouldn't be a machine."

More discussion revealed that, of the dozen children in this discussion group (ages nine to ten and a half), only Matt thought that a robot could be constructed that would actually have real thoughts. I urged the others to produce an argument that might convince Matt he was wrong. And I suggested to Matt that he might think of an argument to win over the others.

Ross and Sam remained pessimistic about settling this question with an argument. There is no proof one way or the other, they kept saying. They were inclined to agree with Nick that a robot with a living brain, if such a thing were possible, wouldn't really be a robot anyway. But Sam was skeptical that such a thing could be put together. He seemed to be concerned about whether one could make all the needed connections so that the living brain could tell the robot body what to do.

I persisted in my request for an argument. "Can anyone think of an argument to prove that something like Tiktok [the robot in the story above], that isn't alive, cannot have real thoughts?" I asked.

Finally Paul obliged. "A way of proving it," he said, is this. The only thing that can think is a brain. And the only things that have brains are people and animals. And even if we did put a brain inside a computer, like Nick said, it wouldn't be a computer anymore, or a robot.

Paul's statement of the case wowed me. Elegant reasoning like that is what I hope to get from my university students, but seldom do. It was presented with the confidence of a professional.

Of course Paul didn't formulate his argument unaided. He developed it out of the preceding discussion. But that is part of what made the argument impressive. It puts together succinctly and perspicuously all the main considerations the group discussion had turned up. I was pleased with it on two levels. On the most basic level, I was glad for the confirmation that Paul and some of the others in the group had come to understand the value in trying to find premises from which one could put together a logically compelling argument for the conclusion one is interested in defending. People in our society certainly have the idea of an argument as an outspoken disagreement. If you say that bad-minton requires more skill than table tennis, and I insist, perhaps vociferously, that the reverse is true, we have an argument, but not in the sense of *argument* that a philosopher is most likely to be interested in. Paul, though not yet ten years old, showed that he knew exactly what I wanted when I asked for an argument. Moreover, he was able to use the general discussion to provide him with the materials he needed for his argument. Furthermore, the argument he was able to come up with, drawing on the discussion of those nine- and ten-year-olds, fits right in with what many professional philosophers are saying these days. As John Searle puts it in his book *The Mystery of Consciousness*,[10]

> We know that human and some animal brains are conscious. *Those living systems* with *certain sorts of nervous systems* are the only systems in the world that we know for a fact are conscious. We also know that consciousness in those systems is caused by quite specific neurobiological processes.

Of course there are philosophers, good philosophers, who disagree with Searle. But the point I want to make is that Paul and the other children in that group were fully able to join the contemporary discussion of consciousness—the discussion of what consciousness is and of which entities might have it. They do not have to wait until they become university students to take part in that conversation. And a classically Socratic children's story, like the one about Tiktok, can be the stimulus for awakening their intuitions and stimulating their reasoning generators.

SUBVERT THE DOMINANT PARADIGM

Here is my conclusion. There is a rich vein of children's stories that prob-lematize important concepts, such as the concept of art, the concept of a cause, the concept of an essence, and the concept of consciousness. Children, even young children, can enjoy these stories and even enjoy thinking about and discussing the philosophical issues they raise. But to invite a discussion of these matters with children is to subvert the epistemological dominance hier-archy we assume in our society. I say that we should prize these stories and let them open up for us adults and our children a thoughtful discussion of the is-sues they raise. We should, in the words of the popular bumper sticker, "sub-vert the dominant paradigm"; in particular, we should subvert the assumption in our society of adult epistemological authority. One of the best ways I know to do that is to read Socratic children's stories with our kids and encourage discussion with them of the issues those stories raise.

NOTES

1. Bernard Wiseman, *Morris the Moose* (New York: Scholastic Book Services, 1959).

2. (New York: Harper Collins, 1989).

3. This volume, page 31.

4. For the contrast between "success" or "achievement" words and "task" words, see Gilbert Ryle, *The Concept of Mind* (London: Hutchinson's University Library, 1949), 149–52.

5. (New York: Atheneum, 1979).

6. Ludwig Wittgenstein, *Philosophical Investigations*, trans. G. E. M Anscombe (Oxford: Basil Blackwell, 1967), 301.

7. (New York: Dell, 1971).

8. (New York: HarperCollins, 1972).

9. L. Frank Baum, *Ozma of Oz* (Chicago: Rand McNally, 1907), 40–46.

10. (New York: New York Review of Books, 1997), 170.

11

Of Batcaves and Clock Towers: Living Damaged Lives in Gotham City

James B. South

My parents taught me a different lesson. . . . Lying on this street—shaking in deep shock—dying for no reason at all—they showed me that the world only makes sense when you force it to.

—*Bruce Wayne in* Batman: The Dark Knight Returns[1]

I made a promise to my parents that I would rid the city of the evil that took their lives.

—*Bruce Wayne in* Batman: Dark Victory[2]

In Darwyn Cooke's *Batman: Ego*, we are given an account of a young Bruce Wayne's Christmas day and evening. The day starts nicely enough with gifts, family cheer, and Bruce's excitement over his new Zorro action figure. However, at Christmas dinner, Bruce's father, Dr. Thomas Wayne, receives a phone call updating him on a patient's health. He decides he must go visit the patient and has Bruce ride along with him. The patient dies, and as Dr. Wayne is covering the body, Bruce walks into the room and sees the dead body. Back in the car, Bruce expresses his confusion following his first experience with death, and the following exchange occurs:

> BRUCE: Are you and mom going to die?
> DR. WAYNE: Well, yes we will, Bruce. Everyone passes on. But not before our time. And that's a long way away.
> BRUCE: Promise?
> DR. WAYNE: I promise son.[3]

235

The sequel to this part of the story is well known: A few weeks later, the Wayne family goes to a movie, and, after the show, Dr. and Mrs. Wayne are shot and killed by a robber, leaving Bruce an orphan. Dr. Wayne was unable to keep his promise. This story points out the fact that promises are remarkably fragile human actions: ones made to specific people in particular circumstances, and which envision a future that may or may not come to pass. So, for example, one need only think about the high divorce rates in Western industrialized societies to recognize how "utopian" promises can be and how recalcitrant reality can be in knocking down the future envisioned by promises.

In this chapter, I want to try to juxtapose the stories told by some comic books, those set in Gotham City and involving Batman, Batgirl, and Catwoman, with issues raised by this fragility intrinsic to promises. I want to argue that these comic books provide us with an image of what I will call, following J. M. Bernstein, "fugitive ethics," that is, a kind of ethical action of which promises are paradigmatic.[4] While a positive description of what such ethical actions are available at the end of this chapter, for now it is sufficient to note two of their central features. First, fugitive ethical actions are actions that are available to us only under the conditions of late modern capitalism. As a result, fugitive ethical actions are ethical actions that are available to lives that are best characterized as damaged in a sense still to be specified. In what follows, I first characterize the understanding of modernism relevant for my discussion, and I then proceed to consider the ways in which lives lived under the conditions of modernism can be called damaged. After that, I will turn to a more extensive description of fugitive ethics. Throughout this chapter, I am providing an approach to the relation between philosophy and popular culture, one that points to a very close convergence of the aims that certain forms of philosophy possess and those aims that certain forms of popular culture possess.

I need to offer one methodological consideration before proceeding. Umberto Eco has talked about the dreamlike quality of superhero comic books, referring to the fact that there is always something more to be said with each new issue, while, nonetheless, "before" and "after" remain hazy.[5] There is a kind of eternal present involved in the experience of reading comic books. This makes talk about "continuity" between comic books very difficult. Geoff Klock has extended Eco's insight about comic book continuity by pointing to the way that "strong work comes to define truth."[6] In other words, certain comic books within a series tend to take on additional weight due to a variety of factors such as their especially high quality, their disproportionate influence on subsequent issues in the series, and their reception as canonical for a series. Many of the comics I discuss below have managed to attain to this level of strong work as generally recognized by the community of comic book writers, artists, and readers. Without disputing the account of strong works within a series, I would add this point: what constitutes strong work can be indexed to the concerns the reader brings to the texts. Thus, I have chosen these comics in part because they help illustrate my point, in part because they are generally recognized as among the best recent work in comics, and in part because of my experience of them. In Eco's dreamlike world of the history of comics, I am certain I could have found other books to illustrate my argument, just as I am sure there are comic books that point in a direction I do not follow here. More importantly, though, the comics I discuss here are comics that have made a strong impression on me, that have come to define a "truth" for me about the universe in which these comics take place and the light that universe sheds on our universe.[7] Yet, while the selection of comics to be discussed is thus ineluctably personal, that fact does not make the conclusion I want to draw idiosyncratic, though I recognize this as a promise to the reader that I can hope to fulfill only by providing the following discussion.

GOTHAM CITY AND MODERNISM

At the beginning of *Batman: Year One*,[8] we see Lieutenant James Gordon, newly appointed to the Gotham City Police Department, arriving in the city via train. Paralleling his arrival, we see the return of Bruce Wayne via airplane to Gotham City after an absence of twelve years. Gordon's arrival is drawn in black and white—gray sky, gray train; it's all wires, bridges, trestles, and train tracks. His internal thoughts in this first panel: "Gotham City. Maybe it's all I deserve now. Maybe it's just my time in Hell." In the second panel, we see the interior of the train: it's overcrowded, people are standing in the aisle, luggage weighs down the caging that is overhead. Gordon continues: "Train's no way to come to Gotham . . . in an airplane from above, all you'd see are the streets and buildings. Fool you into thinking it's civilized." When we see Bruce Wayne, it's from outside his plane. We see him as if he were alone without any of the overcrowding of the train. His thoughts: "From here, it's clean shafts of concrete and snowy rooftops. The work of men who died generations ago.

From here, it looks like an achievement. I should have taken the train. I should be closer. I should see the enemy."[9]

I now want to develop a conceptual apparatus that will help us to understand these two scenes and that will set the stage for a discussion of life in Gotham City. I begin with a definition of modernism. Since any such definition is likely to be contentious, I simply want to stipulate one for purposes of discussion, though it is one with which I agree. I borrow the description of modernism from John Patrick Diggins:

> What, specifically, is modernism? As a way of reacting to the modern world, modernism is the consciousness of what once was presumed to be present and is now seen as missing. It might be considered as a series of felt absences, the gap between what we know is not and what we desire to be: knowledge without truth, power without authority, society without spirit, self without identity, politics without virtue, existence without purpose, history without meaning.[10]

There are two aspects to this account of modernism that I want to emphasize. First, Diggins mentions a series of absences that cluster around the fact that meanings previously available to human beings are no longer available. One characteristic way of discussing these absences is by talking about the "disenchantment of the world."[11] As we shall see, the traditional resources for moral evaluation and commitment are among the most prominent of our losses and foster our disenchantment in a particularly significant manner. Second, while Diggins does not try to provide any content for the rather neutral term *feeling*, it seems worthwhile to have at our disposal a thicker, more descriptive understanding of the feeling generated by the absence of meaning. In fact, Diggins subsequently speaks of the "intellectual wounds of modernity," and I want to draw attention to that phrase.[12] Certainly, *wound* conveys content considerably less neutral than *feeling*, and it seems right that the feeling engendered by the disenchantment of the world be characterized by this richer, less neutral term. Moreover, this richer term begins to provide us with some sense of what is at stake in modernist understandings of our predicament.

For his part, Bernstein has delineated the ways that the good life as traditionally understood is no longer possible for us under the conditions of modernism. On his account, our lives as we currently live them are damaged.[13] There are two situations that stand behind this claim, one having to do with the social conditions in which we must live, the other having to do with the

way in which the scope of ethical action has been increasingly "privatized."
The foundational description of the social conditions under which we must
live our lives privileges Weber's concept of rationalization, and the most obvious success story of rationalization is science. Science is masterfully effective
and successful, and this effectiveness bestows on science an aura of authority.
The success of science breeds more success until, finally, we come to believe
that anything can be understood in principle, that is, that "we can master all
things by calculation."[14] This rationalization process is a key factor in the disenchantment of the world so keenly described in modernist thought. The second situation leading to damaged lives is Weber's famous "bureaucratization"
thesis wherein social relations are rendered calculable in accord with the ruling ethos of science. Under this condition, no social relation remains uncon-
taminated by considerations of efficiency, calculation, and the like. Indeed,
these considerations concerning efficiency coupled with the disenchantment
of the world account for Weber's description of the "iron cage" of rationality
that ensnares us all, warping our experience of the world and trapping us in a
set of social relations that can only be described as "wounding."[15] Given this
understanding of disenchantment, it makes perfect sense for James Gordon to
express skepticism toward the idea that Gotham City is "civilized," and perfect
sense for Bruce Wayne to view the city as "the enemy."

DAMAGED LIFE

If Gotham City can be viewed as representing a rationalized world—one that
wounds—then it should follow that its inhabitants are leading damaged lives.
How, though, can we best represent the notion of a damaged life? Bernstein
presents a compelling framework for this task by focusing on what he calls "affective skepticism": "a systematic separation between the rational and univer-
salistic norms of a rationalized practice, on the one hand, and the concrete,
unique agent-specific motivation for pursuing that practice on the other."[16] In
Alan Moore's famous *Batman: The Killing Joke*,[17] we can see a representation
of such affective skepticism.

This comic gives us an origin story for the Joker, one of Batman's most famous foes. In a series of flashbacks, we learn that the Joker, whose real name
we never learn in the comic, was a down-on-his-luck would-be stand-up comedian before the series of events that turned him into the Joker. He was married, and there was a child on the way; he had left a "good job" as a lab assistant

at a chemical plant in order to pursue his dream of becoming a comedian; and he was thus forced to prove himself as a husband and father. To try to provide for his family, he has involved himself with a couple of low-level criminals who are planning to rob a playing-card company. The most direct access to the playing-card company is through the chemical plant where the future Joker once worked. On the day of the robbery, the future Joker is told that his wife had a fatal accident at home. His two criminal cohorts force him to continue his part in the robbery. When the robbery goes wrong, his two cohorts are shot by the police. At that moment, Batman arrives, has the cops stop shooting, and goes in pursuit of the soon-to-be Joker. Batman pursues him until his only possible escape is to jump into a vat of chemicals. When he is flushed out of the vat into a sewer away from the plant, thereby escaping Batman, he discovers that the chemicals have left him permanently disfigured: his skin is white, his hair is green, and his face is permanently disfigured. This "one bad day" creates the Joker. The conjunction of his disastrous attempt to prove himself and the accidental death of his wife is more than he can take. He describes the result of this one bad day: "When I saw what a black, awful joke the world was, I went crazy as a coot."

The idea of proving something recurs in the Joker's criminal plan that unfolds in the book's present, with equally disastrous results. His plan is to prove to Batman that he and Batman are no different—indeed, that any person is simply a series of bad events away from craziness. This radical contingency is continually represented by imagery of cards and card playing, especially the joker card—what happens to us, it seems, is accidental. Without some master narrative for us to tell ourselves about the world and its sense, there simply is no sense; and the Joker has lost any narrative that could make the world sensible. The Joker mocks Batman in their final confrontation in an abandoned amusement park: "You have to keep pretending that life makes sense, that there's some point to all the struggling."[18] Before arriving at this final point, he had gone to Commissioner Gordon's apartment and had shot his daughter Barbara, he had stripped Barbara of her clothes as she lay paralyzed on the floor and had taken pictures of her, and he had kidnapped the commissioner. Later, in the abandoned amusement park, he tortures Gordon and shows him pictures of his naked, helpless daughter in an attempt to drive him mad, thereby proving his point that we're all just one bad day away from insanity. When Batman arrives at the park, he discovers that Gordon has not gone crazy, that, indeed, Gordon is determined that the Joker be brought in "by the book" to "show him that our way works." Batman confronts the Joker, who argues his case: "It's all a joke. Everything anybody ever valued or struggled for. It's all a monstrous demented gag. So why can't you see the funny side? Why aren't you laughing?" Batman responds: "Because I've heard it before and it wasn't funny the first time."[19] Once defeated, the Joker, former failed stand-up comic, tells a joke to explain why he can never let Batman help him:

> See, there are these two guys in a lunatic asylum . . . and one night, they decide they don't like living in an asylum anymore. They decide they're going to escape! So, like, they get up onto the roof. And there, just across this narrow gap, they see the rooftops of the town, stretching away in the moonlight. Stretching away to freedom. Now, the first guy, he jumps right across with no problem. But his friend, his friend daren't make the leap. Y'see . . . y'see he's afraid of falling. So then the first guy has an idea . . . he says, "Hey! I have my flashlight with me! I'll shine it across the gap between the buildings. You can walk along the beam and join me!" B-but the second guy just shakes his head. He suh-says . . . he says, "Wh-what do you think I am? Crazy? You'd turn it off when I was halfway across."[20]

The comic ends with both the Joker and Batman laughing at this joke.

It is clear that the Joker has succumbed to affective skepticism on a rather massive scale. If it makes sense to say that there can be a coherence in madness—and Joker's perfectly "rational" plan to prove that everyone is "one bad day" away from being like him certainly seems coherent—then the only motive he has for acting comes from features internal to his madness. And yet the proof he's offering bears all the hallmarks of an experiment. The Joker may be mad, but he understands and accepts the rudiments of rationalized thought. More formally, the Joker has lost touch with any values external to his practice, as is evident from his willingness to kill, wound, and torture people in an effort to prove his point. As an interpretation of the joke at the end of the story, I read the asylum as representing the disenchanted world that we all live in as a result of rationalization and bureaucratization. The challenge we face can be summed up nicely by recognizing that while it is possible to escape the asylum by various forms of flight, those forms are at the same time remarkably unstable strategies. The fear of falling is real, but the strategies available to us in a rationalized, disenchanted world are only various forms of fantasy, about as stable as a flashlight's beam.

One concrete way that Bernstein shows the damage done to us in our living lives under the conditions-of-modernism involves the debate between internalists and externalists in moral theory.[21] In brief, externalists hold that justifying reasons for moral actions and motivating reasons for such actions are in principle distinct, while internalists hold that they ought to converge. The externalist will try to justify a moral norm by appealing to abstract principles that are universally applicable in an attempt to show that (a) such moral norms apply to everyone and that (b) they transcend self-interest. Thus, in condemning theft, the externalist might provide reasons that work on an abstract level, say, respect for property or maximization of the greatest happiness for the greatest number, but that still leave me wondering why *I* should not steal. Part of the problem here is that, as Bernstein points out, any such justification aimed at everyone is likely to be "agent neutral"; but if the reason is not compelling to an agent, it need not be compelling to *me*. Moreover, it is simply part of our intuitive notion of morality that it should provide reasons that go beyond what may currently motivate me to act. Thus, the argument against theft should work even for those who are inclined to steal; but, again, that means there will be a disconnect between the set of beliefs and desires that motivate me to steal and the argument against stealing. It is difficult to see how to connect those two sets of reasons. Internalists argue that the only way to do so is by rejecting the externality of justificatory reasons. That is, any reason for action must be one that motivates me from the inside, as it were.

A standard objection to such a view is that any reason that is internally motivating to me must be one I can *already* accept, thus limiting my moral point of view to that sphere within which I have comfort, or, to put it another way, all my moral reasons would be ones that do not challenge *me*. The potential for a self-satisfied morality is all too clear. Bernstein's move, at this point, is very interesting. He essentially denies that there's any substantive moral difference between these two views, pointing out that pretty much any set of external reasons can be internalized:

> The fundamental objection to externalist theories, which in fact supports the claim that they are external, is not that they cannot in principle be incorporated into individuals' motivational sets (almost anything can) but that they are representative and functional components of a generalised experience of disenchantment and societal rationalisation that *hurts*.[22]

In other words, internalism as a position in moral theory is best viewed not as a theoretical demand, but as an expressive response to the disenchantment brought about by rationalization, a response that is necessary because the gap between motivational reasons and justifying reasons hurts us as we try to make our way through the world in morally responsive ways.

Given this experience of hurt, which is manifested philosophically in moral theory as a need for justificatory and motivational reasons to converge, it might be useful to think about responses to this experience of hurt. Bernstein mentions several expressions of this hurt brought about by disenchantment. Direct expressions of the pain we feel include disillusionment, alienation, boredom, and anger, while indirect expressions of this hurt manifest themselves in cynicism, focusing on one part of life in an attempt to make the whole meaningful, religious fundamentalism, obsessive consumerism, and a valuing of pure experience of an erotic or aesthetic sort.[23] Returning to *Batman: Year One*, it is worth noting what we see in the panels immediately following the ones that introduce us to Gordon and Wayne: Gordon is accosted by a religious cultist as he's getting off the train, while Wayne, the rich, single playboy, is accosted at the airport by television reporters. Here we see two of the most obvious forms of flight associated with the hurt of modern rationalized society: religious fundamentalism and an obsession with lifestyle.

Even if we can view Gotham City and its problems as the work of disenchanted reason, a further question remains. Why does scientific thought result in a disenchanted world? The answer to that question comes down to the fact that the overwhelming tendency of reason is to advance what Bernstein calls "identity thinking." The central feature of such thinking involves subsuming particulars under universals, where universals have the function of simplifying, making coherent, explaining, and unifying particulars. The dangers here are pretty obvious, since particulars are always richer than the universal under which they are subsumed. That is, universals, whether they take the form of concept terms or scientific explanations, leave out something about the particular that resists unification and identity.[24] Two items may be identical as they fall under a universal, but they are not identical as particulars. The tension, then, turns on whether one wants to criticize scientific rationalism for its omission of the relevant nonidentity characteristics of items, or accept science and lose the particular characteristics. Obviously, criticizing scientific rationalism is a risky act. If you focus, for example, on the way in which scientific rationalism has some nonrational foundation—a focus central to much twentieth-century philosophy from Heidegger to Kuhn—you simply fail to close the gap between justificatory and motivational reasons for acting. So, for example, if you want to say that the legitimacy of science rests on some historical accident, or the way in which it is inextricably tied to a discredited onto-theology, then motivational reasons will be *reasons*, but ultimately irrational. That is, the two sorts of reasons are not connected. But if that is the case, then motivating reasons are still subject to criticism from reason; that is, affective skepticism still looms as a likely result.[25] Of course, the other possibility that awaits is Joker-like: simply accepting the irrationality. Batman may laugh at the Joker's joke, but it is clear that he is the one who has jumped across the gap between the asylum and the world. How might he have done this, and, more importantly, how might he have done this while not giving into madness?

One possible response canvassed by Bernstein is that we may criticize rationality not because it is rational, but because it is not rational enough:

> Only an expansion of reason, rationality, and cognition will answer the dilemma of disenchantment; and if this expansion is to be keyed to the diagnosis of scientific rationalism as a process of systematically negating particularity in favor of universality (the movement of rationalization as identity thinking), then the direction of expansion will be the inclusion in reasoning of ineliminable moments of dependency and particularity.[26]

The features of dependence and particularity are crucial. By making reason recognize the contours of the world in ways that block identity thinking, it might be possible to rescue the intrinsic rationality of motivating reasons; that is, it might be possible to connect justification and motivation. However, the generality of this suggestion is problematic. What we need are examples of "ineliminable moments of dependency and particularity." One place to find such examples is by considering human actions that are irreducible to general principles and their application. The practice of promising is one such type of action.

PROMISES, PROMISES

In *Batgirl: Year One*,[27] we find out how Barbara Gordon becomes Batgirl (this is the same Barbara Gordon who, after retiring from her duties as Batgirl, is shot by the Joker). She is a successful, very bright young adult who is living a very unsatisfying (to her) life as a librarian. Her days behind a bank of computers at the library are hounded by a paralyzing tedium. She is misperceived routinely by others; that is, others are failing to see her particularity by their focus on her job, or her height, or even her status as daughter. She tries several ways to break out of her constrained life—she applies to the police academy and the FBI—but is rejected by each. She is looking for "anything that will get me out of where I am. Where I don't want to be."[28] For a costume party, she decides to go wearing a female variation of a Batman costume. By the end of the evening, she's been dubbed "Batgirl" and has come to the attention of Batman. When asked why she wants to be a costumed crime fighter, she responds, "You may have all the tools of the trade, but you don't have a monopoly on wanting to help. I'll tell you why, you big scary goon. Because I can." And she immediately adds, "I can see Gotham's future. And without people like you and pixie boots and me, this place doesn't have much to look forward to."[29]

On the surface, this portrayal of Barbara Gordon's motivation for becoming Batgirl would seem to contrast starkly with Bruce Wayne's story. When young Bruce Wayne saw his parents brutally murdered by a robber, he promised that he would rid Gotham City of such evil. For a long time, he saw this as a necessity forced upon him, something about which he had no choice. In his internalization of such an external demand, Bruce Wayne is the very embodiment of the damage done by a disenchanted world. Eventually, though, he came to see it as a choice he made: "I thought I didn't have a choice about being the Batman. That Gotham City chose me to protect her. That is wrong. Ever since the night my parents were taken from me, *I* made the choice. It is a *good* choice."[30] The circumstances under which Bruce Wayne came to see that he had made a choice involved the renunciation of a chance at a romantic relationship. In denying one future, he claims the present and its future for himself. In short, I think there is a nice parallel here between the choice Barbara Gordon makes ("because I can") and the choice Bruce Wayne makes. Why I think this is significant will take a bit of working out, but will involve two points, one having to do with the purely human status of Bruce Wayne and Barbara Gordon, while the other has to do with the intension of the word *can* in Barbara Gordon's motivation for her decision.

One way into the first issue is to ask why it is that Bruce Wayne and Barbara Gordon choose to help in the way that they do. After all, they have no superpowers but are purely human. That is, it's not the case that by their very nature they somehow cannot fit into standard roles and practices. Bruce Wayne could become, say, a policeman. His choice to protect Gotham City takes, let's face it, a pretty counterintuitive and bizarre form: dressing up like a bat and working outside normal legal channels. So, too, in the case of Barbara Gordon: why this choice and not some other? If we remember the context of their choices—living damaged lives in a disenchanted world—it is easier to see what might be going on. In addition, we must keep in mind the ineliminable particularity of Bruce and Barbara as agents. While the police *can* protect and serve, and while policemen *can* be honest and trustworthy—although the *Batman* comics give us many examples of corrupt cops—nonetheless, the police, indeed the entire set of justice institutions, are complicit in the rationalized, disenchanted world that is Gotham City. If Batman were a policeman, he would be doing little more than offering consolation to the citizens of Gotham City, when what they need is the promise of something more, the promise of some sort of experience that is not deformed by disenchantment and that holds out some promise for hope. In a crime-ridden and corrupt city such as Gotham City, it is clear that traditional authority has lost its luster; what else could be expected in a disenchanted world? As we saw Diggins point out, the absence of authority and its replacement with power is a basic condition of modernity. Thus, what the disenchanted world needs is the reestablishment of authority without its juridico-legal context, which would render that authority prey to skeptical reason. Batman and Batgirl can be seen as sources of authority precisely by the choices they make that set them outside the legal context.

But there is another lesson, I think, that can be learned from Barbara Gordon's story. After all, she becomes someone with not only one superhero identity, but two. *Batgirl: Year One* tells the story of Barbara's becoming Batgirl, but it also points to her future, one that she has no way of perceiving at the time of *Batgirl: Year One.* The reader knows that Barbara Gordon both is and is not "divining" her future in her taking on the persona of Batgirl. In the dreamlike world of comic continuity, the Batgirl who comes to be now is also the Batgirl who is shot and permanently paralyzed by the Joker in *The Killing Joke* and later emerges as Oracle, information gatherer and crime fighter. She even becomes a lead character in her own comic series, *Birds of Prey.* While Barbara may not know her future, the book is filled with references to it. She starts by talking about the nature of Cassandra's oracles, portending a future that she was powerless to have an effect on. In trying to anticipate her own future, Barbara states, "I have to find another path. Divine my own future. One uniquely mine. Not a page from someone else's book. Not a fate that begins and ends on page one. . . . To dad, I'm all talk about digging for information. I won't be some glorified 'answer lady' for the cops. I want to be in on the action. Anything that will get me out of where I am. Where I don't want to be."[31] In the very panel in which Barbara expresses her desire to be anywhere but where she is, we see her sitting behind computers in the library, looking out through a window on a scene that clearly calls to mind her bank of computers in the clock tower where she lives and operates as Oracle.

One way to understand a promise is to recognize it as consisting of three elements: (a) it takes place in the present and its context; (b) it imagines a future that is not imaginable from the present except by the very fulfillment of the promise; and (c) it is powerless in relation to what might happen in the future.[32] In Barbara Gordon's story, we have the very nature of a promise playing out in front of us. Her promise ("because I can") does in fact take place in the present, imagines a future (one in which she helps), and is nonetheless powerless in relation to what reality, in the form of the Joker, has to offer. The fragility of promising is made concrete in the fragility of Barbara Gordon in the face of the Joker's bullet. Her "because I can" thus doubly represents "hopefulness in the teeth of intransigent reality."[33] Her promise to become Batgirl is at the very same time her promise to find ways of keeping that promise when the promise has been thwarted by reality. Within her promise to be Batgirl, her promise to be Oracle is inscribed as well. Both the nobility of the promise and its fragility are held up for the reader's inspection.[34]

FUGITIVE ETHICS

Bernstein plausibly argues that the only way authority can be experienced is on the back of fugitive ethical acts: "Certain empirical events have the status of both actualizing a possibility and in so doing making a promise about the future. . . . Since such events both flee from ordinary empirical experience and are intrinsically ephemeral and transient, I consider them 'fugitives.'"[35] That is, what would give Batman and Batgirl authority, as opposed to the power of the police, is precisely the way in which their actions embody a fugitive character, one that is represented concretely by their working outside the law, but which can be philosophically explicated in the convergence of motivating and justifying reasons.[36] This convergence manifests itself in their promising. In considering one more example from the Batman universe, I hope to tie together all the threads of my discussion.

Consider Selina Kyle, the once-and-future Catwoman. In Darwyn Cooke's *Selina's Big Score*,[37] we see Selina trying to pick up the pieces of a life that had spiraled out of control, leaving her no choice but to fake her own death. On returning to Gotham City, she meets Chantel, the girlfriend of a mobster named Falcone. Chantel has overheard Falcone talking about a big chunk of money, and she wants Selina to help her "to rip these fools off."[38] After some questioning by Selina, her motives become clear:

> Me? I know who I am . . . what I am. I'm not ashamed of it, right? 'Cause when it's time, everybody does what they have to to get over. I look at you and I know you hear what I'm sayin'. You spent some time at it, but you got clear—and that's what I want . . . to get clear . . . clear of this pig Falcone. I want to erase every sickening thing I've had to do to hold it together. I could feed you a pile about my kid, but that's none of your nevermind. I could blubber about my old sick mama and get all country and western on your ass, but the stone truth is it's me. I'm sick of it. Like I'd rather die, right? So maybe by doing one more really bad thing I can make something good happen. For me, for my little girl. I'm not talking about right or wrong. I'm talking about basic human dignity.[39]

These words remind Selina of a time when they were spoken to her. Over the course of the book, which inaugurated a new Catwoman comic series, Selina commits to a new sort of life while trying to understand the idea of basic human dignity. While this new life is not one of conventional morality, to be sure, it is one committed to helping others, especially those in the East End of Gotham City. When she returns to Gotham City after killing off her Catwoman persona, she has a particularly harrowing adventure capturing a man who had been killing hookers. It is then that she's able to reclaim her Catwoman persona, but for a different purpose. Her words:

> For a long time, all I could think about was pain—my own and my family's. And that pain defined who I was, and ultimately just caused more until there was nothing left for me beyond that. But today I'm not thinking about the crooked cops and politicians. I'm not thinking about the wife-beaters and rapists, the

mobsters. I'll get to them eventually. No, right now, all I can think about is how good I'm going to feel when that sun goes down. And you can't argue with happiness, can you?[40]

What is so compelling about Selina's story is that it provides a perfect representation of a disenchanted, damaging world in which the major ethical feat available to humans is not being crushed by others. At the same time, these passages and their accompanying images promise the realization that while futures may be grim and lives may be damaged, moments of true happiness are possible, and moments of genuine ethical acting are available. As Bernstein states, "The world is disenchanted, but it is not utterly closed in on itself: there are moments of happiness (and not just pleasure or illusory happiness), and there are the fragmented and heterogeneous that do not fit with the course of the world."[41]

Indeed, I think it striking that despite the difficult and damaged lives led by Bruce Wayne, Barbara Gordon, and Selina Kyle, one of the most notable features of the comics I'm talking about concerns their happiness. In almost every book, this happiness takes a specific form: the characters fly through the air, literally defying gravity. The expression of freedom on their faces and the joyousness of their flight are repeatedly depicted in the face of the monstrous and irrational crimes they see enacted and try to prevent. Fugitive ethical acts are acts that can cause happiness in otherwise damaged lives. Yet at the same time, there are reminders that the happiness and the acts that cause it exact a price. The price is most visible in the fact that none of them maintains a long-standing relationship; they have given up the usual forms of private satisfaction. Also, it is notable that none of them lives in an ordinary place: Batman spends more time in his cave than in Bruce Wayne's mansion; Selina lives at the top of an abandoned tenement in Gotham City's seedy East End; and Barbara Gordon, no longer Batgirl after being shot and paralyzed by the Joker, now lives in a clock tower where she helps Batman and others as Oracle. But of course this graphical depiction of happiness is just that—a graphical depiction of the happiness that results from doing what is in accord with "basic human dignity," or, to put it another way, the experience of having one's motivational and justificatory reasons coincide, or, to put it another way, by making a promise—"because I can."

By way of conclusion, I will point out a lesson this chapter discloses. I've shown that the lives of Bruce Wayne, Barbara Gordon, and Selina Kyle, as graphically represented in some comic books, are representations of lives led in possibility, a possibility that transcends current practices. Thus, while their lives are represented as lived under the conditions of modernism, with all the damage and hurt entailed by those conditions, they also are represented as exemplifications of promise, as exemplifications of the possibility of fugitive ethical acts. While recognizing the fictional nature of these characters, and the problems of continuity, what remains from my reading of these books is the claim that these characters' actions are revelatory of an experience of possibility. Of course, on one understanding of philosophy, the revelation and explication of this experience of possibility is also one of philosophy's tasks.[42] Indeed, in a disenchanted world, the representation of these possibilities in popular culture may be one of few chances for us to view them in a thematic and not merely fugitive manner. Yet the very oddity of the medium's characters—superheroes—reinforces how out of the ordinary such experiences are these days. And while the characters in *Batman*-related comics are not represented as *explicating* this experience of possibility, they can be read as *revealing* it. In this way, at least, a task of philosophy can be performed in a medium of popular culture.[43]

NOTES

I'd like to thank William Irwin and Jorge Gracia for comments on an earlier version of this chapter, and Kelly A. Wilson for her efforts in pulling me inside the world of comic books.

1. Frank Miller, Klaus Jansen, and Lynn Varley, *Batman: The Dark Knight Returns* (New York: DC Comics, 1986), 192.

2. Jeph Loeb and Tim Sale, *Batman: Dark Victory* (New York: DC Comics, 2002), 388.

3. Darwyn Cooke, *Batman: Ego* (New York: DC Comics, 2000).

4. J. M. Bernstein, *Adorno: Disenchantment and Ethics* (Cambridge: Cambridge University Press, 2004), 437–51.

5. Umberto Eco, *The Role of the Reader: Exploration in the Semiotics of Texts* (Bloomington, IN: Indiana University Press, 1979), 141. This passage is cited in Geoff Klock, *How to Read Superhero Comics and Why* (New York: Continuum Publishing, 2002), 5.

6. Klock, 31.

7. It will become clear to the reader that in my discussion of selected comic books, I am not providing a theory of comic book heroes, nor am I providing an in-depth analysis of particular comic book heroes, say, Batman. Indeed, given the issue of continuity across decades, or, more accurately, the notorious lack of such continuity, this would be something of a fool's goal. And, as William Irwin points out in his essay for this volume, it is not a task of the philosopher to provide insight into the intention of the creators of popular culture.

8. Frank Miller, David Mazucchelli, and Richmond Lewis, *Batman: Year One* (New York: DC Comics, 1987).

9. Miller, Mazucchelli, and Lewis.

10. John Patrick Diggins, *The Promise of Pragmatism: Modernism and the Crisis of Knowledge and Authority* (Chicago: University of Chicago Press, 1994), 8.

11. Charles Taylor provides a very clear genealogy of the process of disenchantment over the last three to four hundred years in his book *The Ethics of Authenticity* (Cambridge: Harvard University Press, 1991).

12. Diggins, 9–15.

13. Bernstein, 14–21. Bernstein's book is an attempt to reconstruct an approach to ethics consistent with the writings of Theodor Adorno. For my purposes, though, nothing hinges on whether Bernstein's account of Adorno is accurate. Bernstein's book is attractive to me not just because of its positions, which I find persuasive, but also because it is reconstructive and systematic. At the same time, I am not unaware of the irony of using an ethic founded on the work of Adorno to discuss comic books in a positive fashion since Adorno is typically taken to have been a stark opponent to the pleasures of popular culture. In his essay for this volume, Richard Shusterman provides some representative passages from Adorno in support of this understanding of Adorno.

14. Max Weber, "Science as a Vocation," quoted in Bernstein, 7.

15. Bernstein, 9–16

16. Bernstein, 11.

17. Alan Moore and Brian Bolland, *Batman: The Killing Joke* (New York: DC Comics, 1988).

18. Moore and Bolland, 38.

19. Moore and Bolland, 39–40.

20. Moore and Bolland, 45.

21. Bernstein, 10–15.

22. Bernstein, 15.

23. Bernstein, 19–20.

24. Bernstein, 30.

25. Bernstein, 30–32.

26. Bernstein, 31. In his essay for this volume, Michael Baur makes a similar point about the deficit of rationality as it relates to self-critique. At the same time, if the world is as disenchanted as modernist thought suggests, Baur may be a bit too sanguine about the possibility of achieving radical self-critique.

27. Scott Beatty, Chuck Dixon, Marcos Martin, and Alvaro Lopez, *Batgirl: Year One* (New York: DC Comics, 2003).

28. Beatty et al., 13.

29. Beatty et al., 94. "Pixie boots" is Batgirl's nickname for Batman's partner, Robin.

30. Jeph Loeb and Tim Sale, *Batman: Haunted Knight* (New York: DC Comics, 1996), 86.

31. Beatty et al., 12–13.

32. Bernstein, 436.

33. Bernstein, 436.

34. I have treated the representation of this promise in more detail in my essay "Barbara Gordon and Moral Perfectionism," in *Superheroes and Philosophy: Truth, Justice, and the Socratic Way*, ed. Tom Morris and Matt Morris (Chicago: Open Court, 2005), 89–101.

35. Bernstein, 419.

36. In language used by Gareth Matthews in his essay for this volume, the actions and identities taken on by Batman and Batgirl are "subversive" in precisely the sense that they call into question the "epistemological authority" of rationalized and bureaucratic society.

37. Darwyn Cooke, *Catwoman: Selina's Big Score* (New York: DC Comics, 2002).

38. Cooke, 15.

39. Cooke, 16.

40. Ed Brubaker, Darwin Cooke, and Mike Allred, *Catwoman: Dark End of the Street* (New York: DC Comics, 2002), 134–35.

41. Bernstein, 438.

42. Bernstein, 443.

43. In making this claim, then, I am not quite saying that these comic books *are* philosophy—a claim that Irwin warns against in his essay for this volume—but I am saying that they do more than provide examples for philosophy.

12

"American Pie" and the Self-critique of Rock 'n' Roll

Michael Baur

More than thirty-five years after its first release in 1971, Don McLean's "American Pie" still resonates deeply with music listeners and consumers of popular culture. In a 2001 public poll sponsored by the National Endowment for the Arts and the Recording Industry Association of America, McLean's eight-and-a-half-minute masterpiece was ranked number 5 among the 365 "most memorable" songs of the twentieth century.[1] In 2002, the song was voted into the Grammy Hall of Fame. In 1997, Garth Brooks performed "American Pie" at a concert in Central Park, and in 2000, pop icon Madonna performed her own version of "American Pie" on the soundtrack of her movie *The Next Best Thing*. In 1999, *American Pie* became the title of a popular—and irreverently comical—coming-of-age movie starring Jason Biggs (the movie *American Pie* was followed by *American Pie 2* in 2001, *American Wedding* in 2003, and *American Pie Presents—Band Camp* in 2005). Like the movie to which it lent its name, the song "American Pie" presents a coming-of-age narrative; and, also like the movie, the song appealed strongly and immediately to its contemporary audience. Three months after its release in November of 1971, the song reached the number one slot on the charts in January of 1972, and it remained in the Top 40 for a total of seventeen weeks (longer than any other single during the year 1972). Unlike the movie, however, the song "American Pie" is highly nuanced and sophisticated, containing multiple allusions and layers of meaning which challenge and heighten our understanding of rock 'n' roll music and the possibility of self-reflection and self-critique in popular culture.[2]

THE TASK OF INTERPRETING "AMERICAN PIE"

Before directly addressing the philosophical issue of rock 'n' roll's self-critique, it is important to make some hermeneutical observations, or observations about how one should—or should not—think about interpreting "American Pie" in the first place.

In approaching "American Pie" from a critical, philosophical point of view, it is tempting to think that one can best interpret the various phrases and moments in the song by linking them—through a sort of one-to-one correspondence—to actual persons and events in rock 'n' roll history. Indeed, dozens of studies—and, more recently, dozens of websites—have identified and established clear linkages between the lyrics of "American Pie" and specific events in the difficult and sometimes dark days of rock 'n' roll.[3] The song's allusions to Buddy Holly are perhaps the most unmistakable of all. For example, the words in the refrain—"this'll be the day that I die"—are clearly an allusion to Buddy Holly's own song, "That'll Be the Day." And the lines about "bad news on the doorstep" and "his widowed bride" refer to news reports about Buddy Holly's death in a plane crash (Holly had been married to wife Maria Elena for less than a year). The ill-fated plane was also carrying two other legends of early rock 'n' roll: Richie Valens (who recorded "La Bamba") and Jiles P. Richardson ("The Big Bopper," famous for his 1958 hit, "Chantilly Lace"). Thus the fateful day was a day on which "the music died," and not just Buddy Holly. The day of the plane crash was February 3, 1959, and correspondingly, McLean specifically identifies the month of the fateful day: "February made me shiver / With every paper I'd deliver."

In another set of unmistakable historical allusions, McLean clearly has Bob Dylan in mind. Consider, for example, the following lines: "the Jester sang for the King and Queen / In a coat he borrowed from James Dean." On the cover of the 1963 album *The Freewheelin' Bob Dylan*, Dylan is pictured wearing a red windbreaker, which is precisely what James Dean wore in the film *Rebel Without a Cause*. And shortly before the release of this album, Bob Dylan had performed several times (in 1962) at the King and Queen Pub, located at 1 Foley Street in London, England. "American Pie" also includes a clear and unambiguous reference to one of the darker days in the career of the Rolling Stones. At their free concert at Altamont Speedway (given on December 6, 1969, in Altamont, California), the Rolling Stones hired members of the Hell's Angels motorcycle gang to work as security guards. During the concert—and reportedly during the performance of the song, *Sympathy for the Devil*—the Hell's Angels beat and stabbed to death an audience member named Meredith Hunter. Referring to this incident, McLean writes, "No angel born in hell / Could break that Satan's spell."

Finally, to give just one more example, "American Pie" refers specifically to an actual cultural-historical event involving the music of the Beatles. The line about "Helter Skelter in a summer swelter" clearly refers to the infamous Manson family murders, which took place in the summer of 1969. On the evening of August 9, 1969, members of a cultlike group of hippies, led by psychopath Charles Manson, murdered pregnant actress Sharon Tate and several of her houseguests at her Hollywood Hills mansion. On the very next evening, August 10, 1969, Manson family members murdered Leno and Rosemary LaBianca in their Hollywood Hills home. The gruesome murder scenes included messages—written in blood on the walls of the victims' homes—with phrases such as "Helter Skelter," "Death to Pigs," and "Arise." It was later determined that these murderous rampages were inspired in part by Charles Manson's interpretations of certain lyrics from the Beatles' 1968 *White Album*, which featured the songs *Helter Skelter*, *Piggies*, and *Blackbird* (in *Blackbird*, one hears the line, "You were only waiting for this moment to arise").

There can be no doubt, then, that a one-to-one correspondence can be established between specific lyrics in "American Pie" and specific persons or happenings in rock 'n' roll history. However, it would be a mistake to conclude that the critical, philosophical meaning of "American Pie" is to be found primarily in such one-to-one correspondences. Indeed, many lyrics in "American Pie" positively resist any such one-to-one correspondence with actual events and thus defy any straightforward or univocal interpretation. One could even go so far as to say that the meaning of several passages in "American Pie" consists precisely in their having multiple meanings at once. The song is full of instances involving multiple meaning, but three examples come readily to mind. First, "American Pie" includes a line observing that "Lennin read a book on Marx." In the liner notes from the 2003 rerelease of the album *American Pie*, one can see that the name is spelled "Lennin," not "Lennon" or "Lenin." It is clear, then, that we listeners (and we readers of the liner notes) are to think not only about John Lennon and his political attitudes in the 1960s (and perhaps also the song *Revolution*, which he performed with the Beatles), but also about Vladimir Ilyich Lenin and the legacy that he bequeathed to American popular culture in the 1950s and 1960s, when the American-Soviet Cold War was at its height.

A second instance of simultaneous multiple meaning—and an instance that similarly involves the mixing of music and politics—can be found in a pair of lines patterned after a nursery rhyme: "Jack be nimble, Jack be quick / Jack Flash sat on a candlestick." On one level, the line about "Jack Flash" alludes to the song "Jumping Jack Flash," which was released as a single by the Rolling Stones on May 24, 1968. But on another level, the line most likely refers to John F. Kennedy during the Cuban missile crisis. In October of 1962, President Kennedy (also known as "Jack") had to be nimble and quick, since he had only days to respond to the Russian threat to send into Cuba shipments of missiles (represented by the image of the "candlestick"). Kennedy's success in quashing the crisis is suggested by the image of Jack's actually *sitting* on the candlestick.[4]

Thirdly, "American Pie" also contains a pair of suggestive lines about a jester and king: "Oh, and while the King was looking down / The jester stole his thorny crown." Here the "jester" most likely refers to both Bob Dylan and John Lennon, who were well known for their sense of humor, wit, and rebelliousness. If the jester is taken to be Bob Dylan, then the king would almost certainly be Elvis Presley. Elvis was famously known as "the King," and his popularity began to wane precisely at the time that Bob Dylan became increasingly famous and popular. Furthermore, Bob Dylan's ascendancy was accompanied by his decision to move away from folk music (with which he began his career) and to perform more rock 'n' roll music (which had previously been the proper territory of Elvis Presley). If Bob Dylan is regarded as the jester here, then he not only borrowed a coat from James Dean, but he also sang—at least at first—in a voice "that came from you and me" (that is, he sang in the voice of folk music's common man). But if the lyrics about the jester and king are allowed to have more than one meaning, then the jester could also be John Lennon, and "the King" Jesus Christ himself. After all, the lyrics refer to the king's thorny crown, and traditional religious artwork typically depicts Jesus as wearing a crown of thorns. John Lennon would have "stolen" the king's thorny crown insofar as Lennon presented himself as the equal—or perhaps even the superior—of Jesus Christ. And indeed, this is precisely what John Lennon did—or at least it is what he was thought to be doing—when he was interviewed by a reporter from the the *Evening Standard* on

March 4, 1966. Speaking of the Beatles' worldwide popularity, Lennon said the following to his interviewer, Maureen Cleave:

> Christianity will go. It will vanish and shrink. I needn't argue about that; I'm right and will be proved right. We're more popular than Jesus now; I don't know which will go first—rock 'n' roll or Christianity.[5]

Lennon's now-infamous words shocked the American public and provoked many Americans to boycott Beatles music and even burn Beatles albums in the streets. In his interview, Lennon had predicted that history would eventually prove him right. And as if in direct response, McLean tells us in the very next line of "American Pie" that the jury is still out: "The courtroom was adjourned / No verdict was returned."[6]

The preceding observations have suggested that the lyrics of *American Pie* may very well have multiple and simultaneous meanings—even if these meanings are connected to clearly identifiable persons and events in the early days of rock 'n' roll. But there is another important hermeneutical point to keep in mind as well. While on one level "American Pie" is McLean's attempt to speak for his entire generation, it is on another level a deeply personal and intimate account of his own thoughts, hopes, feelings, and experiences. For example, McLean alludes to his own early thoughts and desires about becoming a musician: "I knew if I had my chance / That I could make those people dance." And McLean's references to the death of Buddy Holly incorporate personal information about his own childhood job as a paperboy: "February made me shiver / With every paper I'd deliver" and "Bad news on the doorstep / I couldn't take one more step." In other words, the song explicitly intertwines the personal and the public, or the particular and the universal. Indeed, the strategy of the song is to undermine any attempt at disentangling its personal and public levels of meaning. With such a strategy, McLean seems to be saying that the general message of "American Pie," about rock 'n' roll's self-understanding and self-critique, is inextricably tied to his own personal experiences. The song's general message is simply inseparable from the intimate and personal meaning that it has for its author: "Something touched me deep inside / The day the music died." It's almost as if McLean wishes to say that what he endured so personally and intimately in the 1950s and 1960s was actually just the concentrated experience of his entire generation, and, conversely, that what his generation experienced as a whole came to accurate and precise expression in him as an individual spokesperson for the times.

Even the song's title—"American Pie"—illustrates the strategic intertwining of the private and the public which characterizes the song as a whole. "American Pie" is a term of McLean's own invention, and so it denotes nothing in general. But it does call to mind the notions of "Miss America" and "apple pie." And so while it is McLean's own term, "American Pie" also readily connotes a general sense of all that is good, redeeming, and beautiful in American culture. Anyone can immediately infer that to say goodbye to "American Pie" is to bid farewell to the sense of optimism that had permeated the younger generation before rock 'n' roll's turbulent coming-of-age in the late 1950s and 1960s. A similar intermingling of the particular and the universal can also be found on the inside cover of the album *American Pie*. On the inside cover, one reads an ode by McLean to one of his personal heroes, television cowboy Hopalong Cassidy. In the ode, McLean addresses his hero directly:

> No matter how scary life got I could depend on you
> You had that easy smile and white, wavy hair
> You were my favorite father figure with two guns blazing. . . .
> My hat's off to you, Hoppy
> Say goodbye to all the boys at the Bar-20
> The black and white days are over
> So long Hopalong Cassidy.

Some commentators—having noticed in "American Pie" the technique of intertwining the personal and the public—even suggest that the song's well-known refrain conveys a generalized message while simultaneously playing with allusions of unique significance to McLean himself. The famous refrain tells us that "them good old boys were drinking whiskey and rye / Singing this'll be the day that I die." But if one listens carefully, McLean seems to be singing "whiskey in Rye," not "whiskey and rye." If this is what McLean is singing, then his famous refrain could actually contain an allusion to the town of Rye, immediately adjacent to McLean's own hometown of New Rochelle (both just outside of New York City).[7] Of course, the possible connection between the song's refrain and McLean's boyhood environs is a matter of unverified (and perhaps unverifiable) speculation. But there is at least one regard in which the refrain does figure into McLean's technique of combining the personal or particular with the public and universal. Each verse of the song ends with words about "the day the music died," and each verse leads into a refrain recounting the composer's hearing of eerily similar words: "This'll be the day that I die." If the day on which the music died is the same as—or is associated with—the day on which the composer (McLean himself) is to die, then an interesting lesson readily suggests itself: the *music* of the generation and *Don McLean himself* are closely connected or even identified in some sense. Once again, McLean is implicitly suggesting that he himself *is* the music of his generation—or at least is the spirit of such music—and that he can speak for his generation precisely by speaking for himself through his own composition.

Along these lines, McLean has suggested that in his writing of "American Pie," it was unclear to him whether he was composing the song or the song was composing itself through him. In a 2003 interview with Paul Grein, McLean compares his writing of the song to the activity of Mickey Mouse in Walt Disney's movie *Fantasia*.[8] In the movie's episode about "The Sorcerer's Apprentice," Mickey Mouse undertakes to guide and control the magical forces that the sorcerer has left at Mickey's disposal. At first, Mickey believes that he has succeeded in his task, for he sees himself directing and controlling the movements of the stars, the seas, and other terrestrial and extraterrestrial phenomena. By the end of the episode, however, it becomes clear to Mickey that his experience of directing and being in control was illusory. As a matter of fact, Mickey had only been dreaming, and his own activities—far from being in control of the phenomena outside of him—were in fact only the consequences or effects of the phenomena operating outside of him and upon him. In short, Mickey was not so much directing and controlling the sorcerer's magical forces as he was being directed and controlled by them. The lesson of the episode is that Mickey's experience of complete self-possession and independence was nothing but a dream. In a BBC Radio 1 interview, McLean harkens back to this theme, observing that his "American Pie" could accurately be called "the first Rock dream."[9]

THE SELF-CRITIQUE OF ROCK 'N' ROLL

The hermeneutical or interpretive issues raised in the preceding section are relevant to the larger question to be addressed in this chapter, that is, the question of how the culture of rock 'n' roll—or any culture or tradition, for that matter—can engage in genuine self-critique. As we have already seen, McLean

presents "American Pie" as much more than a particular song written by a
particular individual at a particular time. While he certainly did write the song
as an expression of his own personal reflections on rock 'n' roll music in the
1950s and 1960s, McLean equally—and perhaps more importantly—claims
that the song is an instance of the generation's self-expression through him.
But this sort of claim raises an important philosophical problem. On the one
hand, McLean presents himself as the embodiment and spokesperson of his
generation's social and cultural experience. On the other hand, he claims to
take a critical and reflective stance toward this generation and its cultural
commitments. But how can McLean and the song be genuinely reflective and
critical of the rock 'n' roll generation if they are an instance of that generation's own embodiment and self-expression?

There can be no doubt that "American Pie" presents a critical perspective
on what the culture of rock 'n' roll has become. As indicated above, McLean's
language about a "jester" and "King" conveys the worry that rock 'n' roll music has become a usurping substitute religion. And McLean expresses the same
sort of concern elsewhere in the song, for example when he asks, "Do you believe in rock 'n' roll? / Can music save your mortal soul?" But the worry is not
just that rock 'n' roll music has become something of a substitute religion; it
has also grown to exercise a negative—and perhaps even demonic—influence
on American youth and culture. In another allusion to the Rolling Stones'
deadly concert at Altamont Speedway, McLean put himself in the position of
a concertgoer and describes what he sees:

> And as flames climbed high into the night
> To light the sacrificial rite
> I saw Satan laughing with delight
> The day the music died.

"American Pie" further suggests that rock 'n' roll's usurpation of religion was
accompanied by other ills, for example, widespread drug use ("the half-time
air was sweet perfume"); violence in war and in antiwar protests ("in the
streets the children screamed"[10]); selfishness and competition within the music industry itself ("the players tried to take the field / The marching band refused to yield"); and public discussions about God himself being dead and
gone ("The three men I admire the most / The Father, Son, and Holy Ghost /
They caught the last train for the coast"[11]).

But how can McLean present "American Pie" as a critique of what is wrong with rock 'n' roll while at the same time presenting it as the expression and embodiment of that very same music and culture? Or how can McLean achieve a genuinely critical stance with respect to American rock 'n' roll, when his own beliefs and his own activity in writing "American Pie" are themselves so deeply indebted to that very same culture? It would seem that McLean—in his very attempt at critique—runs the risk of being co-opted by the very culture that he wishes to criticize. That is, he runs the risk of unconsciously re-asserting—and thus unwittingly reinforcing—the very problems that he seeks to address. Of course, the issues that we are raising about McLean's "American Pie" can be discussed in connection with any culture's or any tradition's at-tempt at self-critique. Doesn't the very idea of self-critique imply that the "tools of critique" are derived from—and thus virtually useless with respect to—the culture or tradition being scrutinized? In three revealing lines from the penultimate verse of "American Pie," McLean touches upon these very problems:

> Oh, and there we were, all in one place
> A generation lost in space
> With no time left to start again.

In all likelihood, McLean's mention of being "all in one place" is a reference to the Woodstock musical festival, which in August of 1969 brought together over thirty of rock music's leading bands and attracted nearly 500,000 fans. And there can be little doubt that McLean's phrase about being "lost in space" is an allusion to the 1960s' science-fiction television show of the same name.[12] But the most important point to be gleaned from these lines is McLean's im-plicit epistemic point: in the midst of rock 'n' roll's heyday, an entire genera-tion found itself lost and confused and realized that it was now too late—there was "no time left"—to make a fresh and unbiased start of things. Any attempt to "start again" would inevitably be too late, for every member of the genera-tion—and every would-be reformer—had already acquired a set of problem-atic attitudes, opinions, and beliefs. No truly "fresh start" was possible, since any new start would inevitably take its direction from the very beliefs and un-derstandings that had led the rock 'n' roll generation into its present difficulty.

The problem being raised here is a problem that potentially affects any cul-ture's or any tradition's attempt at self-critique.[13] Within the philosophical tradition, it was René Descartes, the so-called father of modern philosophy, who attempted to "start again" by doubting everything that could be doubted, and by accepting as his firm new foundation for knowledge only that which could not be doubted whatsoever. As Descartes famously argued, there is indeed one knowledge claim that cannot be coherently doubted, since the very act of doubting it would inescapably confirm the truth of the knowledge claim. This foundational and indubitable knowledge claim is the claim that "I think." Because doubting is itself a species of thinking, Descartes reasoned, it is not possible for me to doubt that I think without performatively demonstrating (through the very act of such doubting) that I think. And if I can know beyond all doubt that I think, then I can arrive at the foundational and indubitable truth that I am a thing that thinks. It is this foundational and indubitable truth ("I am a thing that thinks") which provides the starting point for Descartes' project of critically grounding the entire edifice of human knowledge, including knowledge of God and knowledge of an external, material world.

But, echoing McLean's concerns about the self-critique of rock 'n' roll, one might reasonably ask whether the Cartesian project of "starting again" was itself begun "too late." For in spite of his stated intentions, isn't it the case that Descartes actually had to accept at least some alleged truths borrowed from the very culture or tradition that he sought to criticize? As others were later to argue, if one really doubts all that can be doubted and refuses to accept any truths except those that are beyond doubt, then one cannot legitimately arrive even at the seemingly uncontentious knowledge claim that "I am a thing that thinks." For this knowledge claim (if accepted as presented in Descartes' argument) presupposes the objective validity of the concept of "finite substance."[14] But this concept has been borrowed uncritically from the very tradition that Descartes sought to criticize, and its objective validity has not been demonstrated. Accordingly, the Cartesian inference from the proposition that "I think" to the claim that "I am a thing that I thinks," as well as his later inferences (e.g., about God and the material world), are not justified with the sort of rigor required by the Cartesian project itself. The Cartesian project of criticizing the tradition and setting it upon a new and firm foundation harbors opposing tendencies within itself and ultimately fails on its own terms.

Like the critics of Descartes, McLean rejects any "foundationalist" or "externalist" approach to the self-critique of rock 'n' roll music. As a generation "lost in space," those who would criticize and reform the culture of rock 'n' roll music simply have no access to a privileged, independent, external Archimedean point for conducting such critique and reform. The broader point is that we are all emotively and cognitively indebted to the cultures and traditions within which we live and think, and so our critical examinations and attempted reformations of our cultures and traditions must always operate from within the medium of—and must utilize the "tools" of—those cultures and traditions themselves. In spite of our best attempts at identifying an entirely independent, objective, or external criterion for our theorizing and criticizing, we inescapably make use of the concepts, discourses, presuppositions, and strategies of that which we inherit from the traditions and cultures to which we belong.

But McLean goes further. He suggests that even the very desire to find a privileged, independent, external Archimedean point for the critique and reform of rock 'n' roll culture is not as innocent as it may first appear. Recall that McLean presents himself in "American Pie" as the personification of his generation and its music. Working within this conceit, McLean explains how the tribulations affecting his generation and its music have led him to search for answers outside the culture of rock 'n' roll, for example in the alternative but related culture of blues music. One might think that the turn to blues music (one of rock 'n' roll's earliest sources) can lead to answers which are rooted in a purer, more genuine form of expression from earlier times. McLean sings,

> I met a girl who sang the blues[15]
> And I asked her for some happy news
> But she just smiled and turned away.

This potent set of lyrics contains a threefold message. First and most obviously, these lyrics tell us that to search for comfort and guidance from a source just outside the boundaries of rock 'n' roll itself is to search in the wrong place. A "girl who sang the blues" is clearly not the sort of person who is well-positioned to be a source for "happy news."

Secondly, these lyrics suggest that this strategy of searching in the wrong place tends to intensify and exacerbate, rather than alleviate, the seeker's sense of anxiety and unfulfilled longing. The blues-singing girl from whom comfort is sought evidently knows that the seeker's quest is misguided—hence her (knowing) smile. But rather than divulging this potentially helpful truth, she turns away, thus leaving the seeker even more perplexed; the seeker not only lacks an answer to his initial query, but he now also has to wonder about the girl's strange silence. The problem here is not just that the search for an external and independent criterion or foundation always fails (as noted above); the deeper problem is that this centrifugal search amounts to a kind of flight from self-knowledge, and thus ends up intensifying the seeker's sense of confusion and disenchantment. Notice the vicious circularity that ensues. The searching in the wrong place yields no answers and thus convinces the seeker that he or she is truly disoriented, and this intensified sense of disorientation convinces the seeker all the more fully that he or she can find answers only by fully escaping the limitations of his or her own culture and adopting the wholly independent, external, and "objective" perspective of an Archimedean observer. That is, the misdirected searching seemingly confirms the (wrongheaded) belief that one can find answers only by looking for them in an external source or point of origin (which is precisely in the wrong place), and thus one remains (unwittingly) trapped in a vicious circle of one's own making. This, briefly stated, is the vicious circularity which affects all "foundationalist" or "externalist" attempts at cultural reform. When one begins with an unrealistic, foundationalist ideal, then one's failure to live up to that ideal (that is, one's failure to achieve the desired Archimedean perspective) only seems to confirm the belief that one's own culture (and one's own thinking) is so badly in need of reform that it cannot reform itself except by reference to an independent, externally derived foundation or criterion. But this conclusion only restates the wrongheaded foundationalist belief with which one began in the first place.

Thirdly and perhaps most importantly, these lyrics suggest that the supposedly purer origins out of which "decadent" rock 'n' roll emerged were not so pure and perfect, after all. The bygone days of early rock 'n' roll and its immediate precursors were certainly not devoid of their own forms of disenchantment and disorientation. In looking back to the earliest days of rock 'n' roll, McLean not only reminds us about "the blues"; he also tells us something about difficult personal experiences, which—as we have seen—are representative of the experiences of his entire generation. For example, he relates the painful experience of seeing that the girl after whom he had been longing is now dancing with someone else:

> Well, I know that you're in love with him
> 'Cause I saw you dancing' in the gym.

And in a similar pair of lines, McLean candidly confesses,

> I was a lonely teenage broncin' buck
> With a pink carnation and a pick-up truck.

The line about "a pink carnation" is clearly an allusion to the 1957 Marty Robbins song, "A White Sport Coat (and a Pink Carnation)," which refers to the typical dress code for high school dances in the 1950s. But, more importantly, this allusion reminds us that life in the early days of rock 'n' roll was also filled with moments of anxiety, pain, and loss. The original lyrics of the Marty Robbins song declare,

> A white sport coat and a pink carnation
> I'm all dressed up for the dance.
> A white sport coat and a pink carnation,
> I'm all alone in romance.
> Once you told me long ago
> To the prom with me you'd go
> Now you've changed your mind it seems
> Someone else will hold my dreams.
> A white sport coat and a pink carnation,
> I'm in a blue, blue mood.

Perhaps most revealing of all are the central lyrics of the 1957 Buddy Holly tune, "That'll Be the Day,"[16] which resonate throughout McLean's "American Pie." By alluding to this classic Buddy Holly song, McLean subtly reminds us that the supposedly better, purer days of early rock 'n' roll were also prone to cynicism and darkness, for "That'll Be the Day" represents the perspective of a man who is not the "traditional" 1950s gentleman, but rather a smug and detached lover who is willing to use, and then abandon, the object of his supposed affections:

> Well, you give me all your lovin'
> And your turtle dovin'

Ah, all your hugs and kisses, and your money too.
Well, uh, you know you love me baby,
Still you tell me maybe,
That someday well I'll be blue.
Well, oh, when cupid shot his dart
He shot it at your heart
So if we ever part, then I'll leave you.

Significantly, McLean makes repeated use of a particular line from the famous Buddy Holly song—the line about "the day that I die." The implication here is that early rock 'n' roll (personified by Buddy Holly, just as later rock 'n' roll is personified by Don McLean) contained the seeds of its own eventual destruction and thus anticipated its own demise.

Now while rock 'n' roll music—from the days of Buddy Holly onward—has always contained a dark, destructive, and sinister side, there is a tendency within the culture's own self-understanding to forget this fact and to pretend that the reform and salvation of rock 'n' roll depends on appealing to an external, Archimedean perspective, one that becomes available if one looks to the culture's earlier, purer (predecadent) origin or foundation. But the idea of a better, purer "state of nature" or an unadulterated, "original" Archimedean perspective—free of all tension, uncertainty, and ambiguity—is illusory. And as we have seen, the desire to glimpse such a pure "state of nature," or to achieve such an "external," Archimedean perspective tends to exacerbate—rather than to alleviate—the disorientations and disenchantments to which a culture or tradition is prone. Of course, this is not to suggest that the genuine self-critique of rock 'n' roll culture (or of any culture or tradition) is impossible—far from it. The point, rather, is that genuine self-critique becomes possible only on the basis of a nonfoundationalist or nonexternalist approach. Genuine self-critique takes place within the medium of the culture or tradition being criticized, and it does so by appealing to the culture's or tradition's own concepts, vocabulary, memories, presuppositions, ideals, and values. Accordingly, McLean's message about rock 'n' roll music is not just a critique of rock 'n' roll music; it is a critique that is articulated and presented precisely within the medium of rock 'n' roll music itself.

What emerges from these reflections is a broader Aristotelian point. The point is that the self-critique of cultures and traditions ought to be conceived, not on the model of the technical sciences, but rather on the model of the moral (or prudential) sciences.[17] The technical sciences operate upon matter that is given as external to the activity of the technician. Accordingly, the technician subjects that externally given matter to a rule (or technique) with a particular end in view, and thereby transforms that externally given matter without (necessarily) transforming himself or herself as technician (of course, such self-transformation may take place incidentally, but it is not the aim or end of the technician's activity qua technician). By contrast, the moral (or prudential) sciences—instead of operating upon matter that is given as external to the agent—aim rather to transform the agent himself or herself, and thus aim to facilitate the agent's own self-constitution *as* a moral agent. Following the model of the moral sciences, one recognizes that the critique of one's culture or tradition is never a form of critique aimed at an externally given subject matter; it is never a form of critique which approaches its subject matter from the external, independent, "foundationalist" perspective of an Archimedean observer. Following the model of the moral sciences, one rightly regards the tradition or culture that is the subject matter of one's critique as itself the source of one's own (often unexamined) emotive and epistemic commitments. And thus, in criticizing one's culture or tradition, one is indirectly criticizing oneself and one's own thinking. But this is not all. For this critique of oneself is conducted within the medium of the culture or tradition to which one belongs, and so this critique of oneself is equally (even if minimally) a participation in and contribution to one's broader culture or tradition.

Notice how this account of a culture's self-critique depends on the rejection of the "foundationalist" or "externalist" paradigm discussed earlier. Precisely because one's culture or tradition is the (often unacknowledged) source of one's emotive and epistemic commitments, the activity of identifying and grappling with the problems, limitations, and tensions endemic to one's culture or tradition is simultaneously *both* an exercise in individual self-critique *and* a participation in one's own broader culture or tradition. On the prudential (as opposed to technical) model, one criticizes the culture to which one belongs, not by observing such culture from the perspective of an allegedly external, Archimedean observer who has access to an unshakeable foundation or criterion, but only by participating in the culture so as to identify, expose, and grapple with the culture's internal contradictions, tensions, and limitations. Of course, no culture or tradition is entirely free of internal contradictions, tensions, and limitations; but it is possible, even from within a very imperfect culture or tradition, to become aware of such contradictions, tensions, and limitations—and in thus becoming aware, to transcend them.

The importance of participation is implicitly recognized and addressed by McLean's "American Pie," insofar as the song subtly elicits the listener's own participation. In its opening moments, the song's lyrics are sung by a solitary voice and accompanied by a spare, folksy-sounding guitar. In its midsection, the song shifts into a faster, more percussive and electronic mode. But at the end, just as it leaves us with its final message, the song returns to an acoustic sound; but this time the acoustic guitar's strumming is accompanied by a sing-a-long featuring many ordinary-sounding voices—like those that would belong to you and me—so that McLean's voice is no longer distinguishable from our own as we are induced to sing along.

As a final concern, one might wonder whether the preceding account of the self-critique of cultures and traditions is overly optimistic. Can't one belong to a culture or tradition that is so corrupted and so degenerate that it becomes altogether impossible to criticize it from within? This is, of course, a theoretical possibility, but as a matter of fact, if one actually did belong to such a culture or tradition, then one could never know it, and one could never even speculate about it. For if a culture or tradition were entirely corrupted or degenerate (and thus beyond all possible reform), then it would be impossible for anyone from within that culture or tradition even to speculate and raise questions about its being so corrupted or so degenerate. And thus the very fact that someone—like McLean, or you, or me—can pose such questions about his or her own culture or tradition indirectly demonstrates that the culture or tradition is not beyond all self-critique and reform. Within a fully corrupted or degenerate and unreformable tradition, every scruple about corruption, degeneration, and possible reform will have disappeared. As the good Edgar astutely observes in Shakespeare's *King Lear,*

> And worse I may be yet. The worst is not,
> So long as we can say, "This is the worst."

NOTES

1. According to this poll, "American Pie" was topped (in rank order) only by Judy Garland's "Over the Rainbow," Bing Crosby's "White Christmas," Woodie Guthrie's "This Land Is Your Land," and Aretha Franklin's "Respect."

2. For extended discussion of what constitutes an allusion and the role of allusion in popular culture, see Theodore Gracyk, "Allusion and Intention in Popular Art," in this volume.

3. Two of the more useful websites dedicated to "American Pie" and its cultural-historical allusions are the following: www.levitt.co.uk/interpret.html (authored by Saul Levitt) and www.understandingamericanpie.com/index.htm (authored by Jim Fann).

4. According to the nursery rhyme, Jack did not *sit* on the candlestick but successfully jumped over it: "Jack be nimble / Jack be quick / Jack jump over / The candlestick."

5. The complete *Evening Standard* interview can be found at the following web address: www.geocities.com/nastymcquickly/articles/standard.html.

6. My suggestion here is that McLean's lyrics about a jester and king are probably meant to refer simultaneously to both the Dylan-Presley pairing and the Lennon-Jesus pairing. There is yet a third possible meaning which I will not explore here. A third meaning might be connected to the Rolling Stones' 1968 song "Jumping Jack Flash." For in that song, singer Mick Jagger seems to identify *himself* as someone who wears a thorny crown: "I was crowned with a spike right through my head."

7. For more on this possible connection, see the website authored by Saul Levitt: www.levitt.co.uk/interpret.html.

8. The section of the interview containing McLean's reference to Mickey Mouse and *Fantasia* can be found in the liner notes to the 2003 rerelease of the album, *American Pie.*

9. For more on this, see Saul Levitt's website: www.levitt.co.uk/interpret.html.

10. This line could refer to the antiwar protests in American streets, but since the song was released in 1971, it cannot refer to the unforgettable black-and-white photograph (taken on June 8, 1972, by Associated Press photographer Huynh Cong Ut, also known as Nick Ut) depicting several Vietnamese children (including a naked young girl) screaming and running in the streets to flee a napalm attack near the village of Trang Bang.

11. The religion section of the October 22, 1965, issue of *Time* magazine featured an article about a group of young American theologians—led by Emory University professor Thomas J. J. Altizer—who called themselves Christian atheists and claimed that God was dead. The issue's front cover depicted nothing but a single provocative question—"Is God Dead?"—printed in large, white letters against a stark, black

background.

12. The television show was created by Irwin Allen and ran from 1965 to 1968. The show's plot—while unlikely to the point of being almost comical—is suggestive and clearly echoes some themes in "American Pie." In a futuristic scenario, planet Earth has become overpopulated and so Professor Robinson, his family, and Major West are sent into space in order to establish a colony for future settlement by Earthlings. The evil Doctor Smith is sent by an enemy government to sabotage the mission. After having reprogrammed the ship's robot, Doctor Smith becomes trapped on board. Because of the extra passenger and weight, the ship becomes lost, and the passengers must struggle to survive and find their way back home. When juxtaposed to the themes of "American Pie," the lesson of this science fiction plot seems rather straightforward: an entire generation of rock 'n' roll adherents finds itself in the midst of a journey or project that harbors within itself the dangerous seeds of its own undoing.

13. Indeed, the problem faced by rock 'n' roll music in its self-critique is a specification of the problem faced by any culture or tradition that has become disenchanted or disillusioned with itself. Another instantiation of this problem is the problem of the disenchantment of modern reason (or modernity in general), which is discussed by James South in "Of Batcaves and Clock Towers: Living Damaged Lives in Gotham City," in this volume.

14. This sort of anti-Cartesian argument was made by thinkers of widely divergent philosophical perspectives, from the extreme rationalist Spinoza to the extreme empiricist Hume.

15. This line about "a girl who sang the blues" is almost certainly an allusion to Janis Joplin, who—at only twenty-seven years of age—died of a drug overdose on October 4, 1970, shortly before McLean wrote the song "American Pie."

16. Interestingly, the catchphrase "That'll Be the Day" was made famous by John Wayne in his 1956 film *The Searchers* (directed by John Ford). Throughout the film, this catchphrase is used by John Wayne's character (Ethan Edwards, an embittered, sarcastic loner who had fought on the side of the Confederacy in the American Civil War and who now finds himself on a mission to rescue two white women who have been kidnapped by members of the Comanche Indian tribe). It was this catchphrase that reputedly inspired Buddy Holly and the Crickets to write and record their song of the same title. In one famous scene, the character Martin Pawley (played by Jeffrey Hunter) shouts at Ethan Edwards, saying, "I hope you die," to which the latter responds, "That'll be the day." The genealogy that links Don McLean to Buddy Holly

and John Wayne may be significant: in spite of its apparent valorization of an ideal past, Don McLean's "American Pie" reminds us of the less-than-ideal forms of "love" that prevailed in the 1950s (as depicted in Buddy Holly's "That'll Be the Day"); and in turn, Buddy Holly's song reminds us of the less-than-ideal relations that prevailed in the late nineteenth century between the North and South, and between Americans of different races (as depicted in *The Searchers*).

17. The distinction that I am drawing here between the technical and prudential model for the self-critique of cultures and traditions goes back to Aristotle's distinction (in book 6 of the *Nicomachean Ethics*) between *techne* and *phronesis*.

18. See *King Lear*, Act Four, Scene One.

13

Photography, Popular Epistemology, Flexible Realism, and Holistic Pragmatism

Peter H. Hare

From its beginnings, photography has been linked with democracy. Before photography, only the wealthy were able to own portraits of themselves. With the invention of the daguerreotype, almost overnight millions of people had their pictures taken. A worldwide craze was born, even though each daguerreotype was a unique, nonreproducible image. With the advent of the "mechanical reproduction" that Walter Benjamin makes so much of, the democratic character of photography became more pronounced. Persons of modest means could assemble albums of images—images of family members, images of the most exotic places in the world, or images of famous works of art. We could display ourselves and our family members in countless copies. Common people gained access to treasures of geography and art hitherto unavailable to them. With the invention of the Kodak and roll film, another dimension of democratization arrived. Anyone, even children, could *take* photos as well as collect them; and they could be taken and collected in great quantity. For example, in about 1900, my Great Uncle Bill put together several albums of pictures of himself and his friends at the beach or on boats. A favorite of mine that I keep on our living-room table is of Bill clinging to the top of a sailboat's mast—stark naked except for a stylish cap on his head.

Later, Polaroid took popular culture by storm. Andy Warhol took Polaroids and by signing them created expensive works of art. With the inception of the digital camera (teamed with the Internet), the democratization of photography reached extremes that some regard as absurd and even dangerous. An untutored person can produce a virtually unlimited number of images at negligible cost, and these images can be distributed around the globe cost free. If anyone doubted the cultural potency of photography, surely they were disabused of those doubts in May of 2004, when digital photos of Iraqis being tortured in Abu Ghraib prison were publicly released and overnight electronically transmitted to computer and TV screens as well as to newspapers and magazines in even remote regions of our planet. Not the work of photojournalists, these photos were taken by American soldiers using compact cameras they carry everywhere. This radical democratization of photography has myriad philosophical implications, most of which I haven't space to discuss in this chapter. I shall focus my attention on how the mass-cultural phenomenon of photography has created an army of amateur epistemologists, that is, legions who believe they understand how our photographical representations are related to reality as clearly as they understand how a home run is achieved in baseball.

POPULAR EPISTEMOLOGY

The "popular epistemology" (or what cognitive scientists might call "folk epistemology") of photography consists of two tenets:

1. A photographic image is a mirror image of reality.
2. A photographic image is a manipulation of reality.

In the years since photography's birth in the 1830s, the comparative strengths of these tenets has varied. In the early years, (1) was more powerful. Recently, (2) has been dominant. However, the historical evidence is overwhelming that both intuitions are and always have been embedded in popular culture. Published pronouncements have often been misleading on this point. Time and again, an author has stated that (1) is true and (2) is false, or visa versa, but if one watches an author's everyday practice in responding to photographs, one finds that both tenets are firmly held. In support of (1), we have only to cite the fact that in legal proceedings, photographs are accepted as evidence of what occurred in a way that no painting can be. A variety of metaphors and similes are used to bolster the plausibility of (1). Photography is said to be an imprint or transfer of the real; it is a photochemically processed trace causally connected to the real in a way analogous to the way that fingerprints and footprints are connected to real fingers and feet, or to the way a ring of water left on a table is causally connected to a cold glass that recently rested on the table. Another common way of expressing the idea is to say that by means of the camera, *nature paints itself.* Here the metaphor points up the fact that in the causal sequence between the real and the image of the real, no human being intervenes, though a human agent begins the causal process by releasing the shutter.

But this commonsense intuition of "photographic realism" is easily countered by considerations that favor tenet (2). (1) can be undermined by citing the fact that painting is sometimes as "realistic" as photography. In some paintings can be found subtleties of shading and precision of perspective equal to that found in photographs. Though realism is undeniably easier to achieve with a camera, what *in principle* difference exists between realism in painting and in photography? If the difference is merely one of technological means available to a particular person at a particular time, why should we consider photography any less manipulative of reality than painting? Can the realism of photography be nothing more than a democratically available form of the realism achievable in painting only by artists with special skills and equipment?

This question has suggested to many that the crucial difference between photography and painting lies not in the degree of manipulation but instead in what devices are used in the manipulation. Photographic images are produced by *mechanical* means, as paintings are not. No matter how distorted and how misleading the information about the real provided by a photograph, the causal processes involved in producing it are fundamentally different from the causal processes that result in a painting.

A PROSTHETIC DEVICE

The plausible suggestion is sometimes made that we can best understand the manipulative realism of photography by thinking of a camera as a prosthetic device, by conceiving of photography as an aid to seeing, just as mirrors, telescopes, and microscopes are aids to vision.[1] Photography aids our vision in many ways, most notably by allowing us to see into the past. Such vision of the past is no more odd than telescopic vision of a star's explosion millions of years ago. Why should we consider photographic seeing of our deceased grandfather any more *indirect* than our seeing the ground in front of our feet thanks to images on our retinas? All seeing is mediated in one way or another. What could it be about photographic mediation that makes it incompatible with realism when so many other forms of mediation of vision are not? The claim that in normal vision all that we see, strictly speaking, are our sense data has long been discredited. Why should we take any more seriously the claim that in seeing our dead grandfather through a photograph, we are, strictly speaking, seeing only a piece of paper with an image on it?

It must be recognized that photographic seeing is *not necessarily* what the scene would have looked like to us if we had observed it at the time and place of the shutter's release. Many photographs, to be sure, are attempts to approximate seeing unaided by a camera. Seeing Uncle Bill photographically is an approximation of what I would have seen (minus color) if in 1900 I had been standing behind the camera and looking in the direction of the top of the mast. Such photographic approximations of unaided seeing can serve important purposes. A photograph taken at a crime scene, for example, can show what the accused was able to observe from a certain location. Such approximation is not, however, a necessary condition of being a photograph. Photographic seeing is a distinct form of perception, just as, for example, viewing through a microscope is. We properly speak of seeing an individual blood cell through a microscope even though no one supposes that seeing a blood cell on a glass slide in that microscopic way approximates seeing the same blood-stained slide unaided by a microscope.

Photographs cannot always be distinguished from paintings by the way they look. As Kendall Walton points out, the *appearance* of *Self-Portrait*, a painting by Chuck Close, is indistinguishable from the *appearance* of a photograph of the painter. We experience the *illusion* of seeing Close via photography. Note that this is different from an illusion that we are seeing Close directly, that is, unmediated by photography, as in a trompe l'oeil illusion. Other types of illusions further complicate our attempts to understand the epistemology of photography. What appears to be a photograph by John de Andrea of a man and woman is actually a photograph of a life-size statue. Here the appearance of being a photograph is no illusion, but we are deceived as to the nature of the object photographed.

The many possibilities of deception and illusion in no way undermine, however, the viability of the notion of photography as a mode of seeing no less genuine than seeing via mirrors, telescopes, and microscopes. Nor is this notion of photography threatened by any lack of accuracy found in photographs. To be sure, a high degree of accuracy can be valuable in certain contexts (e.g., legal contexts), and the ease and permanency of accuracy in photographs is also important for many purposes. But the value of accuracy in some photographs does not conceptually entail that some degree of accuracy is a necessary condition of photography as a mode of seeing—no more than the fact that some persons have defective nonphotographic vision shows that they lack genuine vision.

PHOTOGRAPHY AND KNOWLEDGE

More generally, there is no logical connection between photography and *knowledge* of the world, if we understand *knowledge* as professional epistemologists traditionally do, as "justified true belief." Even if we suppose that photographs are usually more reliable, more trustworthy in the information they provide than other sorts of pictures, nothing follows from that supposition about the nature of photography. Like other modes of seeing, photography varies greatly in its information production. A severely myopic person gains more information about the world while wearing prescription glasses than while seeing the world without spectacles, but that does not imply that without prescription lenses he or she lacks genuine vision. Similarly, any greater trustworthiness that photographs may generally have over other pictures does not imply that relative trustworthiness is a necessary condition of being a photograph.

CAUSAL ORIGINS

As I have noted, it has often been claimed that the distinctive causal origins of photographs account for the distinctive nature of photography as compared with other forms of representation. The appearance of a photograph may be indistinguishable from, for example, the appearance of a painting. Photographs are said to be mechanically and automatically produced, whereas paintings are handmade. For philosophers, the parallels with causal theories of perception are obvious. Though we cannot here debate the competing theories of visual perception, it is widely accepted that visual perception is at least partly to be understood in terms of the manner in which a visual image is caused. A parallel causal approach to understanding the nature of photography seems fundamentally sound, but various confusions and false implications must be avoided.

It won't do to say that no persons are involved in the causal production of the photograph of Uncle Bill, that is, to say that the causes are only mechanical and automatic. Uncle Bill's lean and sculpted body was surely part of the cause, as was the friend who released the shutter. Nor will it do to say that there are no fundamental differences between photographs and other pictures since the actions of persons are intimately involved in both. Even if Uncle Bill's Kodak-wielding friend had every bit as much "a subjective point of view" as Picasso would have in painting the same scene, this shared subjectivity does not obliterate crucial causal differences. The "subjectivity" of persons commonly affects nonphotographic vision without undermining its status as vision. If my ophthalmologist puts drops in my eyes to dilate my pupils, he drastically changes my vision, but he would be worried if I complained that I could no longer see at all. Similarly, a "pictorialist" photographer produces an image that is undeniably expressive, but that expressiveness should not be allowed to obscure the fact that the causal origins of such a photograph are crucially different from those of a painting. Nor do the particular ways in which we construct cameras and process film imply that photography is more akin to painting than it is to nonphotographic vision. Unquestionably, there are many conceivable ways to construct cameras and process film that would result in significantly different images, but that is not a good reason to deny that the causal origins of a photograph are akin to those of a nonphotographic visual image and not to those of a painting. When I first encountered a convex side mirror on a car, I was misled in my perception of how far other cars were behind me, but this mistake hardly meant that I didn't see anything behind me until I learned to read such a mirror. If it were possible to change some of the cognitive hardware of my brain so that my visual images were different from what they are now, this would not rob me of vision. Analogously, even if we consider the ways we construct cameras and process film to be in some respects *arbitrary*, this arbitrariness cannot undercut the claim that photography is a mode of seeing.

Much more can be said about how photographs can be distinguished from other pictures in terms of the causal process by which they give us information about the scene depicted. Suppose we are in the office of a real estate agent who is showing us photographs and drawings of homes for sale. In trying to acquire information about the homes by looking at drawings, we must rely on the *beliefs* the artist has about the properties of the homes in a way that we need not rely on the beliefs the photographer has about the homes' qualities. In the case of the photographs we must assume that the camera's machinery was not designed in a radically nonstandard way and that the film processing was not intended to deceive prospective home buyers. With the introduction of the digital camera and Photoshop, we are sometimes more reluctant to make these assumptions than we were when only photochemical photography was available. It seems that nowadays anyone can cut, paste, shade, and rearrange images with ease. Some want to call this "artography." What are we to make of these technological developments? A professional filmmaker friend of mine asserts flatly that so-called digital photography is not genuine photography. He concedes that in digital photography there is a photo*electric* causal chain from the scene depicted to the image produced, as there is a photo*chemical* causal chain in traditional photography, but he thinks that the possibilities of manipulation are now so extensive as to replace photography. A thought experiment about nonphotographic vision will show that greater powers of manipulation and a change from chemical to electrical causation do not amount to a departure from photography. Suppose brain scientists make fundamental changes in the causal processes that produce our visual images. Suppose further that these scientists are able to provide us with devices attached to our brains that allow us, by pushing a few buttons, to manipulate our visual images in almost unlimited ways. We could still, I submit, be properly said to see the world. Only when the *beliefs* of other persons are involved in the causal production of our visual images does genuine vision disappear. If the brain scientists were able to push the buttons on my device on the basis of their beliefs about the scene, then I would no longer be seeing the scene before me. In normal digital photography, beliefs play no such causal role. However, if at some time a "camera" is invented where the image-producing causal process can be directly affected by "belief zaps" from bystanders, the resultant images will not be photographic or images in any other mode of seeing.

DIAGNOSTIC IMAGING

But what are we to say about diagnostic imaging devices—MRI, CAT scan, CT scan, ultrasound/sonography, PET scan, and old-fashioned X-ray? If we put aside the need sometimes for image interpretation by experts, these ubiquitous machines have come to have standing in our culture as democratic as the standing cameras have enjoyed for more than 150 years. All of us (or at least those of us with generous health care plans) have our "pictures taken" by these devices. One wonders what Daguerre's reaction would be to the fact that in the twenty-first century a person's first portrait is often a sonogram taken in the womb. Parents lovingly compile albums of sonograms of their unborn children. No longer is it necessary to have a sonogram taken in a hospital or physician's office. Photo studios are being established that specialize in sonograms. At present, few of us have the expertise and equipment to take these pictures ourselves. But that was true also in the earliest years of photography. Surely that will change, and it won't be long before "Kodak Brownie" versions of the ultrasound machine and the PET scanner will be available, and we'll all be able to watch in real time what's going on inside our bodies without the help of a radiologist. What could be a more intimate self-portrait than that?

I wish to argue that these are all modes of seeing. They are visual prosthetic devices as fully as conventional cameras are. However, they are *not* forms of *photo*graphy. A necessary part of photography, including digital photography, is light reflected from the object being imaged—whether the light is emitted by a distant star or reflected by a human face three feet in front of the camera. This crucial difference is reflected in some of the names given to the new types of imaging. Ultrasound testing and recording is called "sonography." This term points up the fact that the imaging is produced by *sound waves* instead of light rays as in *photo*graphy. The chief purpose of these devices is to make it possible to see tissues, structures, and processes inside the human body where it is not feasible to make use of reflected light. Early in the twentieth century, this nonphoto seeing was first done with X-rays. Today, CAT and CT scanners make the most sophisticated use of X-rays. Neuroscientists continue to find new ways of causally linking internal states of affairs to visual images. MRIs use radio waves and magnetic fields. PET scanners rely on the emission of positrons. By injecting different chemicals into the bloodstream, one can PET scan different features and processes. This is analogous to a photographer using different lenses, shutter speeds, apertures, and lighting.

Sometimes these devices use film. In CAT scanning, as X-rays pass through the body, they are absorbed or attenuated (weakened) at differing levels, creating a profile of X-ray beams of different strength. The X-ray profile is registered on film as a visual image. However, in the more recently developed CT scanning, film is replaced by a detector which measures the X-ray profile. I see no reason to suppose that the use of film makes the process a form of photography. Film is, to be sure, a feature of chemical photography, but, as we have seen, the lack of film in *digital* photography makes it no less genuine photography.

In short, there are now many forms of seeing that are neither photographic nor of the sort given to us biologically. Although the opportunities of manipulation in the various types of scanning are greater even than in digital photography and Photoshop, that is not a good reason to liken them to forms of representation such as painting and drawing. Scanned images have the causal relations to the objects imaged that distinguish them from other forms of representation. The fact that enormously complex computer hardware and software mediate the images produced does not undermine their status as forms of vision as genuine as my vision of the food on the plate in front of me.

INFERENCES ABOUT THE WORLD

Having briefly given an account of how the nature of photographic representation compares with other forms of representation, we must now grapple with the question of how photographic images are related to claims of knowledge and truth. When I examine a photograph, what inferences can I legitimately make about the world? In making such inferences, what standards, procedures, and criteria should I use, and how are the standards, procedures, and criteria different from those appropriate for use in assessing other forms of visual representation such as painting? We should, as I suggested at the outset, try to find a way to incorporate in a self-consistent epistemology both tenets in the understanding of photography found in popular culture: (1) a photographic image is a mirror image of reality, and (2) a photographic image is a manipulation of reality. Accordingly, I will now sketch what I call "flexible realism."

Part of the problem of developing such an epistemology is that the task of assessing the epistemic value of an image alleged to be photographic is often inseparable from the task of determining whether the image is genuinely photographic. The task of judging the epistemic value of Chuck Close's *Self-Portrait*, for example, cannot be achieved without first determining whether it is a photograph. A case study of photography and popular culture will be helpful in exploring these epistemological issues.

NATIONAL GEOGRAPHIC

Over one hundred years old, *National Geographic* magazine today has an estimated readership of thirty-seven million people worldwide. I know of no more penetrating study of the place of photography in popular culture than *Reading National Geographic* by anthropologists Catherine A. Lutz and Jane L. Collins.[2] In a book that is as empirically thorough as it is theoretically well informed, Lutz and Collins try to answer a host of questions, including the question of what impact the "steady, continual, accessible flow of images from an institution like the *National Geographic*" has on "popular consciousness."[3] They reject "the idea that photos are simply objective documents that signify no differently than does any unmediated experience of the visual world."[4] The magazine, they argue, "justifies its self-image as a national institution on the basis of its reputation for purveying important scientific knowledge about 'the world and all that is in it' and for safeguarding important American values and traditions. . . . It is a glossy, stylized presentation of a highly limited number of themes and types of images."[5]

Perhaps most fascinating is their account of the complex editorial process "as one of negotiating standards of 'balance' and 'objectivity,' informational content and visual beauty."[6] Also significant is their finding in readers of the magazine "a tension between the desire to know about other peoples and their ways and the wish to validate middle-class American values."[7]

What epistemic conclusions can we derive from these insights into the place of photography in popular culture? It avails us almost nothing to say that we must reject all claims that photographs are objective documents that provide an unmediated reflection of the world. As we have seen, *every* sort of vision is mediated in one way or another. Insistent talk about the unavoidability of mediation in photography is a red herring that distracts us from the genuine problem of sorting out the many types of mediation with an eye to developing appropriate cognitive strategies to be used in responding to photographs. What we need are procedures and criteria that would help us to determine how this or that photograph in this or that context does or does not constitute evidence that warrants this or that assertion about the world we live in. If one prefers to avoid John Dewey's vocabulary of "warranted assertibility," one can instead employ the language of "the ethics of belief" or of "virtue epistemology." Whatever the preferred vocabulary, what is needed is the means to navigate the sometimes rough cognitive waters of photography so as to minimize the chances of shipwreck. Only to point out that the *National Geographic*'s editors intend the images in the magazine to promote middle-class American values does not take us far. That is like driving instructors telling their students to watch closely the erratic movements of drunken drivers with whom they share the road—good advice, but not much help in parking a car in a small space.

WHODUNIT?

Let us begin by addressing the problem of how to determine whether the image before us is a genuine photograph and an image of what it is purported to be an image of. In light of what has already been said about the nature of photographic representation, it is clear that any attempt to answer these questions must seek clues to the conditions under which the image was produced. Sometimes this is easy, sometimes serious detective work is needed, and sometimes the conditions remain mysterious indefinitely.

In May 2004, the editor of a British tabloid was forced to resign when he ran afoul of the epistemology and ethics of photography:

> In a statement, the *Trinity Mirror* board said the newspaper had "published in good faith photographs which it absolutely believed were genuine images of British soldiers abusing an Iraqi prisoner."
>
> "However," the statement said, "there is now sufficient evidence to suggest that these pictures are fakes [actually photos taken in the back of a truck on an army base in England] and that the *Daily Mirror* has been the subject of a calculated and malicious hoax."[8]

In this case, members of the military unit supposedly involved were able to identify objects in the images that were not located in Iraq. A limited number of people had the information necessary to show that the acts of abuse had been staged in England. The image was found to be a genuine photo, but the scene imaged was not what it was presented as being. It took considerable effort and expertise to show convincingly that a hoax had occurred.

In the case of an image in *National Geographic*, the epistemic situation is quite different. The magazine has an institutional reputation of such value that it is unlikely that the editors would knowingly allow an entirely "tricked up" image to be published. No guarantee is possible, however. Such august newspapers as the *New York Times* and the *Washington Post* have sometimes published fraudulent stories by overambitious reporters. The same could happen at *National Geographic*. Although there is a strong presumption in favor of considering an image published in the *Geographic* a genuine photo, it is a defeasible presumption—to borrow a notion from law and technical epistemology. For example, the presumption would be defeated for me if the magazine had hired as a photographer my next-door neighbor whose clandestine hobby is ingeniously making fake "photos." I once inadvertently discovered him enjoying this hobby when I rushed into his basement to alert him to his wife's collapse on their front lawn. Knowing that, a few months before, my neighbor had been on assignment in Cuba, I would be suspicious of the images accompanying a story about Cuba in the issue just published. The presumption would *not* be defeated, however, by the fact that a technically adept friend of mine could, using a scanner and Photoshop, produce an image indistinguishable from the image found in the magazine.

At the other end of the presumption scale are images in the tabloids. But even among tabloids there are important differences. The images found in the tabloid mentioned above have more presumption in their favor than those found in tabloids that are sold at grocery-store checkout counters. The latter are taken seriously only by the utterly naive and by the attorneys of celebrities hoping to win libel suits. Perhaps in the middle range of presumption are images submitted in photography contests. Although the presumption is strengthened by the fact that there are explicit rules in a contest clearly labeled "photography," it is weakened by the fact that the contestants have ample motivation for faking images. If a contestant were a friend one knew to be a technophobe incapable of using Photoshop, the presumption would be greatly strengthened. In short, the problem of determining whether an image is a genuine photograph is strikingly similar to the problem of solving a murder mystery. Sometimes it is obvious who the murderer is, sometimes it requires a Sherlock Holmes to sift through the clues, and sometimes murder mysteries remain unsolved.

Context is crucial. As we have seen, when an image is in *National Geographic*, we can safely make lots of assumptions that it would be risky to make in other contexts. Found in the context of a cache of Al Qaeda propaganda leaflets, the image of an American soldier torturing a woman in Islamic dress has little presumption in its favor as a genuine photograph. Images appearing in American propaganda have more presumption in their favor—so we like to think.

Another important consideration in judging defeasibility is what is at stake. If an allegedly photographic image is submitted as evidence of guilt in a murder trial, defense attorneys appropriately do their utmost to find defeating conditions. Whereupon the prosecution does everything it can to find evidence that defeats the defeating conditions unearthed by the defense. By contrast, when an image having the appearance of being a photograph is seen on the wall of an art gallery, few people are concerned to look for defeating conditions or conditions to defeat the defeaters. Whether the image is a genuine photograph is considered of limited relevance to its aesthetic value.

Needless to say, the deception of seeming to be a genuine photograph of the scene purportedly depicted is only one of a host of ways that an image can be misleading. As Lutz and Collins demonstrate in fascinating detail, resourceful photographers and editors can—without resorting to nonphotographic images or photographic images which purport to be of scenes they are not actually photos of—manipulate readers' attitudes and beliefs about other cultures in an amazing variety of ways. What does this tell us about how we should respond to images, once we have put aside the question of whether they are genuine photos? Should we be cynical about the motives behind all photos? Should we treat all photos as social constructions that cannot provide warrant for any assertions about the world? Should we, with rare exceptions, take all photos at face value? I wish to suggest that we should adopt flexible cognitive strategies. We should become *flexible* realists. In my view, the bane of all epistemologies, both technical and popular, is the notion that "one size fits all." The search for *the* standard of epistemic justification is the epistemic Holy Grail of popular culture as well as of professional epistemology.

We can begin to get a grip on what those strategies might be by putting ourselves in the shoes of Lutz and Collins as they might today respond to images in the latest issue of the *Geographic*. As anthropologists who have exhaustively studied how the magazine's images are produced and interpreted, we are "educated consumers" of photos found in this context. We know in detail the purposes, techniques, and negotiation process that lie behind the images we are looking at. We are equipped to discern in what respects an image provides warrant for assertions about the world and in what respects it does not. With exquisite sensitivity to nuance, we are able to adjust and target our skepticism. In our "reading" of the photography, we can extract the genuine information and discard the bogus. To be sure, even we are fallible in our responses. We, too, are sometimes misled, but our cognitive equipment is so sophisticated and fine-tuned that the inferences about the world that we draw from the images are reliable. Our status approaches that of "ideal observers" of photos. Our "epistemic status," as we may call it, is exceptionally strong.

Should we regret that our epistemic situation is rarely so strong? No. As I have discussed elsewhere,[9] there are many contexts where we are better off with weak epistemic situations, where we do well to believe *beyond* the evidence. There is ample evidence that we are sometimes better off, for example, with overbeliefs about our own abilities. A person with a somewhat generous belief about his skill as a driver can drive a car more effectively than someone with an acute awareness of his failings as a driver. William James pioneered exploration of overbeliefs, and numerous psychologists have confirmed and extended his findings. Is it regrettable that images in the *Geographic* of other parts of the world induce in us overbeliefs that strengthen our confidence in our own culture's values? That's an open question. Most likely, such overbeliefs are sometimes harmful and sometimes beneficial. Only an epistemological ideologue insists that we should always try our utmost to prevent photographs from inducing overbeliefs about the scenes imaged. We should instead be *flexible* in our judgments about the level of epistemic situation appropriate to the context in which we find ourselves.

EPISTEMIC VIRTUE

This is not a recommendation of epistemic laziness. A hockey player who is exceptionally adaptable to changing circumstances—knowing when to pass, when to shoot, when to check, and so on—is not lazy. He adapts the use of his skills to context. So the epistemically virtuous reader of photographs should flexibly adapt to context in applying epistemic standards.

VISUAL LITERACY

What empowers us to be epistemically virtuous in that flexible way? Certainly what is often called "visual literacy"[10] plays a major empowerment role. Lutz and Collins frequently display extraordinary visual literacy in their analyses of photographs. They can tease out the many things going on in and behind an image, as few of us could. Furthermore, visual literacy is something that can be taught, as computer literacy or a foreign language can be taught. But visual literacy of high order should not be used indiscriminately any more than exceptional base-stealing ability should always be used by a baseball player whenever she is on base.

What I am calling flexible realism in response to photographs is the inclination and ability to negotiate our understanding of relations between image and scene depicted in a way that adjusts epistemic standards to the context and warrants assertions about the world accordingly. The context includes my own purposes as well as the social and physical structures of the environment. As I have noted, the context of legal proceedings where murder is charged is different from contexts in which we casually look at photographs in *National Geographic* or a family album. A high order of visual literacy is necessary for a robust form of such flexible realism, but it is hardly sufficient—any more than the ability to pass the ball well is sufficient to be the MVP in the NBA. Epistemic virtue in the world of photographic images has many elements of which visual literacy is only one, albeit an important one.

Also important are the ethical or unethical principles and practices of photographers. This is clearest in photojournalism where a professional code may forbid altering the "meaning" of a scene.[11] Although this is a vague proscription, a history of adjudicated cases ("case law," in legal jargon) gives photographers a reasonably clear notion of what counts as changed meaning. The proscription can also be given teeth by a rule that places the burden of proof on the photographer who claims not to have altered the meaning.

The flexible realist adjusts assumptions about the conditions that produced the image according to what can be reasonably believed about the principles and practices employed by the photographer. Those principles and practices are parts of the context in which cognitive strategies and epistemic virtues must be exercised. Reasonable beliefs of this sort, together with visual literacy, enable a person to navigate the photographic seas without undue risk. But no amount of flexibility and sensitivity to context will *guarantee* safety. Deception is always possible, and we should be prepared to redesign our cognitive strategies so as to minimize the risk of disastrous deception without unnecessarily sacrificing the benefits of overbelief.

GRISLY IMAGES AND HOLISTIC PRAGMATISM

In photography, everyone can be actively engaged in the production of images of reality, and even the most untutored photographer gives some thought to how a photographic image justifies or does not justify inferences about the world we live in. It is not too much to say that photography permits everyone, not just professional philosophers and psychologists, to be practicing epistemologists. But it's a two-way street. Not only does photography bring epistemology to everyone, but the quotidian practice of photography also highlights aspects of epistemology often ignored by philosophers and psychologists. I have remarked on how our everyday experience of photography shows the need for flexible, context-sensitive cognitive strategies and epistemic standards. Additionally, photography helps to show philosophers the folly of isolating the epistemic from the moral, and the sensory from the emotional. Media editors and readers alike are forced to think (and feel) about what inferences are justified by photographs such as those showing the charred remains of American contractors hanging from a bridge behind an exultant mob in Fallujah, Iraq—and about the psychological and social consequences of the publication of such photos. When a newspaper editor, Margaret Sullivan, decides to publish a grisly photograph (and not publish a still more grisly photograph of an enraged Iraqi young man beating a smoldering torso with a lead pipe), she bases her decision on a complex mix of the epistemic and the moral, the sensory and the emotional, which she summarizes by saying that she made "an effort to balance two sometimes irreconcilable differences: sensitivity and truth-telling."[12] The *New Republic* writer, Adam Kushner, who argues that the more grisly photograph should have been published likewise appeals to the epistemic, the moral, the sensory, and the emotional.[13]

Let us sketch an argument Ms. Sullivan might give against another editor's decision to publish the lead-pipe photo:

1. Every newspaper editor, who has an obligation to present the truth, who has an obligation to serve the public welfare, and who publishes something that does serious psychological damage to children, does something that ought not to have been done.
2. The other editor has an obligation to present the truth.
3. The other editor has an obligation to serve the public welfare.
4. The other editor published the lead-pipe photo.
5. The publication of the lead-pipe photo has done serious psychological damage to children.

Therefore,

6. The other editor ought not to have published the lead-pipe photo.

Therefore,

7. The other editor did something that ought not to have been done.

Now Mr. Kushner's argument:

8. Every newspaper editor, who has an obligation to present the truth, and who has an obligation to serve the public welfare, ought to publish whatever is truthful and serves the public welfare more than any other relevant material available.
9. The lead-pipe photo is truthful.
10. The publication of the lead-pipe photo serves the public welfare more than any other photo of the incident available.

Therefore,

11. The other editor had an obligation to publish the lead-pipe photo.

Kushner next states that he *feels* that the other editor had an obligation to publish the lead-pipe photo, saying that any sane person who *has* an obligation to do something will normally feel obligated to do it. Kushner's rejection of (7) is similar to that of a physicist who has a sensory experience that is different from what is predicted by a theory; the physicist has what W. V. Quine calls a recalcitrant sensory experience; Kushner has a recalcitrant feeling of obligation when denying (7). He has a positive feeling of obligation when he confirms (11) and the conjunction leading to it. After denying (7), he may deny the conjunction that logically implies it, amending or surrendering an ethical principle such as (1) or denying a descriptive statement among the premises that jointly lead to the ethical conclusion such as (5), that the lead-pipe photo does serious psychological damage to children. A similar conjunction of the moral, the sensory, and the emotional could be found in the thinking of a government official charged with the task of deciding whether ever more horrific photos of Iraqis being tortured in Abu Ghraib prison should be publicly released.

Photography can help to persuade us of what Morton White calls "holistic pragmatism," the view that "heterogeneous conjunctions of . . . normative sentences and descriptive sentences may be tested holistically. . . . [T]hese heterogeneous conjunctions of sentences are not tested for their capacity to link sensory experiences alone . . . but rather for their capacity to link sensory experiences with feelings or emotions."[14] To test pragmatically and holistically is to test at once, as a group, a heterogeneous and interdependent mass of moral beliefs, epistemic principles, sensory reports, and feelings. Whoever said that the job of a newspaper editor or high government official who takes his or her responsibilities seriously is easy!

NOTES

1. From the early days of photography, it has been held by some commentators that photography is best understood as an aided mode of seeing the world. This account of the nature of photography has been most clearly formulated by Kendell L. Walton. See Walton, "Transparent Pictures: On the Nature of Photographic Realism," *Critical Inquiry* 11 (1984): 246–77. My account of the nature of photography draws much from this rich essay.

2. Catherine A. Lutz and Jane L. Collins, *Reading National Geographic* (Chicago: University of Chicago Press, 1993).

3. Lutz and Collins, 4.

4. Lutz and Collins, 4.

5. Lutz and Collins, 5.

6. Lutz and Collins, jacket blurb.

7. Lutz and Collins, jacket blurb.

8. *New York Times*, May 15, 2004.

9. Peter H. Hare, "Problems and Prospects in the Ethics of Belief," in *Pragmatic Naturalism and Realism*, ed. John R. Shook (Buffalo, NY: Prometheus Books, 2003), 239–61.

10. See Paul Messaris, *Visual Literacy: Image, Mind and Reality* (Boulder, CO: Westview Press, 1994).

11. See Paul Lester, *Photojournalism: An Ethical Approach* (Hillsdale, NJ: Lawrence Erlbaum Associates, 1991).

12. Margaret Sullivan, "In Grisly Photos from Iraq, Balancing Taste and Truth," *Buffalo News*, April 4, 2004. Cf. Susan Sontag, "The Photographs *Are* Us: Regarding the Torture of Others," *New York Times Magazine*, May 23, 2004.

13. Adam B. Kushner, "See No Evil," TNR Online, April 2, 2004.

14. Morton White, "Normative Ethics, Normative Epistemology, and Quine's Holism," in *The Philosophy of W. V. Quine*, ed. L. E. Hahn and P. A. Schilpp (Chicago and La Salle, IL: Open Court, 1986), 650. See also Morton White, *What Is and What Ought to be Done: An Essay on Ethics and Epistemology* (New York and Oxford: Oxford University Press, 1981); and Morton White, *A Philosophy of Culture: The Scope of Holistic Pragmatism* (Princeton and Oxford: Princeton University Press, 2002), chapter 10.

About the Editors
and Contributors

Michael Baur is associate professor of philosophy at Fordham University, and adjunct professor of law at Fordham Law School. He is translator of J. G. Fichte's *Foundations of Natural Right* (2000), and director of Fordham's Natural Law Colloquium (www.lawandphilosophy.org). He has published articles and book chapters on topics including the philosophy of law, the philosophy of popular culture, epistemology, metaphysics, and ethics, and on thinkers such as Kant, Fichte, Hegel, Aquinas, Lonergan, Adorno, Rawls, Heidegger, and Gadamer, Michael is the coeditor of *The Beatles and Philosophy*.

Paul A. Cantor is Clifton Waller Barrett Professor of English at the University of Virginia. He is author of *Gilligan Unbound: Pop Culture in the Age of Globalization* (2001)—named by the *LA Times* as one of the best nonfiction books of the year—and of essays on popular culture that have appeared in *Political Theory, The Independent Review, Perspectives on Political Science, Wilson Quarterly, American Enterprise, Reason,* and *The Weekly Standard.* His essay on *The Simpsons* has been reprinted in *The Simpsons and Philosophy, Prospect* (England), and *Iskusstvo Kino* (in Russian in Russia).

Noël Carroll is the Andrew W. Mellon Professor of the Humanities at Temple University. His recent books include *Beyond Aesthetics* (2001); *Engaging the Moving Image* (2003); and *The Philosophy of Film and Motion Pictures,* coedited with Jinhee Choi (2005).

Ted Cohen is professor of philosophy at the University of Chicago. Among his recent publications are the book *Jokes* (2001) and the essays "High and Low Art, and High and Low Audiences"; "Identifying with Metaphor"; "Metaphor, Feeling, and Narrative"; and "Three Problems in Kant's Aesthetics."

Jorge J. E. Gracia holds the Samuel P. Capen Chair and is State University of New York Distinguished Professor of Philosophy at the State University of New York at Buffalo. Among his most recent publications are *Old Wine in New Skins: The Role of Tradition in Communication, Knowledge, and Group Identity* (67th Aquinas Lecture, 2003); *Companion to Philosophy in the Middle Ages*, ed. (2002); *The Classics of Western Philosophy*, ed. (2002); *Literary Philosophers: Borges, Calvino, Eco*, ed. (2002); *Hispanic/Latino Identity: A Philosophical Perspective* (2000); and *How Can We Know What God Means? The Interpretation of Revelation* (2000).

Theodore Gracyk is professor of philosophy at Minnesota State University–Moorehead. He is the author of *I Wanna Be Me: Rock Music and the Politics of Identity* (2001) and *Rhythm and Noise: An Aesthetics of Rock* (1996). His next book, *Listening to Popular Music*, will be published by the University of Michigan Press in 2007.

Peter H. Hare is State University of New York Distinguished Service Professor of Philosophy Emeritus. He has contributed an essay to Richard Greene and Peter Vernezze, eds., *Sopranos and Philosophy: I Kill Therefore I Am* (2004) and is an amateur photographer, some of whose images have been published. Recent publications in epistemology include essays contributed to Khalil, ed., *Dewey, Pragmatism, and Economic Methodology* (2004), and John Shook, ed., *Pragmatic Naturalism and Realism* (2003).

William Irwin is associate professor of philosophy at King's College in Pennsylvania. He is the editor of *The Death and Resurrection of the Author?* (2002), *Seinfeld and Philosophy* (2000), *The Simpsons and Philosophy* (2001), *The Matrix and Philosophy* (2002) and *More Matrix and Philosophy* (2005), in addition to being the general editor for the Blackwell Philosophy and PopCulture Series. He is also the author of *Intentionalist Interpretation* (1999) and a number of scholarly articles in aesthetics.

Carolyn Korsmeyer is professor of philosophy and department chair at the University at Buffalo. Among her recent publications are *Making Sense of Taste: Food and Philosophy* (1999) and *Gender and Aesthetics: An Introduction* (2004). She has written three books and edited or coedited five others. Her new anthology, *The Taste Culture Reader*, is scheduled for publication in 2005. In the field of philosophy and popular culture, she has written on the movie *The Matrix* (in *The Matrix and Philosophy*, ed. W. Irwin) and the television show *Buffy the Vampire Slayer* (in *Buffy the Vampire Slayer and Philosophy*, ed. J. South). Both popular culture and high/fine art are included in the discussion of contemporary feminist art in *Gender and Aesthetics*.

Gareth B. Matthews is professor of philosophy at the University of Massachusetts–Amherst. He is the author of *Socratic Perplexity and the Nature of Philosophy* (1999), *The Philosophy of Childhood* (1994), and *Thought's Ego in Augustine and Descartes* (1992). He writes a regular column on children's stories for the journal of philosophy for children, *Thinking*. His website is www.philosophyforkids.com.

Richard Shusterman is the Dorothy F. Schmidt Eminent Scholar in the Humanities and professor of philosophy at Florida Atlantic University–Boca Raton. His authored books include *Surface and Depth* (2002), *Performing Live* (2000), *Practicing Philosophy* (1997), *Sous l'interprétation* (1994), *T. S. Eliot and the Philosophy of Criticism* (1988), and *Pragmatist Aesthetics* (1992; 2nd ed., 2000, and translated into twelve languages). He directed a project for UNESCO on popular music and urban culture.

James B. South is associate professor of philosophy at Marquette University and chair of the department. He is the editor of *Buffy the Vampire Slayer and Philosophy*. His essays on late medieval and Renaissance philosophy have appeared in such journals as the *Review of Metaphysics*, *History of Philosophy Quarterly*, and *Rivista di Storia della Filosofia*.